P9-CJF-190

Reading for Results

ELEVENTH EDITION

Laraine Flemming

Prepared by

Laraine Flemming

Contributing Writer

Ann Marie Radaskiewicz

WADSWORTH
CENGAGE Learning

Australia • Brazil • Japan • Korea • Mexico • Singapore • Spain • United Kingdom • United States

For product information and technology assistance, contact us at **Cengage Learning Customer & Sales Support, 1-800-354-9706**

For permission to use material from this text or product, submit all requests online at **www.cengage.com/permissions** Further permissions questions can be emailed to **permissionrequest@cengage.com**

ISBN-13: 978-0-495-90822-7
ISBN-10: 0-495-90822-3

Wadsworth
20 Channel Center Street
Boston, MA 02210
USA

Cengage Learning is a leading provider of customized learning solutions with office locations around the globe, including Singapore, the United Kingdom, Australia, Mexico, Brazil, and Japan. Locate your local office at: **www.cengage.com/global**

Cengage Learning products are represented in Canada by Nelson Education, Ltd.

To learn more about Wadsworth, visit **www.cengage.com/wadsworth**

Purchase any of our products at your local college store or at our preferred online store **www.CengageBrain.com**

READ IMPORTANT LICENSE INFORMATION

Printed in the United States of America
2 3 4 5 6 7 14 13 12 11

Reading for Results: Instructor's Manual with Test Bank

CONTENTS

A Note from the Author

From the very first edition, I have tried to make *Reading for Results* a textbook with enough exercises for double, even triple reviews. However, I've taught long enough to know that no textbook is ever quite adequate to the task of instruction. There are always a few more students who could use just a bit more help. This resource package, with its additional exercises and tests, is dedicated to those students and the overworked instructors, who struggle to meet their needs.

It's also dedicated to new teachers who are not quite sure how to go about using *Reading for Results.* For them, I offer chapter-by-chapter suggestions as to how they might introduce the skills and concepts presented in the text. I do, however, have one caveat: If the suggestions don't seem to work, ignore them. *Reading for Results* was meant to be flexible. It can be adapted to any number of teaching methods or styles.

For those instructors who would like to assign Internet exercises for lab or homework, Cengage's companion website for Reading for Results (**www.cengage.com/devenglish/flemming/ RFR11e**) provides three levels of review tests, Getting Down the Basics, Checking Your Progress, and Taking the Challenge, which I wrote to accompany the chapters in *Reading for Results*, 11th edition. Instructors can also find more interactive quizzes at **laflemm.com**, along with a sample syllabus.

Best wishes,
Laraine Flemming

PART I

Suggestions for Teaching and Supplementary Material

CHAPTER 1
Strategies for Textbook Learning

SUGGESTIONS FOR TEACHING CHAPTER 1

1. Tell students that *SQ3R* is only one of many study systems, and that they should feel free to use others that they might have learned about in other courses. The main thing to stress is that textbooks do require a system or method of reading. They can't be read like a magazine or a novel, at least not if the reader wants to understand and remember the material.

2. Consider introducing REAP as well. The letters stand for Read, Encode, i.e., summarize, Annotate, and Ponder. Type "*reap* for study reading" into a search engine and you'll find a lot of materials explaining its use and benefits.

3. In teaching the section on using the Web to do research, emphasize how important it is to critically evaluate sites that are not created by educational or government institutions.

4. Student readers often complain about problems concentrating while reading textbooks. Thus, this chapter is the ideal place to introduce some tips on concentration like the ones introduced in this section of the manual. (Supplementary Materials 1.1)

5. For the procrastinators in your class, you might want to hand out the guidelines for battling procrastination listed in Supplementary Materials 1.2.

6. Lots of students don't realize that different texts require different reading strategies. To make your students more aware of the strategies available, hand out the reading strategies checklist. (Supplementary Materials 1.3)

7. Research shows that many students aren't aware of and don't utilize the textbook devices authors include to aid comprehension. If you want to make your students more aware of what's available to them in their texts, give them the questionnaire titled *Assessing Your Textbook*. (Supplementary Materials 1.4)

SUPPLEMENTARY MATERIALS

1.1   TIPS FOR IMPROVING CONCENTRATION

1. Work in the proper physical setting, which includes the following:
   a. an uncluttered desk or table
   b. comfortable, straight-backed chair
   c. proper light
   d. quiet atmosphere
   e. materials such as pen, dictionary, paper, etc.

2. Study in the same place at the same time each day. After a while, the tendency to concentrate at this particular time and in this particular place will become a habit.

3. Establish a specific purpose for each assignment. Know exactly how many pages you expect to cover and how much time you want to spend.

4. Begin work immediately after you sit down. At this point, you are most vulnerable to interruptions. Don't take any chances. Avoid anyone or anything that might distract you.

5. Keep physically active while studying. Outline, take notes, or recite the information to yourself.

6. Take regular breaks. Work for a half-hour. Then take a five-minute rest. Breaks are important. They help avoid the mental fatigue that destroys concentration.

7. Study alone or with other students who are also committed to doing well in school. Avoid anyone likely to disturb your concentration.

8. Each time you finish a study session in which you have maintained concentration, congratulate yourself for improving your study habits.

1.2 BREAKING THE PROCRASTINATION HABIT

People who procrastinate usually have long-term goals they want to achieve. The problem is they are always putting off the daily work necessary to fulfill or reach those goals. In short, they are always procrastinating.

Battling procrastination is tough, but it can be done if you're willing to follow these guidelines.

1. **Know what you want to accomplish.**
   Target one specific project that you want to accomplish within a specific period of time.

2. **Let other people know what your project is and when you plan to finish it.**
   Tell several people you respect what you intend to accomplish. In particular, try to find the kind of people who will ask how your work is coming along.

3. **Divide and conquer.**
   Divide your project into a series of subtasks and give yourself deadlines for each and every one. Make sure that the first task on your list takes no more than fifteen minutes to accomplish. Complete that task within twenty-four hours of making your list. After completing that first brief task, cross it off your list and congratulate yourself.

4. **Maintain your momentum.**
   Go on to the next task immediately after completing the first one. Each time you complete a task by its deadline, congratulate yourself or give yourself some unexpected reward. When you do not finish a task by its deadline, penalize yourself *not by feeling guilty* but by doing something you hate, like cleaning your room or doing your laundry.

5. **Analyze the causes for postponing your work.**
   If you find yourself slacking off and falling into your old predictable ways, you need to discover *why* this is happening. You may have taken on a task that is too difficult to accomplish during the time you allotted. If so, rework your schedule to make it more realistic and doable.

6. **Do not become discouraged by relapses into old habits.**
   It is quite natural to fall back into your old habits when you are trying to create new ones. Don't be surprised or angry if you can't stop procrastinating overnight. However, when you find yourself reverting to old forms of behavior, tell yourself that you *can* kick the habit of procrastination; it's just going to take a little time.

7. **Never forget the consequences of procrastination.**
   Anytime you feel yourself starting to procrastinate, sit down and list for yourself some of the consequences of this seemingly harmless habit: a constant sense of guilt, a mediocre career, unfulfilled potential, and a life of indecision. Is it really worth it?

1.3 STRATEGIES FOR READING

Check off the reading strategies you already use. Put an "x" next to those you plan to use in the future.

1. Rereading the same passage two, even three times. _____

2. Drawing diagrams of the steps or stages explained in the text. _____

3. Reading aloud. _____

4. Referring to illustrations of a text while reading. _____

5. Reading very slowly, practically word for word. _____

6. Visualizing while reading. _____

7. Rereading the introduction to better understand what follows. _____

8. Skipping to the last page to read the *summary,* or brief restatement of key points. _____

9. Looking up unfamiliar words, then rereading. _____

10. Asking questions like "What's the point here?" _____

11. Discussing the text with a friend or an instructor. _____

12. Imagining situations similar to the one being described. _____

13. *Paraphrasing* or translating the author's words into simpler, more familiar language. _____

14. Looking for patterns like *cause and effect, comparison and contrast.* _____

15. Breaking individual sentences into parts. _____

1.4 ASSESSING YOUR TEXTBOOK

Directions: Portions of this questionnaire can be completed after you preread. One or two questions can be answered only after you have begun reading. If you wish, you may complete the questionnaire after you finish the chapter.

Textbook Title: _____

Date: _____

1. Does the chapter open with any of the following?
    a. lists of questions
    b. an outline of topics or issues
    c. a list of learning objectives
    d. an overview of the chapter
    e. other: _____

    Did you find this material useful? Why or why not?

    _____

    _____

2. Does the author include any review questions or statements *between* chapter sections?

    _____

    If you answered "yes," did you also make use of this material? _____

    Was it helpful? Why or why not? _____

    _____

3. Does the author use any of the following to highlight key points or terms?
    a. boldface
    b. italics
    c. colored ink
    d. boxes
    e. illustrations
    f. other: _____

4. Describe and give two examples of the way key terms are introduced and highlighted in the chapter, i.e., boldface, italic, colored ink, and so on.

    _____

    _____

5. Does the chapter contain illustrations? _____

   If you answered "yes," did you study the illustrations carefully? _____

   Why or why not? _____

6. In most chapter sections, do the headings give you a clue to the ideas introduced in the chapter sections? _____

   Does this make your reading
   a. easier
   b. harder

7. How would you rate the writing in this chapter?
   a. easy to understand
   b. hard to understand
   c. somewhere in between

8. Look at the list of reading strategies introduced on page 19. Which ones did you use most often while completing this chapter?

   _____

   _____

   _____

   _____

Research source: Darren J. Smith, "Common Ground: The Connection between Reader-Response and Textbook Reading," *Journal of Reading, 35*(8) (1992): 630–634.

CHAPTER 2
Building Word Power

SUGGESTIONS FOR TEACHING CHAPTER 2

1. In teaching this chapter, stress that using context is *not* a substitute for using the dictionary. Rather, it provides a way to discover an *approximate meaning* so that the reader doesn't spend too much time looking up words.

2. Emphasize how important it is to avoid constant interruptions while reading. Many students think they are doing the right thing if they look up every unfamiliar word, not realizing that too many interruptions can sever their connection to the author's train of thought.

3. Ask instructors in other disciplines to supply words, such as *root, property,* and *base,* that have one meaning in general conversation and another specialized meaning in their field. These word lists can then become part of the vocabulary instruction.

4. Make working with words a part of every class, and spend the first five or ten minutes reviewing the vocabulary introduced or footnoted in the chapter.

5. Keep telling students to create a list of specialized vocabulary for each course.

SUPPLEMENTARY MATERIALS

2.1 STRATEGIES FOR LEARNING NEW WORDS

You already know that reviewing vocabulary through self-testing is a critical part of vocabulary building. However, there are a number of other strategies for expanding vocabulary that you should know and use on a regular basis.

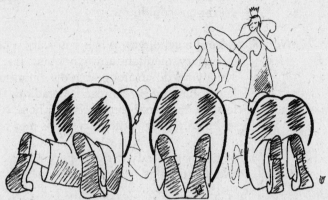

1. **Create a visual image.** For example, to remember that *monarchy* means "rule by one person," imagine someone wearing a crown and sitting on a throne while everyone else in your mental picture kneels on the floor.[*]

Mal **is a good example of a prefix that contributes to many words, e.g., malign, malignant, malefactor.**

2. **Make a map of words sharing a common prefix or root.** Periodically, go through your notebook looking for words derived from a common root or prefix. Then make a map like the one below to highlight the words' common origin.

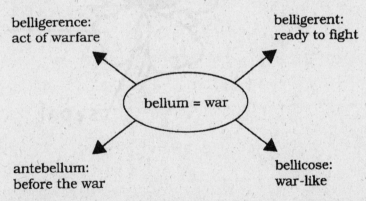

Other examples you might use are polygamy and monogamy.

3. **Include antonyms.** To learn the word *endogamy,* meaning marriage restricted to members of the same group, learn as well the **antonym,** or word opposite in meaning. In this case, the word *exogamy*— meaning marriage restricted to those outside a particular group—is the appropriate antonym.

This is the first reference to paraphrasing. You might want to stress how important paraphrasing is to both reading and writing.

4. **Create your own definitions.** If, for example, an author defines the word *hypothesis* as a "tentative explanation," paraphrase it by translating the definition into your own words—say, "initial guess" or "unproven theory." Then record the author's definition as well as your own. The more you *use your own language to re-create word meaning,* the more easily you can remember new words.

---

[*] The art was supplied by Ulrich Flemming.

5. **Personify the word.** When we personify something, we speak of it as if it were a living being. To personify the word *pugnacious,* for example, meaning "ready to fight," we could make up a sentence like this one: "Rain or shine, pugnacious was always ready to fight." This strategy is even more effective when you personify and link words together, as in "Reticent always dreaded going to parties, but gregarious couldn't wait.

6. **Record a synonym.** When you learn a new word, check to see if the dictionary mentions any synonyms. If it does, write the synonym (or synonyms) down along with the definition. For example, you already know that *belligerent* means "ready to fight or argue," and you just learned the word *pugnacious.* Those two words should be linked together in your vocabulary file as they are below:

    belligerent = ready to fight or argue
    Syn: pugnacious.

7. **Make a sketch.** Particularly for words in the sciences, drawing can be a useful memory aid. Need to remember the words that refer to parts of a flower like *stamen, carpel, petal,* and *sepal?* If you do, make a sketch like the one below.

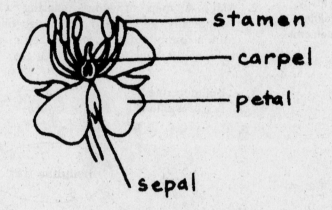

MATCH THE STRATEGY TO THE WORD

When learning new vocabulary, try not to rely exclusively on one strategy over all others. Instead, match the strategy to the word or words. The word *benevolent,* for example, includes the prefix *bene* (meaning "well" or "good"), which has found its way into numerous other words like *beneficiary, benefactor,* and *benign.** Thus, a word like *benevolent* all but cries out for a map of related words, and that strategy would be perfect in this instance. However, a different word might well call for a different strategy. Especially in the sciences, for example, finding a visual image to match a word can be of great value. A quick sketch like the one below could certainly help you remember a specialized term like *systole,* the period of heart contraction.

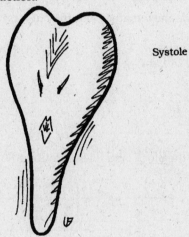

Systole

Link *systole* to a picture and definition of *diastole,* the period when the heart expands and fills with blood, and you will never forget the meaning of these two words.

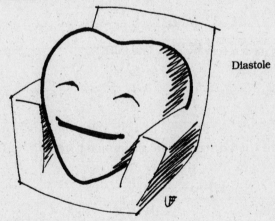

Diastole

---

* There is some dispute about whether *bene* should be classified as a prefix or a root. Since more reference words label it a prefix, I have followed their lead.

2.2 USING CONTEXT

Directions: Each of the following sentences contains an underlined word, and the meaning of that word can change dramatically depending on the context in which it appears. Add one or two more sentences that illustrate some of those changes in meaning.

Example: There was a <u>foul</u> odor coming from the garbage can.

The umpire cried, "Foul!"

They use the foulest language on that show.

Example: Do you get a <u>pickle</u> with your hamburger?

He's in a pretty pickle right now; he's thirty thousand dollars in debt to a loan shark.

She tried to pickle the tomatoes, but they just came out sour.

1. Her <u>form</u> in tennis is really good.

_____

_____

2. It is the last house on the <u>block</u>, and it is surrounded by a picket fence.

_____

_____

3. Just <u>flip</u> through the pages of that book to find the answer.

_____

_____

4. Can you <u>book</u> me a reservation for late fall?

_____

_____

5. Canada and the United States share a common <u>border</u>.

_____

_____

2.3 USING THE DICTIONARY

Directions: You will need to use a hardbound dictionary to answer the following questions; a paperback edition will not contain all the information asked for in this exercise.

1. What did the word *bicker* originally mean?

     _____

     _____

2. According to the dictionary, should the word *semipro* be used when writing a formal composition?

     _____

     _____

3. Write the diacritical marks for the word *harangue.*

     _____

     _____

4. The phrase *sub rosa* means "in secret." What is the history of the word? How did it come into the English language?

     _____

     _____

     _____

     _____

5. How many syllables are there in the word *sidereal?*

     _____

6. According to the dictionary, does the first syllable in *heinous* rhyme with the word *hay* or *hi?*

     _____

7. What part of speech is the word *crag?*

     _____

8. Is the word *submiss* still in use today?

    _____

9. Which syllable receives the accent in the word *cranny*?

    _____

10. What are some other forms of the word *lessen?*

    _____

2.4 BORROWED WORDS AND PHRASES

Directions: This exercise presents words borrowed exclusively from Latin and French. Although the words and phrases included in this list are seldom part of ordinary conversation, they do appear in scholarly writing or speech. If you learn them now, you will avoid being confused or puzzled when you encounter them in textbooks or hear them in lectures. Start by reviewing the list, then complete the sentences that follow.

Latin

1. *ad hoc*   Literally, "toward this"; refers to something devised or created for a particular situation or purpose.

2. *ad infinitum*   Literally, "to infinity"; suggests that someone or something will continue indefinitely.

3. *a posteriori*   Literally, "from the subsequent"; indicates that reasoning is based on experience, that one may argue from facts to general principles.

4. *a priori*   Literally, "from the previous causes"; indicates that reasoning is based on theories or general principles rather than on experience or factual knowledge.

5. *bona fide*   Literally, "in good faith"; means that something is genuine or authentic.

6. *in loco parentis* Literally, "in the place of a parent"; indicates that some group or institution substitutes for absent parents.

7. *in toto*   Literally, "in sum" or "as a whole"; indicates that something should be taken totally or altogether.

8. *prima facie*   Literally, "on first appearance"; refers to a first impression formed before any closer inspection.

9. *non sequitur*   Literally, "it does not follow"; points to an irrelevant or illogical conclusion or statement.

10. *quid pro quo*   Literally, "something for something"; indicates an equal exchange.

French

11. *carte blanche*   Literally, a "blank card"; signifies unrestricted power or unconditional authority.

12. *déjà vu*   Literally, "already seen"; refers to the experience of going through something that seems to have happened before.

13. *double-entendre* Literally, "double meaning"; indicates that a word or phrase has two meanings, one of which has sexual overtones.

14. *entrée*   Literally, "entrance"; can refer to the main course of a meal; can also indicate the right of entrance to a select group.

15. *idée fixe*   Literally, "fixed idea"; suggests that an idea has become an obsession.

16. *fin de siècle*   Literally, "end of the century"; refers to the end of the nineteenth century and suggests a climate of sophistication and boredom.

17. *noblesse oblige*   Literally, "nobility obligates"; signifies that responsible behavior is considered the obligation of all aristocrats.

18. *nom de plume*   Literally, "pen name"; means the same as "pseudonym."

19. *raison d'être*   Literally, "reason for being"; refers to the sole or essential reason for existence.

20. *vis-à-vis*   Literally, "face to face"; can indicate two things or persons that are opposite or corresponding; can also mean "in relation to."

Fill in the blanks with one of the Latin or French words introduced in the previous list.

1. I have such a feeling of _____; it is as if all this had happened to me before.

2. The _____ evidence suggests that he is guilty, but we won't know for sure until we can look more closely at all the facts.

3. They decided to form a(an) _____ committee to elect the president.

4. Even after almost a century, Vienna still has a certain _____ charm.

5. Since his wife's death that child is his _____.

6. George Eliot was the _____ of Marian Evans, the famous novelist.

7. _____ is the motto of my very proper and aristocratic uncle.

8. An aspiring young artist, she arrived in New York hoping for a(an) _____ into the most talented circles.

9. His original belief in the importance of regular exercise has become a(an) _____; even if he is tired or ill, he always spends at least two hours working out.

10. I am so bored after two hours; I really believe this lecture may continue _____.

11. I don't understand how that follows; to me what you say is a complete _____.

12. We want a straightforward _____ agreement; we will accept a cut in wages if management will increase our benefits.

13. I don't like that joke. It is a sly, unflattering _____.

14. Is he a(an) _____ member of that exclusive club?

15. To argue from past experience is to argue _____.

16. For years, schools tried to act _____, but at the present time they have just about given up; they could not give the same level of care provided in the home.

17. When I offered you the use of my home, I did not give it to you _____.

18. If that's what an individual membership costs, what will it cost if we take the group _____?

19. You will have to argue the existence of God _____.

20. _____ the Calvinist tradition in America, Ralph Waldo Emerson was clearly a rebel.

2.5 SOME ADDITIONAL INFORMATION ABOUT DICTIONARIES

Every dictionary entry tells you how to spell, pronounce, and define a word. However, many entries tell you even more than that. To make effective use of those entries, you need to familiarize yourself with the following labels.

Special Context Labels

Labels like *Music*, *Law*, *Chemistry*, and so on, tell you what a word means within a special context or field of study. Look up the word *base*, for example, and you're likely to find definitions that tell you what the word means within the context of baseball and architecture.

> *Baseball.* Any one of the four corners of an infield, marked by a bag or plate.
>
> *Architecture.* The lowest part of a structure, such as a wall.

Usage Notes

Some words are tricky to use. To express a comparison, for example, which is correct—*different from* or *different than*? The **usage note** in the *American Heritage Dictionary* explains that *different than* is considered incorrect by many people, even though some writers use it. If you want to be on the safe side, the *American Heritage* recommends *different from* as the better choice.

Makers of dictionaries generally know what words are likely to be misused. To help their readers avoid mistakes, they include usage notes that explain how to use a word correctly.

Warning Labels

Labels such as *Informal*, *Colloquial*,* *Substandard*, *Vulgar*, and *Slang* warn you to use certain words carefully. The words carrying these labels are generally not considered appropriate in a formal speech or paper.

Idioms

Some entries include *idioms*. Idioms usually don't make sense to non-native speakers. That's because the individual words in an idiom don't add up to an understandable message or to a message that can be taken seriously. For example, *Keep your chin up* is an idiom. But if someone says that to you, the person doesn't really expect you to lift your chin. He or she wants you to keep your spirits up.

Similarly, people talk about an experience making their *blood run cold*. Yet, blood doesn't run hot or cold. This is an idiom suggesting the experience was terrifying.

Obsolete and Archaic

The label *Obsolete* tells you a word is no longer in use. For example, the word *ward*, when it means "to imprison," is usually labeled *Obsolete*. Although the word might appear in one of Shakespeare's plays, it would no longer be appropriate to use it when you speak or write.

The label *Archaic* tells you a word or meaning was once quite common but is now rare. The word *anon*, for example, meaning "at once," is usually labeled *Archaic*.

---

* colloquial: language typical of conversation rather than writing.

2.6 IDIOMS

Note: Idioms are expressions that cannot be taken literally but nevertheless make sense. They often vary from language to language.

Directions: Here is a list of common English idioms. First, review the list and add any that you do not already know to your vocabulary file. Then, complete the sentences that follow the list. *Note:* Occasionally you may have to change the tense of a verb to make the phrase fit the blank.

1. *ivory tower:* To be isolated from life, not in touch with the real world.
   Sample sentence: By secluding herself, she lived in an *ivory tower* and didn't know what was really happening in the world.

2. *to raise Cain:* To cause trouble or make a fuss.
   Sample sentence: If he did not get the promotion, he was determined to *raise Cain.*

3. *to gild the lily:* To praise excessively or unnecessarily.
   Sample sentence: His agent insisted on *gilding the lily* and telling everyone how talented he was—as if two gold medals hadn't already made that clear to all concerned.

4. *to steal someone's thunder:* To get ahead of someone by doing what that person had planned to do before he or she could accomplish it.
   Sample sentence: I had intended to present a new plan for saving company time, but my assistant *stole my thunder* and presented it before me.

5. *to whitewash:* To hide faults or defects.
   Sample sentence: The press did not try *to whitewash* the corruption that was rampant in city hall.

6. *on tenterhooks:* In a state of high anxiety.
   Sample sentence: She was *on tenterhooks* waiting to know if she had been elected.

7. *on the bandwagon:* To join the group, follow the crowd.
   Sample sentence: He had a hard time thinking for himself; all too often he just jumped *on the bandwagon* and did what everybody else was doing.

8. *the writing on the wall:* An event or incident that makes quite clear what will happen in the future.
   Sample sentence: When all four of the other managers were let go, I could see *the writing on the wall.*

9. *bring down the house:* To do something that causes a lot of excitement and enthusiasm.
   Sample sentence: When Marilyn Monroe sang "Happy Birthday" to President Kennedy, her performance *brought down the house.*

10. *a white elephant:* Something no longer valuable.
    Sample sentence: People just do not buy that style of house anymore; it has become a real *white elephant.*

11. *in the doldrums:* Depressed, bored.
    Sample sentence: He's really been *in the doldrums* since his divorce.

12. *blow hot and cold:* To be indecisive, being very positive about something one minute and very negative the next.
    Sample sentence: She is still *blowing hot and cold* when she talks about running for class president.

13. *tilt at windmills:* To waste time in a hopeless task or venture.
     Sample sentence: They are circulating a petition to lower property taxes. I admire their effort, but they are just *tilting at windmills.*

14. *show one's hand:* To let others know your plans.
     Sample sentence: I think the governor has decided to run, but he still refuses to *show his hand.*

15. *turn thumbs down:* To signal rejection.
     Sample sentence: The employees wanted to strike, but union management *turned thumbs down* on the idea.

16. *take the bull by the horns:* To face a problem directly.
     Sample sentence: Eliot Ness decided to *take the bull by the horns* and go after Al Capone.

17. *the lion's share:* The largest amount.
     Sample sentence: Having planned the robbery, she demanded *the lion's share* of the loot.

18. *split hairs:* To make overly fine and fussy distinctions between words or ideas.
     Sample sentence: Do we have to *split hairs* about the meaning of this word?

19. *off the beaten track:* Unusual, not ordinary.
     Sample sentence: His projects are always *off the beaten track.* That's what makes them so interesting.

20. *rule with an iron hand:* Rule sternly, allowing no opposition.
     Sample sentence: The old Communist leadership still wanted to *rule with an iron hand,* but their day was past; the people would no longer tolerate it.

Directions: Fill in the blanks with the appropriate idiom.

1. She always liked to _____ by giving the punch line to my jokes.

2. They tried to _____ the governor's failures, but the panel continued to ask critical questions.

3. He was on _____ waiting for his blind date.

4. After Bill Clinton won votes by appearing on television talk shows, other candidates for public office _____ and did the same.

5. Author Nadine Gordimer has always refused to live in an _____ and pretend that apartheid was not a cruel and inhuman system.

6. When her child began withdrawing, losing weight, and staying out late, she knew she had to read the _____. Her child was in serious trouble.

7. The performer _____ with his imitation of Madonna.

8. With so much office space going unrented, I guarantee you that building will be a _____.

9. The president has been _____ about his chances for reelection. One minute he's sure he'll win; the next minute he's just as sure he won't.

10. Demanding political reform is not just _____; we can make a difference.

11. The press tried to get the mayor to admit she was going to resign, but she refused to _____.

12. Having been a top-ranking movie star for a decade, he was understandably _____ over his failing career.

13. The body builder had received so many compliments on her physique, even her agent did not want to _____ and tell her she looked good.

14. The vice-president did most of the work, but somehow the president always got the _____ of the credit.

15. The scholars at the meeting started _____ over the meaning of the opening sentence.

16. Business school bored her, so she decided to do something that was _____. She became a bee keeper.

17. When management decided to cut their hours, the men and women in the union decided it was time to _____ and threaten a strike.

18. The architect thought his design was first-rate, but the board of directors _____ on the project.

19. On a personal level, she was charming and generous. But on a professional one, she tended to _____.

20. At this point, the government needs to _____ and work out a plan for national health care.

2.7 VOCABULARY PRACTICE: SOME COMMONLY CONFUSED WORDS

Chapter 4 introduces the word *flouting,* along with a definition, "showing contempt for or disregarding." But there's something else you should know about this word. It is often confused with a similar-sounding word that has a very different meaning, *flaunting. Flaunting* refers to the act of showing off or exhibiting shamelessly, as in the sentence "She was fond of flaunting her newfound wealth." Unfortunately, because the words sound so much alike, they are often confused as they are in these two sentences: (a) "Flaunting all tradition, he arrived at the funeral wearing bright colors and a Mouseketeer hat." (2) "Flouting her newly acquired authority, the supervisor told her managers they would need to work late that night and refused to offer them an explanation."

To make sure you know the difference between the two words, fill in the following blanks with the words *flaunt* and *flout.*

1.   She wasn't about to _____ her good luck, particularly since her best friend was currently miserable, and she didn't want to make him feel worse.

2.   Always a rebel, he liked to _____ the coach's rules every chance he got.

Now write two sentences of your own, with each one illustrating the correct use of *flaunt* or *flout.*

  1.   _____

  2.   _____

There are many other words in the English language that sound alike but mean something altogether different. For example, look up the words *allusion* and *illusion.* Read the definitions for both. Then fill in the blanks.

a.   He was under the _____ that having a lot of money was the same as being happy.

b.   To show that she was well-informed about Cuban history, the young reporter made several _____ to people like José Marti and Tomas Estrada Palma.

Do the same for *discreet* and *discrete.* Then decide which word goes into which blank.

a.   The reporter made _____inquiries concerning rumors about the president's roving eye. She knew she had to be careful about whom she spoke to because she did not want to lose her access to the White House.

b.   The bees lived in _____communities, which could not be combined. If they were, there would be a battle to the death.

2.8 HANDOUT FOR CONSIDERING CLICHÉS

Clichés are overworked expressions that lack originality and thought. They are to be avoided, particularly in writing, because they suggest that an author hasn't really bothered to think deeply about his or her subject. Some synonyms for the word *cliché: bromide, platitude, truism,* and *commonplace.* All of these words refer to expressions or statements that have been made so often, they no longer excite or stir the mind to thought.

Here are two examples of clichés: "Exceptions prove the rule." "Don't judge a book by its cover." Can you come up with two more clichés?

1. _____

2. _____

2.9 ANALYZING ACRONYMS

The word NASA comes from combining the initials of the words *N*ational *A*eronautics and *S*pace *A*dministration. That word is a good example of an acronym. Sometimes acronyms are formed only from first initials, but they can also be created from word parts as in the word *radar,* which is derived from *ra*dio *de*tecting *a*nd *r*anging.

Find the meaning for each of the following acronyms by either looking in a desk dictionary or using a website like www.acronymfinder.com.

1. Laser _____

   _____

2. NATO _____

   _____

3. JPEG _____

   _____

4. SMS _____

2.10   UNDERSTANDING ALLUSIONS

Allusions are brief references to historical events or famous people, both real and fictional. The references are used as a verbal short cut that implies something about the topic under discussion. For an illustration, look carefully at the italicized allusion in the following sentence:

> Her friends and relatives were worried because her new beau seemed to have an almost *Svengali*-like effect on her normally independent spirit.

This sentence alludes to the fictional character Svengali, an evil hypnotist, who figures importantly in the novel *Trilby,* by George DuMaurier. Readers who recognize the allusion to Svengali immediately get the point of the sentence: The woman's new friend seems to be controlling her thoughts in unusual and unpleasant ways. Readers who don't recognize the allusion to Svengali will probably have a less clear idea of what the sentence means.

Allusions like the one illustrated above are powerful clues to meaning. Thus, it's in your interest to pay attention to them when they turn up. If you don't understand an allusion, don't ignore it. Instead, jot it down and look it up later on. Then go back and reread the passage in which it appeared.

Fortunately, most good desk dictionaries will give you definitions for famous literary, historical, or mythological figures. In addition, there are books like *Merriam-Webster's Dictionary of Allusions, The Dictionary of Global Culture,* and *The Dictionary of Cultural Literacy,* all of which offer brief definitions for common allusions. Most libraries will have at least one of these resources available, so there is no excuse for not building a solid store of allusions that will help you in your reading.

Read each passage and look at the explanation of the italicized allusion. Then circle the letter of the statement that best describes the point of the allusion.

1. The study group met for informal discussions of the course material. Most of the members wanted to keep the meetings simple and informal. But David acted as if he wanted the meetings run according to *Roberts Rules of Order.*

    > **Roberts Rules of Order** is a manual for procedures used in government. It was first produced in 1876 and offers very specific rules as to how members of a group must behave.

    The allusion implies that

    a. David is uncomfortable in groups and doesn't know how to behave. Therefore he needs rules to follow.

    b. David is trying to force the other members of the group to follow certain procedures for their meetings.

    c. David is not a U.S. citizen and he needed to understand how meetings were normally run.

2. In most areas of his life, Nelson was awkward, even clumsy, but as soon as he stepped on a basketball court, he became Nijinksy in sneakers.

    > **Nijinsky**(1890-1950) was a Russian ballet dancer and choreographer, famous for his perfect timing and technique.

    The allusion implies that

    a. Nelson became fluid and graceful when he played basketball, in contrast to how he behaved in the rest of his life.

b.   Nelson was even clumsier on a basketball court than he was in other parts of his life.

c.   Nelson liked to showboat when he was on the basketball court, playing to the crowd at every opportunity.

3.   As the president of the company entered the room, the vice-presidents looked nervously from one to the other. Everyone in the room was expecting the night of the long knives, and no one knew who would have an office the next day. The suspense and the fear had put everyone's nerves on edge.

> **The night of the long knives** originally referred to a massacre carried out by Adolf Hitler against the Brownshirts, a gang of thugs whose leader had begun to assume too much power. Close to a hundred people were killed on Hitler's orders.

The allusion implies that

a.   the vice-presidents were trying to wrest power from the president.

b.   the president knew that the vice presidents were lazy and incompetent.

c.   those sitting in the room were afraid they were all going to be fired

4.   My mother was a lively and energetic woman who was extraordinarily healthy for most of her life. Thus when others were sick, she was not exactly inclined to play the role of *Florence Nightingale*.

> **Florence Nightingale** (1820-1910) was an English nurse, who was the driving force behind some important medical reforms in a military hospital, where she worked as a nurse.

The allusion implies that

a.   the author's mother was more concerned about other people's health than she was about her own.

b.   the author's mother had always wanted to be a nurse in some branch of the military.

c.   the author's mother wasn't particularly sympathetic to other people's ill health.

2.11 BORROWING FROM THE FRENCH

The word *entrepreneur* (on-tra-pren-ur) is a French word that has found a home in English, and it's not alone. We have borrowed other words from the French, for example, the word *entourage*. The word refers to a person's attendants or associates and is mostly used to describe the people surrounding someone famous or important, as in this sentence: "To the reporter's surprise, the title-winning boxer arrived without her entourage."

Then there's the French phrase *déjà vu* (day-zhah voo), which literally means "already seen." It's used to describe the feeling that we have had an experience before and are going through it again. Here's an example of the phrase in context: "Although she had never before been in the old house, she had a strong sense of déjà vu."

You may also encounter the French phrase *coup de grâce* (koo day grahs). It translates "blow of mercy" and is used to describe an event that marks the end of a situation or experience. "For the young doctor, losing his right to practice the medicine of his choice was the coup de grace; he decided to leave the clinic and strike out on his own."

And you may already know the word *carte blanche* (kart blahnsh). Originally, the French used it to refer to a white card belonging to a person of great authority. Now, they, and we, use it to mean the power to take whatever action seems appropriate. "The failing company gave the consultant carte blanche when it came to hiring and firing."

Test your understanding by using these four words to fill the blanks below: *entrepreneur, déjà vu, coup de grâce,* and *carte blanche.*

1. He knew they had never met, but when she walked into the room, he had an eerie feeling of

    _____.

2. She liked to think of herself as an _____, but she lacked the nerve to strike out

    on her own and start her own business.

3. When the scientist arrived at the lab, he hoped they would give him _____

    over vaccine research since that was his specialty.

4. The press secretary had been willing to make excuses for the president, but the

    _____ came when he flatly told her to lie; at that point, she quit.

2.12 CONTEXT CLUES AND WORD ANALYSIS

Part A: Using Context

Directions: Each of the following sentences contains an italicized word you may not know. However, the context of the word should help you infer an approximate definition. Write that definition in the blank. Then identify the type of context clue that appears in the sentence by filling in the blank with one of these four letters: *E* (Example), *C* (Contrast), *R* (Restatement), and *G* (General Knowledge).

1. It's very *imprudent* to run up big credit card bills when you are not sure that you will have a job in six months.

    Definition: _____

    Context Clue: _____

2. The assassin had the kind of *nondescript* appearance that allowed her to blend easily into a crowd; because there was nothing individual or special about her, nobody ever remembered seeing her.

    Definition: _____

    Context Clue: _____

3. Early in his career, the faith healer had been a *charlatan,* but after he became a born-again Christian he changed his dishonest ways and never again made false claims about his ability to heal the sick.

    Definition: _____

    Context Clue: _____

4. One of the symptoms of the disease was a terrible *lassitude*; most of the time, she could barely find the strength to get out of bed.

    Definition: _____

    Context Clue: _____

5. There is very little scientific proof for the *efficacy* of herbal medicines, yet many consumers don't care that there isn't much scientific evidence for herbs' effectiveness. They just assume that herbs are a part of nature and must be beneficial.

    Definition: _____

    Context Clue: _____

6. With the passage of time, the protesters grew increasingly *strident* in their demands; the more time that went by, the louder and more aggressive they became.

    Definition: _____

    Context Clue: _____

7. When doctors began prescribing the drug called Zeitung, they assumed that it would, like all drugs, have some side effects, but no one ever expected the side effects to be as *deleterious* as they turned out to be. At least 1,000 people experienced side effects that ranged from nausea and vomiting to permanent hair loss and facial twitches.

   Definition: _____

   Context Clue: _____

8. Multiple births were once considered an *anomaly,* but nowadays, they are becoming more and more common.

   Definition: _____

   Context Clue: _____

9. Fashion magazines make readers think that being thin is the norm, but most of us are a good deal more *corpulent* than those magazines suggest.

   Definition: _____

   Context Clue: _____

10. The manager of the computer company hired his nephew, niece, and grandmother to fill all of the new openings. He doesn't seem to realize that *nepotism* is frowned upon in the business world.

    Definition: _____

    Context Clue: _____

Part B: Context Clues and Word Analysis

Directions: Each of the following sentences contains one of the roots or prefixes listed below. Each sentence also contains a context clue. Make use of both to determine the meanings of the italicized words.

> 1. Trans (Latin prefix) across, beyond
> 2. Vita (Latin root) life
> 3. Sequ (Latin root) follow, following
> 4. Sent, Sens (Latin root) feel
> 5. Ten, Tain (Latin root) hold, holding fast, extend
> 6. Pre (Latin prefix) before

11. In Shakespeare's play Julius Caesar, Caesar's wife has a *presentiment* about his death. She dreams that her husband is murdered. The next day, her dream becomes reality, and Caesar is assassinated.

    Definition: _____

12. As an actress, she wasn't all that good, but she had the kind of charm and *vitality* that make for stardom.

    Definition: _____

13. Great athletes are possessed of great talent, but just as important, they also possess spiritual *tenacity*. When the going gets rough, they dig a little deeper and refuse to give up.

   Definition: _____

14. Franklin Delano Roosevelt, the thirty-second president of the United States, faced his greatest personal crisis in 1921. When Roosevelt was stricken by polio, his friends and family urged him to abandon his plans for a political career. But he insisted that he could *transcend* his illness to be an effective statesman; he would not let it defeat him.

   Definition: _____

15. The first official attempt to *traverse* the Arctic began in 1881. The goal of the mission was to look for evidence of meteors. Three years after the group set out, seventeen of the original members were dead of cold and starvation. The remaining ones had to be rescued by boat.

   Definition: _____

16. On a series of undercover missions, the CIA tried to discover the degree of anti-government *sentiment*. Once the agency established the general feeling of the population, it would know whether or not the country was ready to explode as had been rumored.

   Definition: _____

17. From a scientific standpoint, his position is simply not *tenable*. One cannot just take his word for it that he has personally spoken to people from other planets. In the world of science, taking the position that "my word is good enough" is not defensible.

   Definition: _____

18. When the journalist first interviewed the congresswoman, she appeared to be a party hack who possessed absolutely no ideas of her own. But in their *subsequent* meetings, she seemed to come into her own. On several key issues, she differed from the party leadership and wasn't afraid to speak out.

   Definition: _____

19. The waiter couldn't believe it when the elderly gentleman *tendered* him a fifty-dollar bill to pay for the coke.

   Definition: _____

20. A mounting body of research makes it impossible to claim that animals lack all feeling. On the contrary, they are *sentient* beings who experience and express strong emotions.

   Definition:
   _____

CHAPTER 3

Connecting the General to the Specific in Reading and Writing

SUGGESTIONS FOR TEACHING CHAPTER 3

1. To start a discussion of *general* and *specific* words, you can ask students to explain what they think the two words mean. Usually there are two or three answers that reveal some knowledge of the terms. Use those answers as a starting point for the definitions in the text.

2. Many students have the misguided notion that all general statements or generalizations are bad, the result, perhaps, of comments on their compositions such as "too general," "be more specific," and "needs specific details." Emphasize that communication is most effective when the speaker or writer moves back and forth between general and specific levels of language.

3. Dialogues such as the following help illustrate what communication would be like if we always wrote or spoke on one level of specificity.

Dialogue 1

Marcia: So what was your day like today?

Paul: Well I got up at eight o'clock after not getting enough sleep and then I spilled coffee all over my new suit. Because I had to change my suit, I was late for work, and my boss said he is going to dock my pay. I was so mad at him I couldn't concentrate, and I didn't get my monthly report done.

Marcia: Wait a minute. I haven't got all the time in the world here. You mean you had a bad day. Right?

Dialogue 2

Mother: What's the matter with you?

Daughter: I'm not feeling well.

Mother: What's the matter? Are you sick? Is it your stomach? Your head?

Daughter: I just don't feel too great.

Mother: I don't understand. What's wrong?

SUPPLEMENTARY MATERIALS

3.1   GENERAL AND SPECIFIC WORDS

You'll soon be working with general and specific sentences, but let's begin with general and specific words. Once you learn to distinguish, or see the difference, between general and specific words, it's easy to identify general and specific sentences.

Here are two lists of words, one labeled *general,* the other *specific.* As you read each list, think about these two questions: How do the words in each list differ? What makes one word general and another word specific?

General	Specific
creatures	dogs
silver	nickels
expression	smile
object	statue
liquid	ink
flower	daisy
machine	computer

Did you notice that the words on the left can be interpreted, or understood, in a variety of ways? The word *creature,* for example, is broad enough to include everything from cows to children. The word *dogs,* however, quickly eliminates both the cows *and* the children. We are now talking about a specific type of creature—one that barks, has four legs, and wags its tail.

Similarly, the word *silver* can refer to table settings or to money. The word *nickels,* however, quickly eliminates all other possibilities. It refers to coins rather than forks.

With these illustrations in mind, we can sum up the differences between general and specific words. **General words** are broad in scope. They refer to or include a wide variety of different things and thus can be understood in several ways. **Specific words,** in contrast, are much narrower in focus. They cover less territory and can't be understood in so many different ways. General words expand meaning; specific words narrow or focus it. To make ourselves understood, we need both kinds of words. We need general words to sum up our experiences and specific words to explain or clarify them.

Let's look at two more pairs of words. This time, it's up to you to label them. Write a *G* next to the general word. Write an *S* next to the more specific one.

sound _____   scream _____

dance _____   movement _____

Did you put a *G* next to *sound* and an *S* next to *scream*? If you did, you're on the right track. The word *sound* covers everything from a meow to a giggle. Thus it's the more general of the two.

If you put an *S* next to the word *dance* and a *G* next to the word *movement,* you again labeled the words correctly. The word *movement* refers to many activities, from playing baseball to doing a tango. The word *dance,* however, eliminates playing baseball along with a host of other possibilities, such as kicking a football or waving good-bye.

3.2   GENERAL AND SPECIFIC WORDS

Directions: After each word, list at least three more specific words that could be included under that heading.

Example:

communication

Speech
Signs
Television

Explanation: Because all three words refer to a specific type of communication, we can include all three under the more general heading.

1. feelings

    _____

    _____

    _____

2. music

    _____

    _____

    _____

3. machinery

    _____

    _____

    _____

4. illness

    _____

    _____

    _____

5. fruit

    _____

    _____

    _____

3.3 GENERAL AND SPECIFIC WORDS

Directions: For each group of words, write one word or phrase *general enough* to include all the words on the list.

Example:

academic subjects
_____

American history
English composition
sociology
algebra

Explanation: In this case, all four items can be included under the heading *academic subjects.*

1. _____

   The Scarlet Letter
   Harry Potter and the Goblet of Fire
   The Road
   The Last Symbol

2. _____

   maple
   oak
   dogwood
   pine

3. _____

   monitor
   mouse
   modem
   keyboard

4. _____

   Spongebob Square Pants
   Superman
   Bart Simpson
   Batman

5. _____

   Salon.com
   Slate.com
   AskMen.com
   Cha: An Asian Literary Journal

3.4   LEVELS OF SPECIFICITY

Directions: Fill in the accompanying diagrams with the appropriate letters. The letter of the most general word goes on top. The letter of the most specific word goes on the bottom.

Example:

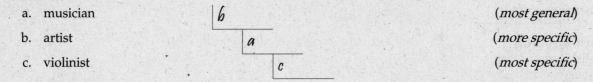

a. musician   (*most general*)

b. artist   (*more specific*)

c. violinist   (*most specific*)

Explanation: The word *artist* can refer to many different kinds of people, for example, painters, sculptors, or writers. It is the most general word and therefore goes on the top level. *Musician* is somewhat more specific than *artist*. It excludes all people who are not concerned with music. Therefore, it goes on the middle rung. *Violinist* is the most specific word because it refers only to people who play the violin.

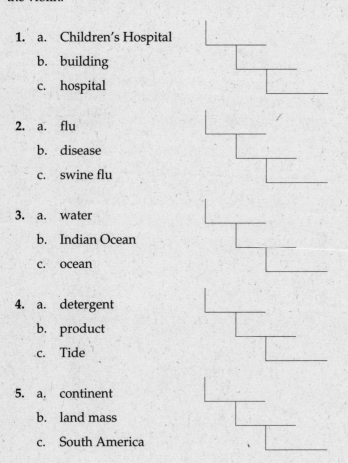

1. a. Children's Hospital

    b. building

    c. hospital

2. a. flu

    b. disease

    c. swine flu

3. a. water

    b. Indian Ocean

    c. ocean

4. a. detergent

    b. product

    c. Tide

5. a. continent

    b. land mass

    c. South America

3.5 LEVELS OF SPECIFICITY

Directions: In each group of four words, write an *S* after the two words or phrases that are on the same level of specificity.

Example:

church _____

building _____

St. Peter's in Rome ___*S*___

St. Mark's in Venice ___*S*___

Explanation: Building is more general than *church,* but the names of the churches are equally specific.

1. object _____

   knife _____

   weapon _____

   gun _____

2. clothing _____

   dress _____

   coat _____

   wedding dress _____

3. product _____

   soap _____

   Ivory _____

   Dove _____

4. machine _____

   automobile _____

   Ford _____

   motorcycle _____

5. insect _____

   butterfly _____

   animal _____

   bumblebee _____

> **Reminder:** Words can be considered general or specific only if they are placed in the context of other words.

3.6 FROM GENERAL TO SPECIFIC

Directions: Arrange the words on each of the rungs so that the most general word goes on the top level and the most specific word goes on the bottom.

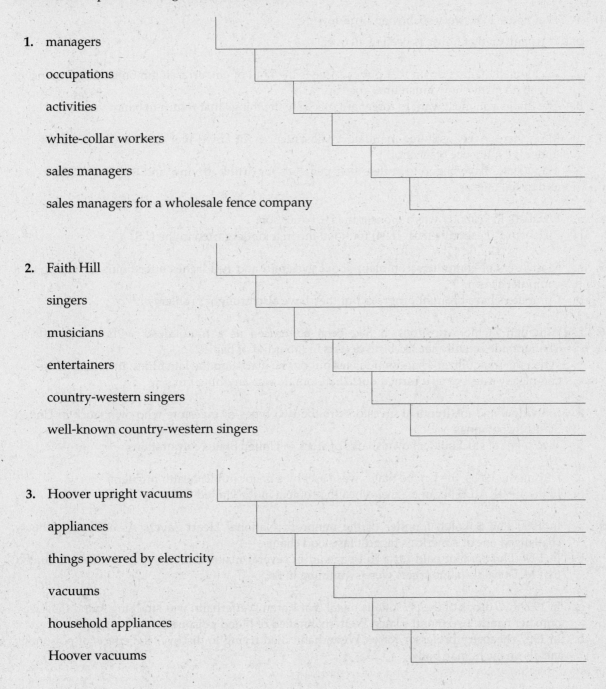

1. managers

    occupations

    activities

    white-collar workers

    sales managers

    sales managers for a wholesale fence company

2. Faith Hill

    singers

    musicians

    entertainers

    country-western singers

    well-known country-western singers

3. Hoover upright vacuums

    appliances

    things powered by electricity

    vacuums

    household appliances

    Hoover vacuums

3.7   GENERAL AND SPECIFIC SENTENCES

Directions: Circle the letter of the more specific sentence.

1. a.   That house looks very shabby and rundown.

    b.   The paint on that house is peeling all over.

2. a.   Accidentally falling down in a public place is the kind of embarrassing moment that you never forget, no matter how much time goes by.

    b.   The things you most want to forget are precisely the things that return to haunt you.

3. a.   Many states have instituted mandatory jail sentences for any driver convicted of driving while under the influence of alcohol.

    b.   Many states have begun to stiffen their penalties for drunk driving, and they no longer treat it as a trivial offense.

4. a.   Elizabeth P. Peabody was a pioneer in U.S. education.

    b.   Elizabeth P. Peabody (1804–1894) founded the first kindergarten in the U.S.

5. a.   Most users of computers complain about eyestrain and headaches after hours of staring at a computer screen.

    b.   Computers have brought progress, but they have also brought problems.

6. a.   Although in the late fifties, it had been advertised as a tranquilizer without side effects, Thalidomide actually caused birth defects in thousand of babies.

    b.   When the tranquilizer Thalidomide was put on the market in the late fifties, it was advertised as completely safe, but as it turned out, Thalidomide was anything but safe.

7. a.   Individual and institutional investors are the two types of investors who own stock in United States corporations.

    b.   Two types of stockholders own shares of stock in United States corporations.

8. a.   During the 1980s, the United States was beset by a major public health problem.

    b.   In the 1980s, AIDS became a major health problem in the United States.

9. a.   In 1990 Phil Sokolof, founder of the nonprofit National Heart Savers Association, publicly challenged one of America's biggest fast-food chains.

    b.   In 1990 Phil Sokolof paid for a full-page ad in several major U.S. newspapers; the ad claimed that McDonald's hamburgers were swimming in fat.

10. a.   In 1997 two drops of the poisonous metal that Karen Wetterhahn was studying found their way onto her hands; two months later, Wetterhahn died of blood poisoning.

     b.   In 1997 chemistry professor Karen Wetterhahn died trying to discover the effects of poisonous metals on the human body.

3.8 GENERAL AND SPECIFIC SENTENCES

Directions: Arrange the sentences on the rung so that the most general sentence is on the top and the most specific on the bottom.

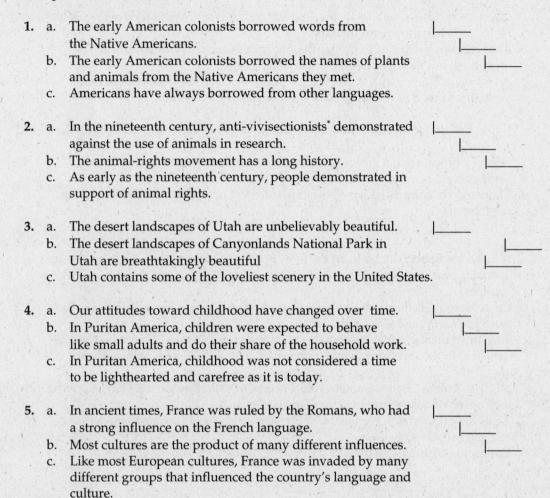

1. a. The early American colonists borrowed words from the Native Americans.
   b. The early American colonists borrowed the names of plants and animals from the Native Americans they met.
   c. Americans have always borrowed from other languages.

2. a. In the nineteenth century, anti-vivisectionists* demonstrated against the use of animals in research.
   b. The animal-rights movement has a long history.
   c. As early as the nineteenth century, people demonstrated in support of animal rights.

3. a. The desert landscapes of Utah are unbelievably beautiful.
   b. The desert landscapes of Canyonlands National Park in Utah are breathtakingly beautiful
   c. Utah contains some of the loveliest scenery in the United States.

4. a. Our attitudes toward childhood have changed over time.
   b. In Puritan America, children were expected to behave like small adults and do their share of the household work.
   c. In Puritan America, childhood was not considered a time to be lighthearted and carefree as it is today.

5. a. In ancient times, France was ruled by the Romans, who had a strong influence on the French language.
   b. Most cultures are the product of many different influences.
   c. Like most European cultures, France was invaded by many different groups that influenced the country's language and culture.

---

*anti-vivisectionists: people opposed to the cutting up of live animals for scientific research.

3.9   GENERAL AND SPECIFIC SENTENCES

Directions: Read the specific sentences. Then look at the general sentences that follow. Put a check next to the general sentence they are likely to support.

Specific **1.**
Sentences

a. If you're curious about the future, one site on the World Wide Web offers visitors a free tarot card* reading.
b. The Ragu spaghetti sauce company sponsors a website overflowing with free recipes, plus a basic course in the Italian language.
c. An Oakland University website lets Internet users transfer hundreds of useful programs to their home computers without spending a penny.

General _____
Sentences

1. Computer users can find a wealth of free information and services on the World Wide Web.
_____ 2. Surveys indicate that a growing number of American families own a home computer.
_____ 3. Thousands of companies have been trying to find new ways to make money on the Internet.

Specific **2.**
Sentences

a. When actor Robert Coates liked the lines in one of Shakespeare's death scenes, he would repeat the scene over and over until angry theatergoers pelted him with oranges.
b. Coates forgot his lines every night, so he made up his own for well-known plays such as *Hamlet* and *King Lear*.
c. England's theater critics laughingly called the actor "Romeo" Coates because he would stop the show to wave to friends and chat with people in the audience.

General _____
Sentences

1. Robert Coates, a nineteenth-century stage performer, may have been the most incompetent Shakespearean actor who ever lived.
_____ 2. Actor Robert Coates played many of Shakespeare's most famous characters during the early 1800s.
_____ 3. Handsome costumes mattered very much to British actor Robert Coates.

Specific **3.**
Sentences

a. A blue fireball exploded above central Siberia when an asteroid hit near the Tunguska River on June 30, 1908.
b. A mushroom cloud bloomed in the air, and trees were uprooted and scorched for dozens of miles.
c. An entire herd of reindeer died because of the heat the asteroid produced, while its impact shattered windows as far away as 600 miles.

---

* tarot card: a card used in fortune telling.

General ____   1. Scientists believe that asteroids are ancient chunks of matter that never clumped
Sentences   together to become planets.

____   2. Most asteroids are grouped into belts that hang in space.

____   3. When an asteroid crashed to Earth in 1908, it caused great damage.

Specific **4.**   a. In sign language, we use hands and other body parts to make gestures that stand
Sentences   for letters, words, and concepts.

b. Morse code requires a wire telegraph machine to produce sounds—dots and
dashes—that are translated into letters, numbers, and punctuation.

c. Often seen at airports, the semaphore, or flag signaling system, works this way:
A person stands holding a flag in each hand, then moves his or her arms to
positions that indicate letters and numbers.

General _____   1. Mass communication means that passages are sent to large audiences.
Sentences

____   2. Some communication methods do not rely on written language.

____   3. Simple writing systems date back to the Sumerians of 3000 B.C.

Specific **5.**   a. Using the milk from 6,000 cows, a 13,440-pound cheese was produced for an
Sentences   exhibit at the 1937 New York State Fair.

b. In 1801, a Massachusetts preacher, John Leland, presented President Andrew
Jackson with a 1,200-pound Cheshire cheese made in Leland's hometown.

c. The Wisconsin Cheese Foundation collected 180 tons of milk for its display in the
1964 World's Fair: a cheese wedge that weighed more than 34,500 pounds and
stood six feet high.

General _____   1. Ancient Romans who created huge cheeses were considered quite eccentric.
Sentences

____   2. Canadians proudly show their skill at cheese making during the annual Toronto
Fair.

____   3. Over the years, cheese-loving Americans have produced some pretty big cheeses.

3.10   GENERAL AND SPECIFIC SENTENCES

Directions: Read each pair of sentences. Then mark the general sentence with a *G* and the more specific one with an *S.*

1. a.   In wintertime, the body temperature of a woodchuck undergoes a steep drop of many degrees. _____
    b.   In wintertime, the body temperature of a woodchuck drops from 90°F to around 40°F. _____

2. a.   The fats found in fish, nuts, and vegetables may actually help protect you from heart disease. _____
    b.   Not all fats are bad; in fact, some may be good for you. _____

3. a.   The temperature of Antarctica is changing; it is not as cold as it used to be. _____
    b.   Current Antarctic temperatures are nine degrees higher than they were fifty years ago. _____

4. a.   Heart disease is the leading cause of death in the United States. _____
    b.   Heart disease is a killer. _____

5. a.   Many records claim that baseball was first played in 1846, but there is evidence suggesting that the game is older than that. _____
    b.   In her 1818 novel *Northanger Abbey*, author Jane Austen refers to a game called baseball, suggesting that the game was played before 1846.

3.11   GENERAL AND SPECIFIC SENTENCES

Directions: Read each general sentence. Then circle the letters of the specific sentences that help explain the general one.

General Sentence **1.** Followers of the Hindu religion divide almost everything in life into numbered categories, or groups.

Specific Sentences

a. More than 80 percent of India's approximately 1 billion residents practice the Hindu faith.

b. Hindus classify sacred writings as belonging to one of four *Vedas*, or collections of hymns, prayers, beliefs, and tales.

c. Hindus believe people have three basic qualities, or *gunas*, that should be kept in balance: goodness, passion, and darkness.

d. According to Hindu lore, energy flows through the body in a pattern that looks like a lotus blossom or spinning wheel.

e. In the Hindu belief system, society is divided into four classes, or castes; they are philosopher-scholars, ruler-politicians, merchant-farmers, and servant-workers.

f. The geography of India is considered holy by Hindus, especially a sacred river, the Ganges, that is said to wash away the sins of anyone who bathes in it.

General Sentence **2.** In the last decade, Americans have displayed a growing interest in haiku, a type of Japanese poetry that must be composed using only three lines and seventeen syllables.

Specific Sentences

a. From 1990 to 1997, the Haiku Society of America grew from a small club to a national group with ten regional leaders.

b. In Japan, haikus are printed on tea cans that are sold in public vending machines.

c. Ancient haikus often celebrated the beauties of nature, but today's haikus might focus on movies, cartoon characters, junk food, or rock bands.

d. When a U.S. newspaper, the *Christian Science Monitor*, sponsored a haiku contest in 1996, editors received 30,000 entries—three times as many as they got in 1986.

e. The World Wide Web hosts hundreds of haiku sites designed by residents of all fifty states, and the number of haikus on Internet bulletin boards increases every year.

f. Haiku fans in Europe throw parties where guests read their poems aloud and compete to write the best haiku in five or ten minutes.

General Sentence **3.** Several famous cities in ancient Greece were reserved for specific purposes.

Specific Sentences

a. The city of Delphi held an important temple where priestesses were said to receive messages from the gods.

b. History records that many rival battles took place near Greek islands.

c. Enthusiastic crowds flocked to Olympia, which was set aside for athletic games and physical contests.

d. Rulers organized Greece into city-states, large areas that were dominated and run by towns at their centers.

e. The teachings of the philosophers Socrates, Plato, and Aristotle influenced Greek citizens no matter where they lived.

f. The ancient city of Corinth earned fame as a busy trading center that linked Greece with the eastern and western worlds.

General   **4.** Because many Americans are fascinated by the idea of life on other planets, Roswell,

Sentence   New Mexico, has become a popular tourist town.

Specific
Sentences

a. Visitors spend $5 million in Roswell each year, hoping to find proof that a flying saucer landed in the desert in 1947 and was hidden by the U.S. Air Force.

b. From 1991 to 1996, more than 100,000 people traveled to Roswell for a glimpse of its UFO* Museum & Research Center.

c. Roswell's annual UFO Festival now draws about 150,000 people; the six-day event includes lectures, concerts, bus tours, banquets, a "spaceship derby," and a costume ball.

d. A book by Kal Korff, *The Roswell UFO Crash*, contends that the damaged spacecraft was actually a classified military balloon intended to track Soviet nuclear tests.

e. When Walker Air Force Base closed in 1967, many of Roswell's 48,000 residents lost their jobs and the town was deprived of its main source of income.

f. Most people who claim to have seen beings from outer space describe the creatures as small, with large heads, gray-green skin, and almond-shaped eyes.

General
Sentence

5. When it comes to public celebrations, the people of Brazil's Rio de Janeiro have no match, and the Carnival that explodes in Rio just before the nation settles down to Lent* has all the music, color, and excitement anyone could ask for.

Specific
Sentences

a. In Cologne, Germany, everyone dresses up for Carnival and heads for the street, anxious to meet friends and neighbors, most of whom will be wearing masks.

b. Ash Wednesday officially brings an end to the Carnival season.

c. In Rio de Janeiro, Carnival officially begins when the mayor hands the keys to the city over to the King of Carnival, who demands only that his subjects eat, drink, and be merry.

d. During Carnival, samba* dancers dressed in fabulous costumes compete for prizes I in the Sambadrome, a 700-yard avenue that is blocked off so the dancers will not be interrupted by traffic.

e. Although Carnival parades throughout the city draw people out of their local neighborhoods, when residents return they can count on finding numerous street parties still underway.

f. The official King of Carnival is often so heavy he can barely move; the King of Carnival in the year 2000 weighed in at 385 pounds.

---

* UFO: unidentified flying object.

* Lent: the forty days from Ash Wednesday until Easter, observed by Christians as a time to fast and repent.

* samba: a Brazilian ballroom dance of African origin.

CHAPTER 4
From Topics to Topic Sentences

SUGGESTIONS FOR TEACHING CHAPTER 4

1. To help students see the difference between the topic and main idea, ask them to imagine they have overheard a conversation in which their name came up repeatedly, but when they asked a friend what the conversation was about, he replied simply, "you." Would they be satisfied with just the topic? Or would they want to know the main idea?

2. Identifying the topic by asking students to track chains of repetition and reference in a paragraph is new to this edition, and I believe this is a concept worth spending time on. In addition to the sample paragraphs introduced in the chapter, take some of the paragraphs in the exercises and ask students to underline all references to the topic they have chosen as an answer. They will be surprised at the many different ways authors thread references to a topic through a paragraph.

3. When students have to identify topic sentences, everything they have learned about general and specific sentences comes into play. Since a topic sentence is more general than most of the sentences in the paragraph—introductory sentences can be as general or more general—students cannot identify a topic sentence without being able to distinguish between general and specific sentences. I emphasize this point because students need to realize that they are building on skills previously learned and need not be intimidated by the new terminology.

4. Spend some time helping students distinguish between the *topic sentence* and the *main idea.* It helps to describe the topic sentence as the author's way of "languaging" a thought in order to communicate that thought to others. Also tell students that the main idea is the *message* to be communicated, whereas the topic sentence is the *means* of communication.

5. If students are still struggling with the distinction between these two terms, tell them anyone can paraphrase the main idea, but only the author can write the topic sentence.

6. Paraphrasing is an excellent way to monitor, or check, comprehension. Tie this idea to a point made in Chapter 1, where students are told to recall after reading. Stress that paraphrasing after reading fulfills two objectives: (1) It helps readers recognize gaps in their understanding and (2) aids remembering. Paraphrasing after reading is a good way of reviewing what's just been read and giving long-term memory a chance to store the new information.

SUPPLEMENTARY MATERIALS

4.1 IDENTIFYING TOPICS

Directions: Identify the topic for each paragraph by circling the letter of the correct answer.

1. High credit card balances could be costing you hundreds of dollars in interest payments each year. To pay off your credit card debts and save yourself money, create and then stick to a strict payment plan. The first step in paying off your debts involves making a firm resolution to do so. Make a promise to rid yourself of the extra expense of owing creditors. As part of this resolution, avoid adding more changes; you may need to destroy your credit cards in order to resist the temptation to use them again. Second, if you have several credit card debts, you may want to consider consolidating them. If possible, use a card with the lowest interest rate to pay off the others, or obtain a lower-interest personal bank loan to pay off all of your cards and to reduce your overall interest rate. Third, always pay more than the minimum balance required by each creditor. This will allow you to pay off the cards more quickly and save more money. Once you pay off all of your debts, save credit cards for emergencies only. Plan to save money to purchase items rather than obtain them on credit.

   a. getting rid of debt
   b. getting rid of credit card debt
   c. credit cards

2. It is strange to think that tobacco, one of the most deadly and addictive drugs known to man, is legally grown and consumed in countries around the globe. Tobacco, smoked in the form of cigarettes or cigars or in pipes, contains the drug nicotine. Nicotine, in addition to being highly addictive, is a poison. It has been estimated that the amount of nicotine present in one pack of cigarettes would kill a nonsmoker if directly injected into his or her bloodstream. In addition to nicotine, tobacco contains many other chemical compounds, called *carcinogens,* which can cause cancer not only in smokers but also in anyone who happens to breathe smoke exhaled by the smoker. Although it is still legal, many restrictions on smoking are being implemented in some countries.

   a. carcinogens
   b. the dangers of tobacco
   c. restrictions on smoking

3. One of the most common mental disorders is a disease known as Alzheimer's. It is found almost exclusively in people over the age of sixty. Characterized initially by a gradual loss of memory and other cognitive functions, Alzheimer's can, in time, rob its victim of both speech and thought. Death comes eventually, usually after the victim has become bedridden and has lost most motor functions. Although there is no known cure, drugs can slow the onset of its symptoms. The only definitive test for the disease has to be done via autopsy.

   a. Alzheimer's disease
   b. drugs for the treatment of Alzheimer's
   c. old age

4. Federal income tax rates are arranged into ascending amounts based on amount of income. In the year 2000, each taxpayer fit into one of five different tax brackets: 15 percent, 28 percent, 31 percent, 36 percent, and 39.6 percent. Some politicians, though, would like to alter the tax structure by reducing the five brackets to four. They suggest the four rates of 10 percent, 15 percent, 25 percent, and 33 percent. Those who favor this new rate structure say that it would not only reduce the amount of taxes owed by all Americans, but it would also allow people with the lowest incomes to keep more of their earnings. Those who oppose the change, however, argue that the new plan would mostly benefit the wealthy and affect middle-income taxpayers very little. Also, some fear that a reduction in the government's tax income could create another national budget deficit. Other

members of Congress have put forth the notion that there should be a flat tax system introduced with every American paying 20 percent of his or her income to the federal government. Supporters of the flat tax claim it's unfair for those who have worked hard and amassed wealth to be taxed more than those who earn less. Critics point out, however, that many people in the highest income brackets have inherited rather than earned their wealth. They also point out that a flat tax would make the tax burden highly unequal. For someone earning $20,000 a year, four thousand dollars is a big bite out of their yearly income. In contrast, someone who earns $200,000 dollars a year is less likely to feel strapped for cash after paying out $20,000 in income tax.

a.   taxing the wealthy
b.   taxes
c.   income tax rates

4.2 IDENTIFYING TOPICS

Directions: Read each paragraph. Then circle the appropriate letter to identify the topic.

1. If you want to lose weight, the most difficult—and most important—step will be starting your new diet and exercise routine. However, you shouldn't overwhelm yourself by focusing on the total amount of weight you want to lose. Instead, set a smaller, more achievable goal of losing 10 percent of your current weight. When you successfully accomplish that first step, you can then set another goal to work toward. To lose that first 10 percent, you'll need to reduce your portion sizes and exercise regularly. You don't have to give up your favorite foods; instead, eat them in smaller quantities, and eat more slowly to enjoy every bite. If you do succumb to the temptation to overeat, don't give up on yourself. Accept the fact that you'll make mistakes, and resolve to resume your diet. Ease into a daily exercise routine by starting slowly and gradually increasing the duration and intensity of your activity. Finally, remember that it will take a while to form new eating and exercise habits. Give yourself time to adjust, and celebrate each time the scale tells you that you've lost a pound. According to Weight Watchers, following these strategies will help you lose weight and keep it off.

    Topic
    a. overeating
    b. the value of exercise
    c. dieting strategies

2. Scientific analysis of a huge, ten-mile wide crater in Mexico indicates that an asteroid six miles wide slammed into the earth sixty-five million years ago. This collision, which caused an explosion with the force and destruction of a nuclear bomb, created a cloud of dust and debris that enshrouded the planet, blocking the sunlight for at least several months and reducing worldwide temperatures to about fourteen degrees Fahrenheit. This cold darkness killed the plant life, the food source for many animals, and created a chain reaction of death among all living organisms. This is the popular, dominant theory about what caused the extinction of dinosaurs.

    Topic
    a. scientific analysis
    b. theory of dinosaur extinction
    c. scientific analysis of asteroids

3. The Halloween holiday originated thousands of years ago in Celtic Britain and France. Every year, the Celts celebrated their New Year on November 1 with the festival of Samhain, the Lord of the Dead, to end the harvest and to acknowledge the beginning of winter. The Celts believed that Samhain called together all dead people on October 31 and that it was possible for the living and the dead to communicate during this turning point in the seasons. During the first century, the Romans invaded Celtic Britain. They, too, celebrated with a festival around the first of November, a holiday known as Pomona Day in honor of their goddess of gardens and the harvest. Eventually, the Celtic and Roman festivals merged into one holiday. By the ninth century, Christianity had spread throughout Britain and Europe, and the Roman Catholic Church declared November 1 a church holiday to honor the saints. This holiday was known as All Hallows. However, people continued to celebrate the old festivals, too, and the October 31 celebration became known as All Hallow Even. That ancient practice, now called Halloween, came to America with Irish immigrants whose customs included remnants of Celtic observances.

    Topic
    a. history of Halloween
    b. the Celts
    c. the Roman invasion of Britain

4. The word *opera* comes from the Italian *opera in musica* (work in music), and it may be defined as a drama, either tragic or comic, sung throughout and presented on stage with scenery and action. The emphasis is on the solo voice, and, like the oratorio, which borrowed the forms from opera, it employs arias [melodic solos] and recitatives [musical forms without melody]. Because opera, of all the musical or dramatic forms, is the most difficult and expensive to produce, it has always been associated with the upper strata of social life. Often, the satisfaction of being able to support an operatic production—that is, sponsor a big, ostentatious display—has been compensation enough for a great many noble and wealthy patrons. Likewise, to be able to understand and appreciate this art form has been, and still is, a prestige symbol with the general public. (Mary Ann Frese Witt et al., *The Humanities,* Volume Two. Boston: Houghton Mifflin, 1997, p. 275.)

Topic
a. definition of opera
b. music
c. Italian opera

5. One simple but powerful mnemonic, or memory strategy, is called the *method of loci* (pronounced "low-sigh"), or the method of places. To use this method, first think about a set of familiar locations—your home, for example. You might imagine walking through the front door, around all four corners of the living room, and through each of the other rooms. Next, imagine each item to be remembered in one of these locations. Whenever you want to remember a list, use the same locations, in the same order. Vivid images of interactions or relationships seem to be particularly effective. For example, tomatoes smashed against the front door or bananas hanging from the bedroom ceiling might be helpful in recalling these items on a grocery list. (Douglas A. Bernstein et al., *Psychology*. Boston: Houghton Mifflin, 1997, p. 259.)

Topic
a. the power of memory
b. mnemonics
c. the *method of loci*

4.3 IDENTIFYING TOPICS AND TOPIC SENTENCES

Directions: Read each paragraph. Circle the appropriate letter to identify the correct topic. Then write the number of the topic sentence in the blank.

1. ^{1}When antibiotics arrived in the 1940s, they were hailed as wonder drugs, capable of curing bacterial-caused diseases like tuberculosis and pneumonia, which had previously posed deadly threats. ^{2}Currently, though, antibiotics, while still essential to curing many diseases, are viewed with a good deal more anxiety and doctors are worried that antibiotics are losing some of their healing power. ^{3}Bacteria can mutate, or change, over time. ^{4}Unfortunately, some bacteria have undergone mutation and adapted to the antibiotics that once destroyed them. ^{5}The presence of antibacterial agents in soap and antibiotics in animal feed haven't helped the situation. ^{6}Bacteria that survive an onslaught of antibiotics breed and pass on their immunity to their offspring. ^{7}As a result, there are some serious super-bacteria roaming the world, and they are much less vulnerable to existing antibiotics. ^{8}Vancomycin, for instance, was once a magic bullet in the war on staph infections. ^{9}But since 1996, a number of untreatable staph cases have been reported as resistant to Vancomycin treatment. ^{10}The hope was that the injectable antibiotic Synercid would step into the breach and kill Vancomycin-resistant bacteria. ^{11}Unfortunately, Synercid has serious side effects. ^{12}More importantly, though, there are already signs that some bacteria can stand up to even this potent antibiotic.

   Topic
   a. overuse of antibiotics
   b. antibiotics
   c. new diseases

   Topic Sentence _____

2. ^{1}Prior to the 1970s, the environmental movement in the United States received relatively little attention or publicity. ^{2}But for many people, the environmentalists became a force to be taken seriously on April 22, 1970—the first Earth Day ever celebrated in the United States. ^{3}On that day, to the surprise of many, 20 million Americans gathered together to celebrate nature and protest environmental pollution. ^{4}The first Earth Day also drew attention to the public's desire for environmental legislation, which helped bring about the Federal Water Pollution Control Act (1972), the Endangered Species Act (1973), and several amendments to the Clean Air Act (1977). ^{5}Perhaps most importantly, Earth Day made lawmakers and politicians realize they had to take preservation of the environment seriously, because failure to do so would anger a large bloc of voters.

   Topic
   a. the first Earth Day
   b. the Clean Water and Clear Air acts
   c. the environmental movement

   Topic Sentence _____

3. ^{1}Do you think that buying a new car will make you happy? ^{2}Are you convinced that marrying your current sweetheart will bring you all the happiness any one person could desire? ^{3}Well, according to Daniel Gilbert, a psychology professor at Harvard, whatever your prediction, it's probably wrong. ^{4}Gilbert, along with psychologist Tim Wilson of the University of Virginia and economist George Lowenstein of Carnegie Mellon University, has studied what's called "affective forecasting"—predicting how one will feel or behave if an event does or does not occur—and the

results are pretty clear: People aren't very good at predicting how future events will affect them. [5]According to Gilbert, Lowenstein, and Wilson, their studies, conducted over several years, show that most of us consistently under- or overestimate the depth and intensity of our emotional reactions. [6]In other words, the things we think will overwhelm us with joy often don't. [7]By the same token, the things we assume will devastate us often faze us far less than we imagined.

Topic
a.   happiness
b.   predictions about effects of future events
c.   studies by Tim Wilson, George Lowenstein, and Daniel Gilbert

Topic Sentence _____

4.   [1]These days, we take spices such as cinnamon, nutmeg, and pepper for granted. [2]To obtain them, we need only head to the nearest supermarket. [3]In the fifteenth century, however, spices were a much sought-after treasure, bringing wealth and power to whoever could obtain them. [4]Thus, in 1497, King Manuel I of Portugal ordered the young navigator Vasco d Gama to find the shortest route between India and Europe. [5]With India a source of every possible spice from ginger to arrowroot, King Manual knew he could feed the European appetite for spices and make a fortune in the process if da Gama accomplished his task. [6]Da Gama did find the shortest route between India and Europe, and, for a while at least, Portugal cornered the market on spices and became a world power.

Topic
a.   Vasco da Gama's accomplishment
b.   King Manuel I of Portugal
c.   spices in the fifteenth century

Topic Sentence _____

5.   [1]Over the years, those tricky computer geniuses, called "hackers," have pulled off some astounding crimes. [2]They have targeted phone companies and computer systems storing   credit card numbers and other valuable information. [3]In 1979, one of the most notorious hackers, Kevin D. Mitnick,[†] stole software valued at $1 million from the Digital Equipment Corporation. [4]Mitnick was on supervised release when he hacked Pacific Bell voice mail computers and ended up having to flee the country. [5]In 1988, another notorious hacker,   Robert Tappan Morris,[†] launched a program on the Internet that copied itself endlessly, filling the memories of 6,000 computer systems—at the time, about one-tenth of the Internet.   [6]Because of Morris's program, systems crashed at major businesses, schools, the U.S.   government, the Air Force, and NASA. [7]In 2002, U.S. federal authorities announced that they had cracked the case of an international hacker who broke into roughly 100 unclassified   U.S. military networks. [8]In 2008, hackers infiltrated websites belonging to Fortune 500   companies and stole information about people who had visited the hacked sites.

Topic
a.   the Internet
b.   Kevin D. Mitnick and Robert Tappan Morris
c.   computer hacker crimes

Topic Sentence: _____

[†] Kevin D. Mitnick is now a security consultant. He specializes in helping businesses learn how to keep hackers and other intruders out of their computers.
[†] Robert Tappan Morris created what is now known as the "Morris worm" while still a student at Cornell. He is now a professor at the Massachusetts Institute of Technology.

4.4 IDENTIFYING TOPICS AND MAIN IDEAS

Directions: Circle the letters of the correct topic and main idea.

1. Want to know what it's like to be thrown from the cockpit of an airplane or to perform live with Janet Jackson? Those are just a few of the experiences you can have if you are willing to enter the computer-generated world of "virtual reality." Put on an electronic glove, for example, and you can experience the illusion of flying. Pull on a computerized suit and you can enter a variety of artificial worlds, ranging from tropical jungles to arctic snows. Special goggles and a headpiece can give you the experience of underwater diving and the thrills of a roller-coaster ride. For those of us who like adventure without any danger, virtual reality offers all the thrills minus the risks.

    Topic
    a. Computers and their uses
    b. Adventures in virtual reality
    c. The experience of flying

    Main Idea
    a. Virtual reality offers adventure without the threat of danger.
    b. Some people like adventure but they don't like the danger that goes with it.

2. Nowadays, Bill Gates, the CEO of the computer company Microsoft, is pretty much considered to be a genius. Everything he puts his hand to seems to turn a profit. But it wasn't always so. Windows, the operating system that made Gates a billionaire, could hardly be called an instant success. In the mid eighties, when Windows first came on the market, it was thought to be a dud—too flawed to be useful. But the determined Gates would not give up on it. Instead, he brought in Neil Konzen, a computer whiz barely out of his teens. In less than six months, Konzen rewrote the entire Windows program. When the new, revised version of Windows 3.0 came on the market, it was immediately successful. Thanks to Konzen's efforts and Microsoft's smart marketing campaign, computer stores could barely keep Windows on their shelves.

    Topic
    a. The introduction of Windows
    b. The life and times of Bill Gates
    c. Microsoft marketing

    Main Idea
    a. Bill Gates knows how to market his products, and that knowledge has made him a billionaire.
    b. Windows, the operating system that made Bill Gates rich, initially looked as if it would be a huge failure.

3. As a child growing up in Switzerland, Hermann Rorschach (1884–1922) played a game called *Klecksography* that used inkblots to tell a story. When he grew up, Rorschach enrolled in medical school and became interested in psychology. Influenced by discussions about psychoanalysis, which emphasized the role of childhood memories on adult behavior, Rorschach began to think about the inkblot game he had played as a child. More precisely, he began to wonder why two people might interpret inkblots in wildly different ways. Whereas one person might see in the blot a bird in flight, another might see a rose with drooping petals. When Rorschach graduated from medical school in 1912, he began to pursue his inkblot research in earnest. In 1921 he published his landmark[*] work, *Psychodiagnostik,* in which he explained how inkblots could be used to explore

---

[*] landmark: an event that identifies an important historical shift.

the unconscious. Although less popular than it once was, the Rorschach test is still used all over the world—and to think, it began with a simple childhood game.

Topic
a. The origins of the Rorschach test
b. The life of Hermann Rorschach
c. psychoanalysis

Main Idea
a. Although it is less popular than it once was, the Rorschach test is still used occasionally.
b. The Rorschach inkblot test grew out of Hermann Rorschach's early interest in a game called *Klecksography.*

4. *The Great Train Robbery* is the name of a famous film. However, what many people don't know is that the film was firmly based on fact. On August 8, 1963, the Royal Mail Train left Glasgow, Scotland, carrying 7.3 million pounds. It was bound for London, England. Suddenly, at three o'clock in the morning, the train came to an abrupt halt, and fifteen masked men boarded and robbed it. At first it looked as if the thieves would get away scot-free. But their abandoned hiding place was ferreted out by the police, who found fingerprints everywhere. Over the next few months, twelve of the gang members were hunted down and caught. All twelve went to prison, although two eventually escaped. The whereabouts of the remaining three robbers, however, remains unknown to this day.

Topic
a. *The Great Train Robbery*
b. The factual basis for *The Great Train Robbery*
c. Famous train robbers

Main Idea
a. Most people aren't aware that the crime enacted in *The Great Train Robbery* actually took place.
b. *The Great Train Robbery* was a popular movie that relied on realistic detail for much of its success.

5. On August 23, 1927, two Italian immigrants, Nicola Sacco and Bartolomeo Vanzetti, were put to death for the crimes of robbery and murder. In the years since their death, it has become clear to many that the two men were executed because of their political beliefs, not because of the evidence against them. Sacco and Vanzetti were anarchists,* and, along with socialists and communists, they were considered a threat to the U.S. government. When they were arrested, both Sacco and Vanzetti had what seemed to be airtight alibis. Witnesses testified that the two men had been nowhere near the scene of the crime. Yet the prosecutor, Frederick Katzenbach, insisted those witnesses were mistaken. He also claimed that a wool cap found at the scene of the crime belonged to Sacco. Later on, it was discovered that the cap had been found the night before the murders. Although Sacco and Vanzetti's supporters had obtained a stay of execution, a special committee appointed by the governor of Massachusetts upheld the execution order, and the two men were put to death.

Topic
a. The treatment of anarchists, communists, and socialists in the 1920s
b. Frederick Katzenbach
c. The innocence of Sacco and Vanzetti

---

*anarchists: people who believe that all forms of government are unlawful.

Main Idea
    a.   To this day, many people believe that Sacco and Vanzetti were executed because of their political beliefs.
    b.   Over the years, innocent people have been executed for crimes they did not commit.

6.   For years, the 1927 film *The Jazz Singer,* starring Al Jolson, has been called the first "talking film." Purists,[*] however, like to point out that, in fact, movies had sound long before Jolson adlibbed his famous line, "Wait a minute! Wait a minute! You ain't heard nothin' yet!" Live music, for example, had accompanied silent films since the 1890s. Throughout the country, movie theaters used a pianist or organist to drum up musical excitement for the movie scenes on the screen. By the 1920s, Bell Labs had linked movies to phonograph records, and the 1926 film *Don Juan* was accompanied by music from the New York Philharmonic. What *The Jazz Singer* actually added to movies was not sound, but dialogue.

   Topic
    a.   Sound in film
    b.   The history of movies in the United States
    c.   Al Jolson

   Main Idea
    a.   *The Jazz Singer* made film history when Al Jolson spoke on screen.
    b.   *The Jazz Singer* was not the first movie to employ sound.

7.   To some degree, the discovery of penicillin was a lucky break. In 1928, Dr. Alexander Fleming, the discoverer of penicillin, was a medical bacteriologist[*] at St. Mary's Hospital Medical School in London. While on duty, he noticed that a staphylococcus[*] culture he was cultivating had been contaminated[*] by mold. He noticed, too, that in the area around the mold, bacteria were dissolving. Fleming isolated the mold and discovered that substances within it—substances he called penicillin—were inhibiting the bacteria's growth. A cautious medical detective, Fleming reported in 1928 that penicillin "appears to have some advantages over the well-known chemical antiseptics."[*] It wasn't until 1940 that additional research proved just how effective penicillin could be in the war against bacteria. In 1945, Fleming was awarded the Nobel Prize for medicine.

   Topic
    a.   The life of Alexander Fleming
    b.   The discovery of penicillin
    c.   The war against bacteria

   Main Idea
    a.   Penicillin proved to be the most effective treatment for staph infections.
    b.   Alexander Fleming's discovery of penicillin happened by accident.

8.   The dark side of being famous revealed itself on the night of March 1, 1932. On this night, the twenty-month-old son of Charles and Anne Morrow Lindbergh was kidnapped from the couple's brand-new home in New Jersey. The kidnapper entered the Lindbergh house by means of a homemade ladder and left behind a ransom note written in broken English. Following the kidnapping, a man with a German accent called and demanded a $50,000 ransom. Although the

---

[*] purists: people who like to be exact.
[*] bacteriologist: one who studies bacteria, microorganisms that sometimes cause disease.
[*] staphylococcus: a type of bacteria.
[*] contaminated: infected; made impure.
[*] antiseptics: substances that get rid of germs by washing them away.

ransom was paid, the baby was not found where it was supposed to be. Eventually, a truck driver discovered the child's corpse buried near the Lindbergh home.

Topic
a. Famous kidnappings
b. The Lindbergh kidnapping
c. Charles and Anne Lindbergh

Main Idea
a. The Lindbergh kidnapping illustrates that fame can have its dangerous side.
b. The Lindberghs never got over the death of their child.

9. In the thirteenth century, a new order of worship came about in the Catholic Church—the order of friars. The order of friars differed from the older orders of monks in several ways. First, the friars' lives and works were centered around the community, while monks remained isolated from the rest of the world. Friars swore vows of poverty and were allowed no personal possessions. Monks, on the other hand, often owned land, and in some cases were quite wealthy. Finally, friars drew their members primarily from the working classes, while monks generally came from the nobility.

Topic
a. Monks
b. Friars
c. The difference between monks and friars

Main Idea
a. In the thirteenth century, monks were the source of all spiritual instruction.
b. Thirteenth-century monks and friars differed from one another in several ways.

10. According to Greek myth, Zeus was the ruler of all the Greek gods, and the only other god he feared was his wife, Hera. Quick to take revenge on those who offended her, Hera was wildly jealous of Zeus's many mortal lovers. Whenever Zeus fathered a child by a mortal woman, Hera did her utmost to ensure that both mother and child suffered and died. Hercules, one of the few of Zeus's out-of-wedlock children to survive, spent his adult life fending off Hera's attacks. Once, Zeus even turned a mortal lover into a cow, so that Hera would not find her. But Hera was too smart for him. She sent a swarm of gadflies to chase the cow around the world and keep her perpetually miserable.

Topic
a. Greek mythology
b. Zeus's power
c. Hera's jealousy

Main Idea
a. Jealous of Zeus's love affairs, the goddess Hera knew how to get her own brand of revenge.
b. In Greek mythology, Zeus was the most powerful of all the gods, but he did not always use his power wisely.

4.5 PARAPHRASING

Directions: Read each passage. Then circle the letter of the statement that better paraphrases the passage. Note: These paraphrases are more formal. They are similar to those you might use for a term paper.

1. On April 14, 1912, on its maiden voyage from Southampton, England, to New York, the cruise ship *Titanic* struck an iceberg and sank to the ocean floor within three hours, killing 1,523 of the 2,228 passengers and crew aboard. (From "*Titanic* Up for Sale," *Philadelphia Inquirer,* February 15, 1998, p. A-10.)

    Paraphrase
    a. On its first voyage out, on April 14, 1912, the cruise ship *Titanic* hit an iceberg and sank in little more than three hours. When the ship sank, more than fifteen hundred people died.
    b. On April 14, 1912, the cruise ship *Titanic* sank to the bottom of the Atlantic ocean. Because it was poorly constructed, the ship sank immediately after hitting an iceberg.

2. Famous stage actor Lionel Barrymore once got so drunk before a stage production of *Hamlet* that he forgot the second half of the line "to be or not to be." After some hesitation, Barrymore finally remembered the line and the play continued. Reviews of the performance praised his delivery of the "to be or not to be" line, saying that he truly seemed to be considering the implications of the words.

    Paraphrase
    a. Actor Lionel Barrymore came from a famous acting family. But like other members of his distinguished family, Barrymore had a drinking problem and it eventually destroyed his career.
    b. Playing *Hamlet,* actor Lionel Barrymore was so drunk he stumbled over the line "to be or not to be." But the mistake worked in the actor's favor when critics praised his thoughtful delivery.

3. Scientists believe that a hormone called orexin is what triggers feelings of hunger.

    Paraphrase
    a. The discovery of orexin, the hormone that triggers hunger, will probably result in a host of new diet drugs.
    b. Scientists now think that a hormone called orexin is what causes the brain to feel hunger.

4. Mountain climbers who climb twenty-five thousand feet or higher are subject to the effects of low blood oxygen, which can cause confusion, dizziness, and exhaustion. One of the most dangerous effects of low blood oxygen is the inability to accurately assess risky situations.

    Paraphrase
    a. It's highly dangerous for a mountain climber to ascend beyond twenty-five thousand feet. Climbers who do are likely to suffer terrible side effects and can, as a result, put their lives and the lives of others at risk.
    b. At twenty-five thousand feet or higher, a mountain climber is likely to suffer the effects of low blood oxygen. Too little oxygen in the blood can make a person confused, dizzy, and tired. Even worse, it can reduce a climber's ability to accurately assess danger.

5. Most parents think their home is a safe place for their children, but in many cases, it's about as safe as a minefield. More than 90 percent of the injuries that bring children to the emergency room happen in the home and are preventable.

Paraphrase

   a. Most of the injuries that bring children to the emergency ward happen in the home.

   b. Most parents have no idea of the trouble their children can get into when they are playing.

6. Memory's ability to offer a series of pretty pictures effectively eases present pains and problems. (Rick Kogan, "Don't Look Back," *Chicago Tribune*, August 2, 1996, p. 2.)

Paraphrase

   a. Memories lie, and they lie a lot.

   b. Memories of happier times often make the present easier to handle.

7. On February 9, 1964, TV variety-show kingpin Ed Sullivan presented the Beatles for the first time to a mass American audience. In a matter of days, it was clear that the group had taken America by storm. Their appearance on Sullivan's show had drawn seventy million viewers—the largest TV audience ever at the time—and from that point on, everyone wanted the Beatles for guest appearances, no matter what their price.

Paraphrase

   a. When Ed Sullivan put the Beatles on his show in February of 1964, they drew the largest audience ever—seventy million viewers—and from then on, they could just about write their own ticket. America was in love with the Beatles.

   b. The Beatles' success on the *Ed Sullivan Show* made it clear that a new era was upon us. What came to be known as "the British Invasion" had begun, and Americans, particularly girls between the ages of thirteen and seventeen, were in love with the Beatles.

8. In *Love, Medicine and Miracles,* Bernie S. Siegel, M.D., asks ailing readers to answer a key question: "Why do you need this disease?" While some consider the question worth asking as a way of probing the connection between mind and body, others are outraged by the suggestion that they have brought about their own illness.

Paraphrase

   a. Bernie S. Siegel, M.D., the author of *Love, Medicine and Miracles,* firmly believes that, in part at least, disease is a symptom of emotional distress. Heal the mind and you cure the body as well.

   b. Bernie S. Siegel, M.D., the author of *Love, Medicine, and Miracles,* poses this question of those who are ill: "Why do you need this disease?" Readers who believe in the mind–body connection usually respond positively to the question whereas others are enraged at the suggestion that they helped themselves get sick.

9. Sales of organic fruits and vegetables have quadrupled since 1990. The driving force behind this sales increase is consumer concern about pesticide use and the effect it may have on their health.

Paraphrase

   a. Because people are concerned about the use of pesticides on produce, they are buying more organically grown fruits and vegetables.

   b. Although studies still have not clarified how the use of pesticides on produce can affect our health, people are concerned enough to buy organic fruits and vegetables. The problem is that the label "organic" does not guarantee freedom from pesticides.

10. A fever announces the arrival of viruses and bacteria. But because the heat of a fever spurs on the body's natural defenses, it also helps to fight off those very same viruses and bacteria.

   Paraphrase
   a. A fever both announces and helps to cure diseases caused by viruses and bacteria.
   b. One theory of fever holds that the elevated body temperature reduces the amount of iron in the blood and stops bacteria from multiplying.

4.6 RECOGNIZING AN ACCURATE PARAPHRASE

Directions: Read each paragraph and write the number of the topic sentence in the blank. Then circle the letter of the most accurate paraphrase. *Note:* These paraphrases are reading paraphrases. Most would be inappropriate for a term paper.

1. [1]For centuries, people have been fascinated by the story of Atlantis, the advanced civilization that, according to legend at least, mysteriously disappeared into the sea. [2]In the fourth century BC, the ancient Greek philosopher Plato claimed that Atlantis was an island located in the Atlantic Ocean, somewhere close to Gibraltar.[†] [3]In Plato's account, the island sinks in a single day, following an earthquake. [4]In the eighteenth century, Atlantis once again became a popular subject, and attempts were made to prove its existence. [5]None succeeded, but failure did not kill the legend. [6]Even today, the story of Atlantis still has its believers. [7]Convinced by books like the 2003 *Atlantis: The Lost Continent Finally Found*, some believe the Atlantis really exists.

    Topic Sentence _____

    Paraphrase
    a. Plato said Atlantis was island close to Gibraltar.
    b. Legend of Atlantis long been object of fascination.
    c. Many people believe Atlantis will eventually be rediscovered.

2. [1]Fourteenth-century poet Geoffrey Chaucer, who penned the famous *Canterbury Tales*, is considered one of history's finest writers. [2]Yet toward the end of his career, Chaucer apologized for the *Canterbury Tales* and declared them "sinful." [3]Worried about the fate of his soul, Chaucer repudiated those works he thought might displease God. [4]Chaucer is not the only artist who later in life disowned his best work; many other great artists have done the same. [5]Chaucer's contemporary, Giovanni Boccaccio, wrote a collection of lively, sexy tales entitled *Decameron*. [6]Then like Chaucer, Boccaccio was embarrassed be the indecent creations of his youth. [7]He even considered burning his earlier works. [8]Fortunately, a friend persuaded him not to set the stories aflame. [9]Sixteenth-century painter, sculptor, and architect Michelangelo also turned away from his art. [10]Fearing for his soul, he wrote, "I now know how fraught with error was the fond imagination which made Art my idol and my king . . . no brush, no chisel will quiet the soul." [11]Aging writer Leo Tolstoy underwent a similar spiritual crisis in the nineteenth century. [12]Turning to religion, Tolstoy called all of his earlier fiction "trash," including the classics *War and Peace* and *Anna Karenina*. [13]In an essay titled "What is Art?" written twelve years before he died, Tolstoy condemned other great artists like Shakespeare, Beethoven, and Dante for infecting people with immoral desires.

    Topic Sentence _____

    Paraphrase
    a. Chaucer rejected *Canterbury Tales*, considering them displeasing to God.
    b. Late in life, several famous artists rejected their finest work.
    c. Boccaccio, like Chaucer, got religious late in life and worried about the fate of his soul.

3. [1]Two kinds of elections are held in the United States: general and primary. [2]A *general election* is used to fill an elective office. [3]The presidential election, for example, is a general election, as are the congressional races. [4]A *primary election* is used to select a party's candidates for an elective office, though, in fact, those who vote in a primary election may not consider themselves party members. [5]Some primaries are closed. [6]In a *closed primary*, you must declare in advance that you are a

---

[†] Gibraltar: a peninsula on the south central coast of Spain.

registered member of the political party in whose primary you wish to vote. [7]About forty states have closed primaries. [8]Other primaries are open. [9]In an *open primary*, you can decide when you enter the voting booth which party's primary you wish to participate in. (Adapted from Wilson and Dilulio, *American Government*, p. 241.)

Topic Sentence _____

Paraphrase
a. While closed primaries require voters be registered in advance, open primaries don't.
b. Around forty states have open primaries, where all voters participate.
c. In the United States, two kinds of elections are held; general elections and open or closed primaries.

4. [1]One early theory likened human memory to a muscle that had to be exercised regularly in order to function properly. [2]This theory was eventually replaced by the idea that remembering was like writing, with experience as the pen and the mind the blank page. [3]But eventually this idea was also rejected. [4]In its place came another theory—that human memory functioned like a complex and well-stocked library. [5]With a key word, you could look up any piece of stored or cataloged information. [6]Over time, that theory has also been discarded. [7]Human memory may, in fact, be too sophisticated and too complex to be explained through any one single comparison.

Topic Sentence _____

Paraphrase
a. No single comparison captures complexity of human memory.
b. Human memory functions like a library.
c. Memories are recorded like writing on a page.

5. [1]The West's exposure to Muslim women is largely based on Islam's most extreme examples of oppression: Taliban-dominated Afghanistan, Wahhabi[†]-ruled Saudi Arabia, and post-revolutionary Iran, regimes where women are forced to cover their faces and bodies or suffer painful consequences. [2]In parts of Afghanistan, even veiled women are forbidden to drive. [3]Yet these Islamic societies, with their emphasis on the repression of women, are not typical of the Muslim world. [4]In Egypt, female police patrol the streets. [5]In Jordan, women account for the majority of students in medical school. [6]And in Syria, courtrooms are filled with female lawyers. [7]"Women are out working in every profession, and even expect equal pay," says Leila Ahmed, Harvard Divinity School professor and author of *Women and Gender in Islam*. [8]Though the atmosphere in Muslim countries is becoming more restrictive, no matter how conservative things get, they can't put the genie back into the bottle. (Adapted from Lorraine Ali, "Reform: Not Ignorant, Not Helpless," *Newsweek*, December 12, 2005, p. 33.)

Topic Sentence _____

Paraphrase
a. Egyptian society allows women more freedom than other societies.
b. Jordanian women majority in medical school.
c. Islamic societies that oppress women not typical of the Muslim world.

[†] Wahhabi: a segment of Islam that allows women few, if any, rights.

CHAPTER 5
Focus on Supporting Details

SUGGESTIONS FOR TEACHING CHAPTER 5

1. Again, this chapter builds on students' understanding of general and specific sentences, and it's important that they realize this. If they can recognize degrees of generality or specificity in the paragraph, they can also distinguish between major and minor details. For many students, this is a reassuring thought.

2. For the most part, the paragraphs included in this chapter are fairly schematic, with major details neatly separated into different sentences. However, students need to know that in more complicated paragraphs, one sentence might contain two or even three details. In these instances, it's up to the reader to mentally sort out the individual details rather than trying to remember them as one big block of information.

3. Ask students to create paragraphs that could be used on an exam testing major and minor details. Hand out some of the paragraphs along with a blank diagram like the one below. Ask them to fill in the diagrams.

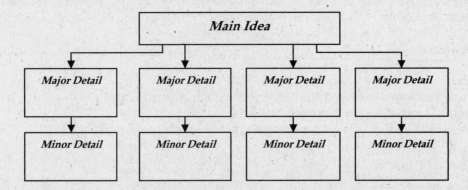

SUPPLEMENTARY MATERIALS

5.1   RECOGNIZING SUPPORTING DETAILS

Directions: Read the topic sentence. Then circle the letters of the three sentences that provide support.

1. *Topic Sentence:* Famed sex researcher Alfred C. Kinsey had a hard and difficult childhood.

    Supporting Details:
    a. Alfred C. Kinsey's book *Sexual Behavior in the Human Male,* published in 1948, was an immediate bestseller.
    b. Alfred C. Kinsey's childhood was dominated by poverty.
    c. Sickly and thin, Kinsey was the target of bullies throughout his childhood.
    d. In social gatherings, Kinsey, no matter how famous, was unable to make small talk.
    e. Kinsey's father was overly stern with both his wife and children.

2. *Topic Sentence:* During the Depression-torn thirties, probably the biggest celebrity in the country was a mud-colored racehorse named Seabiscuit.

    Supporting Details:
    a. Between 1935 and 1938, Seabiscuit won—against all odds—almost every race he entered, and the public loved him for it.
    b. Man O' War was probably the greatest racehorse that ever lived, but Seabiscuit had more heart.
    c. Some of Seabiscuit's extraordinary popularity stemmed from the fact that the Depression-weary public was desperate for someone, even a horse, to be a winner.
    d. By the time he was three years old, Seabiscuit had run and lost sixteen races.
    e. For Seabiscuit, drawing a crowd of twenty thousand people or more was commonplace.

3. *Topic Sentence:* Online therapy is becoming a booming business.

    Supporting Details:
    a. In 1995, only a handful of therapists offered therapy online, but by 2000, an estimated three hundred or so counseling Web sites had emerged.
    b. Aware of the boom in online therapy, the American Counseling Association has issued guidelines for therapy on the Web.
    c. A major drawback to online therapy is the fact that the therapists can't see the patient's expressions or gestures.
    d. The ease and convenience are two reasons why online therapy has become popular.
    e. It's probably a lot easier for patients to lie to a therapist that they have never talked to in person.

4. *Topic Sentence:* Surgery has been around for centuries, but the use of anesthesia is fairly recent.

    Supporting Details:
    a. The use of anesthesia for surgery was America's first major medical contribution.
    b. For centuries, doctors performed surgery without sterilizing their instruments.
    c. In 1842, the American Crawford Williamson Long was the first doctor to use a general anesthetic during surgery.
    d. In 1846, William Morton wrote an article publicizing the use in U.S. hospitals of ether as a surgical anesthetic.
    e. By the 1920s, the use of general anesthesia during surgery had become a generally accepted practice among doctors.

5. *Topic Sentence:* There are alternatives to using fossil fuels like coal and oil.

    Supporting Details:
a.   One alternative to fossil fuels is hydroelectric power, which gets energy from flowing water.
b.   The burning of fossil fuels has contributed to the world's environmental problems.
c.   Solar power uses the sun as a source of energy; some believe it is the best alternative to fossil fuels.
d.   Nuclear power is certainly an alternative to fossil fuels, but it has some serious drawbacks.
e.   Environmentalists worry that protected areas of wilderness will no longer be safe from oil companies intent on drilling for oil.

5.2   RECOGNIZING SUPPORTING DETAILS

Directions: Circle the letters of the supporting details that develop or explain the topic sentence.

1. *Topic Sentence:* There's a wealth of life in just a handful of soil.

   Supporting Details
   a. Soil is filled with bacteria.
   b. In parts of Utah, the soil is a deep, rich black.
   c. Soil contains all kinds of worms, some so small they can only be seen with a microscope.
   d. Many insects make their homes in soil.
   e. Some individuals have a strange disorder that compels them to eat dirt.
   f. Gardens by the sea are tricky to grow because the soil is so salty.

2. *Topic Sentence:* Chinese history includes many references to the flooding of northern China's Yellow River, but one of the worst incidents of flooding occurred in 1938.

   Supporting Details
   a. The 1938 flood began when China's leader, Chiang Kai-shek, destroyed the Yellow River's dikes in an effort to drive out Japanese invaders.
   b. Chiang Kai-shek was a brutal leader who cared little for the people of China.
   c. In the end, Chiang Kai-shek was defeated by the Communist rebels.
   d. When the Yellow River flooded, more than a million Chinese died.
   e. The flood waters destroyed more than four thousand villages.
   f. In 1969 the Yellow River flooded again, despite extensive repairs made to the river's dikes.

3. *Topic Sentence:* Between 1918 and 1919, a dangerous and deadly flu epidemic ranged over the globe.

   Supporting Details
   a. Although the first outbreak of the 1918 flu occurred in the United States, it quickly spread to Europe, Asia, and South America.
   b. Not all historians believe that the 1918 flu epidemic began in the United States; some believe it began in France.
   c. Of all the countries affected, India was the hardest hit by the 1918 flu; at least twelve million people died.
   d. In some countries the flu was so widespread that businesses and transportation had to shut down.
   e. Antibiotics are useless against flu attacks.
   f. Many people rely on home remedies to combat the aches and pains of the flu.

4. *Topic Sentence:* In most groups, three types of leaders are likely to emerge.

   Supporting Details
   a. *Reference groups* help us evaluate our behavior.
   b. *Instrumental leaders* achieve goals by getting members to concentrate on performance.
   c. Some people use their families as a reference group.
   d. *Expressive leaders* work to make members feel good about themselves.
   e. It's very hard to live outside group membership.

f.   Once goals are identified, *laissez-faire leaders** leave group members alone to do what they want.

5.   *Topic Sentence:* An interest group is an organized collection of people that attempts to influence government policies.

Supporting Details
a.   For over twenty years, America's two major political parties have been accused of exchanging influence for money.
b.   Civil rights groups, the American Medical Association, unions, and the National Association of Manufacturers are all examples of interest groups.
c.   Interest groups frequently file lawsuits to further their goals.
d.   When all is said and done, Republican and Democratic representatives are more similar than different.
e.   Interest groups also engage in letter-writing campaigns and work to elect sympathetic candidates.
f.   In Washington, there's always an "in group" and an "out group."

6.   *Topic Sentence:* Some of America's favorite foods appeared in the first two decades of the twentieth century.

Supporting Details
a.   In 1900, Louis Lasser, the owner of Louis' Lunch in New Haven, Connecticut, ground up a pound of lean beef, broiled it, and served his customers America's first hamburger.
b.   Before 1912, if you wanted mayonnaise, you had to make it, but then Richard Hellmann began whipping up batches of his own mayonnaise and selling it in glass containers.
c.   The year 1921 saw the birth of the first hamburger chain, White Castle—the precursor* of today's McDonald's.
d.   Thanks to George Schmidt's invention of the electric shake mixer, America learned to love the milkshake.
e.   It's hard to imagine a world without tuna sandwiches, but they didn't exist until 1907, when A. P. Halftill of San Pedro, California, began packing tuna in cans.
f.   The luncheon meat called Spam first appeared in 1937.

7.   *Topic Sentence:* The modern Olympic Games, even in their earliest years, produced some outstanding athletes.

Supporting Details
a.   In 1896, the Olympic Games were so disorganized that some of the athletes attending didn't realize they were in the Olympics.
b.   On July 16, 1900, former polio victim Ray Ewry of Lafayette, Indiana, won gold medals in the standing high jump, standing long jump, and standing triple jump.
c.   In 1904, George Eyser won three gold medals in gymnastics, as well as two silver and a bronze, despite the fact that he had a wooden leg.
d.   In the 1912 Olympic Games, Jim Thorpe, a Native American from Oklahoma, won the decathlon* and the pentathlon.*
e.   One of the most dramatic moments in Olympic marathon history occurred when athlete Dorando Dretri collapsed at the finish line and had to be helped across.

---

* laissez-faire: French for "let do."
* precursor: person or institution that precedes, or comes before, another.
* decathlon: Olympic event with ten events.
* pentathlon: Olympic event with five events.

f.   In 1924, fights broke out when the French rugby team was unexpectedly beaten by the American team.

8.   *Topic Sentence:* Supporters of using marijuana for medical purposes insist that marijuana can help in the treatment of numerous illnesses.

Supporting Details
a.   In 1996 California voted to allow the medical use of marijuana.
b.   The medical use of marijuana is illegal in every state in the nation except California.
c.   Supporters claim that marijuana can be used to treat the nausea caused by chemotherapy.
d.   More than ten million marijuana users have been arrested since 1965.
e.   AIDS patients say that using marijuana helps increase their appetite and reduce nausea.
f.   In some cases, marijuana has been successfully used to control the symptoms of glaucoma.

9.   *Topic Sentence:* The ivorybill woodpecker, now practically extinct, is famed for both its size and its personality.

Supporting Details
a.   At twenty inches, the ivorybill is America's largest woodpecker.
b.   If they still exist, ivorybills can be found living in swamps.
c.   Ivorybills feed on the grubs that attack dead trees.
d.   Ivorybills are also most likely to be found in old-growth forests.
e.   The ivorybill is known for its courage and defiance.
f.   When famed birder Alexander Wilson captured an ivorybill, it tried to peck its way through a wall in order to escape.

10. *Topic Sentence:* Over the years, a number of Americans have taken some very, very long walks.

Supporting Details
a.   On April 15, 1931, thirty- six-year-old American Plennie Wingo set out from his home in Santa Monica, California, on a journey to Istanbul, Turkey; his goal was to walk the entire way backward.
b.   In 1950 travel writer John Sack decided to visit only the countries that most people ignored as too small to be of interest.
c.   Starting in June of 1970, brothers John and David Kunst of Minnesota walked all the way to Afghanistan, where bandits attacked and killed John Kunst in October 1972. (It took Dave two more years to complete the around-the-world journey.)
d.   The Hungarian Alexandre Kelemen and the Belgian Jan de Vautriel have both attempted walks around the world without success.

e. From 1983 to 1987, Steven Newman of Bethel, Ohio, walked his way around the world.
f. In 1950 Australian Ben Carlin, accompanied by his wife, set out around the world from Montreal, Canada, in a jeep.

CHAPTER 6

More About Inferences

SUGGESTIONS FOR TEACHING CHAPTER 6

1. Spend some time discussing the kinds of inferences we all make in everyday life; inferences, for example, about how people feel or what they think. Once students recognize that drawing inferences is part of their daily life, they are less likely to be intimidated by the thought of drawing inferences in reading.

2. If making students feel comfortable about drawing inferences is the first step in this chapter, the next crucial step is to make them conscious of the difference between *effective* and *ineffective* inferences. When it comes to inferences, students are inclined to think that any inference will do, and they need to realize that inferences in reading have to be solidly based on the author's actual words; otherwise, they will hinder rather than help the reader's search for meaning.

3. I think it's important to do at least one of the exercises in this chapter in class as a group. Students should justify the inferences they select or create by pointing to specific statements in the paragraph. What has to be held in check is the tendency for students to base their inferences purely on personal knowledge.

4. Use quotations and proverbs to show students how important it is to draw inferences in order to create meaning. To illustrate, here are two supplied by Professor Barbara Reall of Rhode Island Community College: "One who wants a rose must respect the thorn" (Persian proverb). "The way to love anything is to realize that it might be lost."

5. I like to spend some time having students analyze the different ways very simple statements, both spoken and written, require inferences to be meaningful. For instance, in the grocery store, the common question, "Paper or plastic"? requires the person addressed to infer the word "bags."

6. Similarly, the following pair of sentences, taken from a discussion of ways to save energy is only meaningful if the reader infers parts of the second sentence: "Closing state offices has cut energy use by 13 percent in Utah. Officials hope to bring that number closer to 20 percent." In just two short sentences, the reader is already expected to drawn an inference so that the second sentence makes sense: "Officials hope to bring that number [referring to the cut in energy use] closer to 20 percent." This kind of reader-inferred information is added to a text constantly as we read.

SUPPLEMENTARY MATERIALS

6.1 DRAWING INFERENCES

Directions: Provided below are three specific sentences, each describing the behavior or appearance of a different person. Read the sentence and then choose the inference that best fits the information given in the specific sentences.

Example: a. Although the man's clothes were old and dirty, it was easy to see that they were well cut and expensive.

         b. The walls of his run-down shack were papered with autographed pictures; many of the inscriptions on the photos contained his name.

         c. Articulate and well read, he liked to talk of the places he had been and of the famous people he had known.

    Inferences
1. The man was an alcoholic.
2. The man was unhappy with his life.
3. The man had not always been so poor.

Explanation: Sentence 1 isn't a good choice because the specific sentences say nothing about the man's drinking habits. There is no evidence to support such a statement. Sentence 2 isn't appropriate because there is no information about the man's state of mind. We know that he likes to talk about his past, but that does not necessarily mean that he is unhappy with his life. Sentence 3 is the correct inference because every sentence tells us that the man had lived another kind of life, one not associated with poverty.

Do the rest of the exercise in the same manner.

  1. a. The student squinted when she sat at the back of the room and looked at the blackboard.

       b. She left out words when she copied anything from the blackboard.

       c. After she read for an hour, she got a headache.

Inferences
1. The student gets excellent grades.
2. The student needs glasses.
3. The student wants to get out of doing any work.

  2. a. Whenever he felt anxious, he went to the refrigerator to find something to munch on.

       b. When he got promoted, he was so happy he managed to lose twenty pounds, and his friend said he was almost too thin.

       c. When he lost his job, he put on thirty pounds.

Inferences
1. He couldn't get the kind of job he wanted because he was too heavy.
2. He was always disgusted with himself after he had eaten too much.
3. His weight fluctuated with his state of mind: When he was happy, he was slender; when he was unhappy, he was overweight.

3. a. Her hands remained clamped to the lectern while she give her speech.
   b. Her voice trembled slightly when she spoke.
   c. She didn't look at her audience once.

   Inferences
   1. She was used to giving speeches.
   2. The audience did not like her speech.
   3. She was not used to giving speeches.

4. a. Sue stood at the edge of the group and smiled timidly at the other children; intent on their game, they did not smile back.
   b. When the game broke up, everyone else walked home in pairs; Sue walked home alone.
   c. When Sue's mother asked if she had enjoyed the group play after school, the child burst into tears.

   Inferences
   1. The child was unhappy because she felt left out and lonely.
   2. The child cried because the mother asked too many questions.
   3. The other children did not like Sue.

5. a. Many cat and dog owners buy their pets clothing, special food, and toys.
   b. A great many men and women talk to their pets.
   c. It is not uncommon for a dog or cat who has died to receive a headstone with a poetic inscription.

   Inferences
   1. Many cat and dog owners treat their pets as if they were human beings.
   2. Most people who like dogs and cats do not like other human beings.
   3. It is unnatural for human beings to treat their pets like humans.

6.2 LOGICAL AND ILLOGICAL INFERENCES

Directions: Circle the letter of the more logical inference.

1. During a job interview, a person has to be very careful about what he or she says. After all, the wrong answer to a prospective employer's question could mean the loss of potential employment. In addition to what one says, what one wears is equally important. Clothes can make or break the interview, and most employers are put off by clothing that is too colorful or too fancy. From their point of view, such clothing suggests that the person wearing it may not be serious and hard working. For that matter, even gestures count, and most employers are reluctant to hire someone whose physical movements do not seem relaxed. Too much fidgeting implies that the person is not confident and at ease, raising an immediate question in the interviewer's mind: Is there some good reason why this person lacks confidence?

    a. To interview successfully, you have to consider just about every detail of your appearance and behavior.
    b. Interviewers like people who are very aggressive, even overconfident.

2. The first thing that strikes tourists arriving in New York City is the number of restaurants. There are so many, offering every conceivable kind of food, ranging from Mexican to Indonesian, with something for every taste. The theaters offer the same kind of wonderful variety. For those who like the classics, there is always a production of Shakespeare to be found. Likewise, lovers of musicals will not be disappointed. Nor, for that matter, will those who like their theater serious or comic. New plays are always being produced on some small off-Broadway stage. Movie lovers will not find a better selection anywhere else in the world, and every kind of movie from every era and every country is available. For tourists arriving in New York, the major difficulty is finding enough time to do everything.

    a. Although most tourists love visiting New York, very few would ever want to live there.
    b. Tourists are usually not disappointed by the variety of entertainment in New York.

3. In Rome, American tourists are usually startled by the sight of the familiar yellow arch announcing the presence of McDonald's; and the Italians, like the Americans, have a taste for Big Macs and double cheeseburgers. Similarly, it is not surprising for an American walking through the country villages of Greece to suddenly hear the sound of Bruce Springsteen belting out "Born in the U.S.A." or Bob Seger singing about life "On a Tightrope." For that matter, tourists strolling down Berlin's famous KuDamm are usually struck by the number of Germans wearing Calvin Klein clothing, whereas visitors to Russia are constantly asked to sell their blue jeans for high prices, and even Russians know the name "Levis."

    a. Europeans resent the degree to which the American way of life makes itself felt in their own countries.
    b. The American way of life is not confined to America; you can also find it in Europe.

4. By the end of the marathon, the majority of the runners had gray faces and blue lips. Some were trembling all over, and others could barely walk over the finish line and did not seem to recognize the family members who greeted them. Sweat-soaked and sunburned, at least six hundred or more walked to the medical tent, where doctors were available to check the runners' hearts and blood pressure. A good many stayed in the tent for the rest of the afternoon, until they felt strong enough to walk again.

   a. Marathons are grueling and exhausting events.
   b. Anybody who runs a marathon is crazy.

5. Almost every automobile advertisement has a gorgeous model somewhere in the background. Usually she does not drive the car. She simply stands next to it and looks beautiful. The suggestion is that the woman goes with the car. Liquor advertisements are also fond of showing breathtaking beauties hanging on the arms of men smart enough to buy brand X whiskey. Even the makers of men's cologne use women to advertise their product. Usually, some lovely young thing is swept off her feet and falls madly in love with the wearer of brand Y cologne.

   a. It is common practice in advertising to suggest that use of a particular product will attract beautiful women.
   b. Using attractive women to sell products is insulting to both women and men.

CHAPTER 7
Drawing Inferences from Visual Aids

SUGGESTIONS FOR TEACHING CHAPTER 7

1. Emphasize that visual aids serve three purposes: (1) They reinforce what's said in the text (2) They provide evidence for the author's point and (3) They add information that might be too time-consuming to supply in verbal form. When readers look at a visual aid, they need to determine what purpose (or purposes) it's serving. Readers need to study not just the visual aid itself but also the title and caption. Then they need to infer answers to these questions: Why is this visual aid present on the page? What's its relationship to what's said in the text? The answers to these questions can be more or less obvious. But the crucial point is this: *The answers are never supplied by the author*. The author never says, "Here's a graph now that supports my claims about the increase in hurricanes due to global warming. I placed it here to convince you that what I am saying should be taken very seriously." It's the reader's job to draw that inference.

2. Open every discussion of a visual aid by describing its most common use or general purpose. For me this has always been a problem with explanations of visual aids: The explanations explain how the chart, table or graph is constructed, but don't explain what it's most likely to be used for or when say a bar graph is more effective to use than a pie chart.

3. I'm a huge fan of books like Darrell Huff's "How to Lie With Statistics." But students don't have to read the book to get the idea: Statistics can mislead. This is an important point to emphasize. Before students accept as true everything they see in chart or graph form, they need to know the source of the figures, what bias might be reflected in the source, and how recent the figures are.

4. In teaching about pie charts, emphasize that they highlight part-to-whole relationships. But you might want to point out as well that they are most effective when the pieces or sectors in the pie are large. Most instruction on how to use pie charts emphasize that lots of little slivers in the pie do not make for easy viewing.

5. For the pie charts and the other visual aids in this chapter, except for drawings or cartoons, go to http://nces.ed.gov/nceskids/index.asp. Tell students to make their own visual aids using personal data or data taken from their textbooks. It's the easiest site on the web to follow, and the graphs turn out great.

6. Bar graphs don't measure part-to-whole relationships. Their purpose is make comparisons between related things or events, usually to indicate differences or changes over the course of time. While sometimes bar graphs and pie charts can be used interchangeably for the same data, for instance, the figures on health care in the Power Point accompanying this chapter, the bar graph is the visual aid of choice when (1) the author is recording the frequency with which something occurs or (2) there are lots of variables, for instance, the tax rates in industrialized countries.

   For a review of bar graphs: http://cstl.syr.edu/FIPSE/TabBar/CONTENTS.HTM

7. While bar graphs can also track changes over time, they can't do it in the subtle way line graphs do, so writers are use bar graphs when they want their readers to see subtle changes. Again, I think it's important to point this out to students so that they have a clear understanding of why an author chooses one kind of visual aid over another.

SUPPLEMENTARY MATERIALS

7.1 This web site offers a brief overview and a quiz on visual aids:

   http://www.tv411.org/lessons/cfm/reading.cfm?num=10&act=2&que=1

CHAPTER 8

Beyond the Paragraph: Reading Longer Selections

SUGGESTIONS FOR TEACHING CHAPTER 8

1. Emphasize that this chapter builds on previous knowledge. Students need to realize that if they can locate the essential elements in a paragraph, they have already taken a major step toward reading and understanding longer selections.

2. Asking students to write a short paper is probably the best way to reinforce the reading instruction in this chapter. Students really begin to understand the relationship between main ideas in paragraphs and the main idea of the entire reading once they have had to create their own interconnected web of ideas. In this case, I also like to use a sentence outline as a first draft; that way students can check the relationship between paragraphs and reinforce what they've learned in Chapter 8—that every main idea of a paragraph must in some way point or refer to the more general main idea.

SUPPLEMENTARY MATERIALS

8.1 Recognizing Thesis Statements

8.2 Guidelines for Summary Writing

8.3 Sample Summary

8.4 Summarizing Exercise

8.1   RECOGNIZING THESIS STATEMENTS

Directions: Underline the thesis statement of each reading.

1.   Female Athletes and Eating Disorders

Statistics show that athletic activities requiring a lean physical body predispose serious, competitive female participants to eating disorders. In figure skating, gymnastics, and ballet, more than half of competitive females report some form of pathological dieting, and as many as 25 percent are dangerously underweight or undernourished (Graber et al., 1996; Zerbe, 1993). This figure is more than double that for other women athletes (e.g., softball or basketball) and many times higher than for women in general. Eating disorders among skaters, gymnasts, and ballet dancers usually take the form of either *anorexia nervosa* or *bulimia.*

Several factors contribute to the prevalence of eating disorders among women in the "lean" sports. Competitive skating and ballet require much practice and pencil-like proportions to make turns and lifts. This sets the stage for excessive exercise and a compulsion to prove one's worth through competitions.

Most winners of Olympic competitions in these sports are teenagers, and the females are five to ten years younger than their male counterparts (Ryan, 1995). They are likely to be slender because some have not yet fully experienced puberty and because intense exercise delays the onset of puberty. Their immaturity makes them less likely to question the intense exercise needed to succeed at skating or gymnastics.

These young females may not seem obviously troubled because their activities support society's gender-role expectations. Both their talent and appearance are what the public often wants to see: a childlike body combined with a competitive spirit, one that performs on demand and does not mind being looked at intently or even erotically (Guttman, 1996; Hesse-Biber, 1996). Under these conditions, it becomes easy to hide an eating disorder. (Adapted from Kelvin L. Seifert, Robert J. Hoffnung, and Michele Hoffnung, *Lifespan Development.* Boston: Houghton Mifflin, 2000, p. 354.)

2.   Mate Selection

Early adulthood is a time when people look for partners, or mates. How do they find them? Many cultural myths lead us to believe that "opposites attract" or that we "will meet a stranger across a crowded room." These myths do not hold up to the scrutiny of scientific study. Similarities are what bring people together into romantic or sexual relationships (Murstein, 1988). Bill and Karen are a good example. They met on the same job on the same university campus and found they came from the same area and knew some of the same people. In the National Health and Social Life Survey (NHSLS), Robert Michael and his associates (1994) found that people's sexual partners were overwhelmingly like them in race/ethnicity, age, and educational level. They varied only in religion, and the couples who married were likely to have the same religion as well.

Most people meet their partners in very conventional ways. They are introduced by people they know well, or they introduce themselves in familiar places where people come together because of their similarities. Although people do sometimes meet in outside settings, such as on a vacation or at a bar, very few go outside of their network to establish sexual relationships and, when they do, the relationships are likely to be short term (Michael et al., 1994). Sixty-three percent of the NHSLS participants who were married had been introduced by family and friends, co-workers, classmates, and neighbors, as were 60 percent of couples living together and 55 percent of couples not living together and in a relationship lasting more than one month. The most common places people met were school, work, a private party, or a religious institution, all places where they were likely to find others similar to themselves. The NHSLS study found that when people in the same social network introduced each other or met each other in a preselected place, each person's friends and family were more likely to approve of the relationship, which helped the partnership to last (Michael et al., 1994).

You may be wondering why, since we meet a lot of people similar to ourselves in familiar places, some relationships "click" while others do not. It appears that we are more vulnerable to falling in love when our lives are turbulent (Hatfield, 1988). If we have experienced the loss of another relationship or are unsettled by life events, we are more likely to be open to romantic love (Bergmann, 1988). Potential partners may be in sight, but we do not notice them unless we are in need of them.

How does sex affect the development of romantic relationships? Getting to know someone as a friend before having sex is more likely to lead to a long-term relationship than responding to passion first and then trying to build intimacy. The more permanent the relationships of the NHSLS participants, the longer the partners had known each other before they had sex (Michael et al., 1994). In 90 percent of the married couples the spouses knew each other more than a month before they had sex, and in about 50 percent they knew each other more than a year. This does not necessarily mean they were dating for a long time before they had sex; rather, like Bill and Karen, they probably knew each other and were friends for awhile before dating. Most people were unlikely to have had sex immediately after meeting, and when they did the relationship was likely to have lasted a month or less. It seems that people proceed differently if they are interested in a casual sexual relationship than if they seek a long-term relationship. (Seifert, Hoffhung, and Hoffhung, *Lifespan Development,* pp. 478–79.)

3.   Affirmative Action Programs

An *affirmative action program* is a plan designed to increase the number of minority employees at all levels within an organization. Employers with federal contracts of more than $50,000 per year must have written affirmative action plans. The objective of such programs is to ensure that minorities are represented within the organization in approximately the same proportion as in the surrounding community. If 25 percent of the electricians in a geographic area where a company is located are black, then approximately 25 percent of the electricians it employs should also be black. Affirmative action plans encompass all areas of human resources management: recruiting, hiring, training, promotion, and pay.

In the beginning, many firms pledged to recruit and hire a certain number of minority members by a specific date. To achieve this goal, they were forced to consider only minority applicants for job openings; if they hired nonminority workers, they would be defeating their own purpose. But the courts have ruled that such quotas are unconstitutional even though their purpose is commendable.[*] They are, in fact, a form of discrimination.

Unfortunately, not all business people are in favor of affirmative action programs, although most such programs have been reasonably successful. Managers not committed to these programs can "play the game" and still discriminate against workers. To help solve this problem, Congress created (and later strengthened) the *Equal Employment Opportunity Commission* (EEOC), a government agency with the power to investigate complaints of employment discrimination and the power to sue firms that practice it.

The threat of legal action has persuaded some corporations to amend their hiring and promotional policies, but the discrepancy between men's and women's salaries has not really been affected. For more than thirty years, women have consistently earned only about 60 cents for each dollar earned by men. (Adapted from Pride et al., *Business.* Copyright © 1993 by Houghton Mifflin Company. Used by permission.)

4.   The Rise and Fall of Rasputin

---

[*] commendable: praiseworthy

Grigori Rasputin, the Russian monk, was an influential member of Czar* Nicholas's court from 1907 until 1916. During that time, he managed to discredit not only himself but the czar's authority as well. Rasputin first acquired power in 1907, when it was discovered that Alexei, the czar's son, suffered from hemophilia, a mysterious blood disorder. Because he appeared able to heal the boy, Rasputin became the czarina's* closest friend. She relied on him for every decision, making him the most influential member of her entourage.*

By 1909, with the help of the czarina, Rasputin dominated the Holy Synod, the supreme body in the Russian Orthodox Church. But he refused to abandon the riotous ways of his youth, and rumors circulated about his drunken orgies. Rasputin, however, did not seem to care, responding with his personal brand of religious credo: "Sin in order that you may obtain forgiveness."

In 1911 Rasputin was so sure of his powers that he began to meddle openly in political affairs. Although Russian aristocrats had at first found him a willing instrument, they soon realized that his power had grown beyond their control. Because he was standing in the way of reforms needed to divert the impending revolution, it was clear that something had to be done.

In December 1916, a group of his former supporters waylaid and assassinated the monk. But if they hoped to ward off the revolution by killing Rasputin, their efforts were in vain. By 1917, the peasants were in revolt, and the Russian Revolution had begun.

---

* czar: male ruler in Russia before 1917.
* czarina: female ruler in Russia before 1917.
* entourage: train or group of followers.

8.2   GUIDELINES FOR SUMMARY WRITING

Guidelines for Summary Writing

1. **Highlight the Essentials.** Underline and mark your text while you read to discover and highlight the essential elements—the overall main idea, the supporting details needed to explain or prove that the main idea, and any other concluding statements that make predictions, offers solutions, or describes consequences.

2. **Introductions Aren't Necessary.** Start your summary with the main idea of the entire reading. Introductions are essential to essays, not bare-bones summaries.

3. **Use Questions to Guide Your Thinking.** Ask yourself which reasons, examples, facts, etc., are absolutely essential to your understanding of the main idea. Generally speaking, your summary should be guided by the same questions that organize the opening paragraphs of newspaper articles. A good summary should tell you *who, what, when, where, why,* and *how.*

4. **Use Your Own Words.** Here again, paraphrasing is essential. Through paraphrasing, you give your mind a chance to rework and rethink the material. If your summary uses the exact same words as the author, you can't be sure you understood the meaning that resides in those words.

5. **Accuracy Counts.** Be as accurate as possible. The need to be selective, for example, doesn't mean you can distort the author's meaning. For example, if the reading talks about two causes of global warming and your summary makes it seem that there is only one, you are distorting the author's original meaning, and that's a mistake. If there are two causes, you need to summarize both. Don't sacrifice accuracy in the name of brevity.

6. **Don't Interpret.** A summary should give an abbreviated version of the author's ideas. It should not include any of your own interpretations or comments. Save those for the margins of your text, where you can comment to your heart's content.

7. **Consider Your Purpose.** If your summary is strictly for your own personal use, you needn't worry about how you refer to the author or title. However, if you are turning the summary in, then the first sentence should indicate your source, e.g., "Writing for *Timeout* magazine (May 19, 2004), Boyle Haddon criticizes Michael Moore's politics but still manages to praise Moore's controversial film.

8.3 SAMPLE SUMMARY

Here to illustrate is a sample reading followed by a summary. Note how much the original text has been reduced:

Hard versus Soft News

Where news is concerned, there are two different categories, hard news and soft news. The former is what most people think of as news. Something actually happens on a particular day—a bank is robbed, a bridge collapses, or civil war breaks out in a foreign land. Time is an important consideration in such stories. They are news because they are the day's fresh happenings in local and world events and must be reported to the public as rapidly as possible.

Soft news, on the other hand, is not so time-critical. It focuses on situations, people, or events that have "human interest." Such stories are seldom based on events that are restricted to a particular day. Thus, they can be used in the news whenever they are needed.

A classic example is the story of a pair of male and female eagles in the Syracuse, New York, zoo. Captured originally as part of a breeding program to reestablish eagles in the wild, the pair finally bred and the mother incubated an egg until a chick hatched. Then the mother died. Observers predicted disaster. Surprisingly, however, the male eagle took over the job of raising the newly hatched infant. The father fed the baby regularly, cleaned it. and so on, until it grew large enough to be released in the wild. The local media and the public loved it, and these events provided an ongoing series of touching stories—a classic example of soft news. (Melvin L. DeFleur and Everette E. Dennis, *Understanding Mass Communication,* 6th ed. Boston: Houghton Mifflin. 1998, p. 243.)

Summary

News can be divided into two kinds, hard and soft. Daily happenings in local, national, and world affairs make up hard news. The collapse of a bridge or the outbreak of civil war is hard news. Soft news need not be particularly current, but it must have human interest. A father eagle who takes care of a fledgling when the mother dies is a good example of soft news.

In this summary, only the absolute essentials remain from the original reading. The controlling main idea remains, as do just enough of the supporting details to make that idea meaningful. In short, the summary has reduced the original material to its bare bones. That's what makes it effective for later reviews.

8.4 SUMMARIZING EXERCISE

Directions: Read the sample selection and summary that follows. Then read and summarize the selection titled "The Christian Music Industry."

Example:

Interethnic Friendships

Friendships between adolescents from different ethnic and racial groups tend to be an exception rather than the rule. One national study of students enrolled in more than one thousand public and private high schools in the United States found that fewer than 3.5 percent of the eighteen thousand friendships identified by students involved friendships between African-American and white teens (Hallianan & Williams, 1989).

However, the social contexts in which potential friendship interactions occur seem to make an important difference. In one study of school and neighborhood friendship patterns among African-American and white students attending integrated high schools, most students reported having a close other-race school friend. But only about one-quarter saw such a friend frequently outside school.

Living in a neighborhood with children from other ethnic groups appears to increase the likelihood of having close other-race friends outside of school. Having a higher proportion of neighborhood friends attending one's school affects other-race friendship. Living in a racially mixed neighborhood can help create positive attitudes toward members of other ethnic groups and provide a meeting ground on which cross-race friendships can develop outside of school. The informal peer activities that occur in neighborhood settings are more likely to promote close friendships across groups than the more formal teacher-directed activities in school. (Adapted from Seifert et al., *Lifespan Development,* p. 394.)

Summary:

Interethnic friendships between adolescents tend to be rare. In one study, only 3.5 percent of the

18,000 friendships observed were between white and African-American adolescents. However,

interethnic friendships definitely seem to be affected by social context. In one study of integrated

high schools, most students reported having a friend of another race. Living in a neighborhood with

children from other ethnic groups seems to encourage interethnic friendships.

Explanation:

The summary considerably reduces the original reading, but it does cover the essentials. It identifies the implied main idea—although interethnic friendships seem to be rare, they tend to increase under the right conditions—as well as the study cited in support of that main idea. Note, however, that the summary also names the social contexts which affect interethnic friendships among adolescents. This, too, is essential because so much of the reading is devoted to explaining the factors that can encourage adolescent interethnic relationships.

Now it's your turn to write a summary of the following article.

The Christian Music Industry

For many years, the Christian music segment of the record business was nearly invisible. Most record stores did not stock Christian albums. Instead, over 90 percent of all Christian music was sold through religious bookstores, usually small, locally owned businesses. The exhibition side of the industry was also separate from the rest of the record industry. Followers learned about Christian artists through one of the hundreds of religious radio and television stations across the United States or from their friends at church.

Today Christian music accounts for more than 3 percent of all album sales, and Christian music has become increasingly mainstream. Christian albums have earned a place in the record racks of chain stores such as Wal-Mart. Christian artists like Kutless Skillet and Switchfoot have branched out from their core Christian music emphasis and gotten main stream exposure.

Recent figures indicated that, in total, Christian music has become a billion dollar a year industry, with Christian music the sixth most popular type of music in the United States. Some artists worry that this commercial success is harming the genre* because major music labels have bought out formerly independent religious record companies. These new owners seem less focused on ministry and more on money. Like artists in other musical genres, Christian artists are finding that in the music business, the emphasis is increasingly less on music and more on business. (Adapted from Turow, *Media Today*, p. 213.)

Summary

_____

_____

_____

_____

_____

_____

_____

_____

_____

_____

_____

* genre: category or class.

CHAPTER 9
Recognizing Patterns of Organization in Paragraphs

SUGGESTIONS FOR TEACHING CHAPTER 9

1. Try to have students write paragraphs or brief papers using all six patterns (actually seven because the time order pattern includes both process and sequence of dates and events paragraph patterns).

2. Stress the extent to which recognition of an author's underlying pattern or patterns can aid remembering. You might even demonstrate by asking students to read some selections in which the underlying patterns of exposition are obvious. Once they are through reading, ask them to recall the key elements of each pattern. Students are usually impressed by how much they can remember if they organize new information according to the underlying pattern.

3. Students should realize that the majority of paragraphs and readings mix patterns. However, practice with shorter passages that rely on one pattern is still useful because it helps students become familiar with the particular characteristics of each pattern.

4. It's very hard to find "pure" paragraph patterns. Process, for example, almost always contains elements of cause and effect, so in teaching Chapter 9, I always tell students that they are being asked for the *primary pattern*. This is the one that organizes most of the sentences in a paragraph. They should not be misled by a *single sentence* that uses another pattern.

5. For years I balked at including simple listing because it so often overlaps with other patterns. But finally, thanks to prodding from my colleague Denice Josten, I gave in and added the simple listing pattern. I think she's right: There are times when it's the only pattern that really applies (for instance in paragraphs telling readers what not to do in a job interview).

   However, I think there will still be times when it's a toss up as to whether, for example, the pattern is cause and effect or simple listing, e.g. "The arrival of blogs devoted to news and politics has posed a number of significant challenges for traditional media." If a student labeled a passage developing that topic sentence, *Simple Listing*, I'd say yes, now tell me the challenges listed. Yet if another student said the pattern was cause and effect because the challenges are the effects of blogs becoming more political than personal, I'd agree with that too and ask the student to paraphrase the challenges.

My point is that I consider the label of the paragraph's organizational pattern less significant than how the student uses that label to derive meaning from the passage, and in this case, I think both labels can get students what they need to know.

6. The only time I'm inclined to call an answer about patterns of organization dead wrong is when the student can only point to a single sentence as evidence of that pattern. Patterns organize supporting details, and the emphasis here is on the plural. As I have said so often to students, one sentence does not a pattern make.

SUPPLEMENTARY MATERIALS

9.1 Identifying Primary Patterns of Organization

9.2 Identifying Primary Patterns of Organization

9.1 Identifying Primary Patterns of Organization

Directions: Circle the letter of the primary pattern used to organize details in each of the following paragraphs.

1. When it comes to holding down a job, working well with others is extremely important for your professional success. Thus it pays to know the five kinds of behavior that can deeply irritate both colleagues and supervisors. Not being self-reliant is high on the list. That means if the copier runs out of paper just as you finish using it, make sure you refill it. Don't leave the job for someone else. Keeping your cell phone on continuously and talking in a loud voice, particularly during a personal call, are both guaranteed to drive everyone you work with to distraction. Therefore, avoid doing either. And if you are sick, stay home. You may feel like a martyr when you go to work with a bad cold. However, your colleagues will see you as a walking germ factory and celebrate your selflessness. It should be obvious, too, that while cleanliness may not really be next to godliness, as the old saying goes, personal hygiene is important. Absolutely no one likes working next to someone who smells as if he or she just lifted weights for an hour and forgot to shower.

    a.   definition
    b.   time order
    c.   simple listing
    d.   comparison and contrast
    e.   cause and effect
    f.   classification

2. The goal of nonassertive behavior is to avoid conflict and tension, and it is often accompanied by statements like "Don't make waves" or "I don't want any trouble." Unfortunately, those who are prone to nonassertive behavior frequently don't get what they want. The goal of assertive behavior, in contrast, is to directly and honestly communicate one's desires and wishes. A person who is assertive takes action rather than just thinking about it and usually ends up satisfied with the results.

    a.   definition
    b.   time order
    c.   simple listing
    d.   comparison and contrast
    e.   cause and effect
    f.   classification

3. A good sales interview begins by the salesperson establishing a relationship, arousing interest, and getting the consumer involved. Then the salesperson explores the customer's needs through probing questions, careful listening, and observation. The next step is to present the product or service and illustrate how it will meet the customer's needs. This step is followed by an acknowledgment of the potential buyer's objections in which the salesperson explores and answers each objection. Finally, at the closing of the sale, the salesperson reiterates the reasons to decide favorably, asks for a commitment, and paves the way for future business.

    a.   definition
    b.   time order
    c.   simple listing
    d.   comparison and contrast
    e.   cause and effect
    f.   classification

4. Throughout their lives, human beings are bound to undergo periods of psychological crisis. However, according to Erik Erikson's theory of psychological development, the threat of death brings about the most profound form of psychological crisis. The threat or possibility of death causes people to evaluate their lives and accomplishments and affirm them as meaningful (leading to a feeling of integrity) or meaningless (leading to a feeling of despair). They also tend to become more philosophical and reflective, attempting to put their lives into perspective. They reminisce, resolve past conflicts, and integrate past events. They may also become more interested in the religious and spiritual side of life. This "life review" may trigger anxiety, regret, guilt, and despair, or it may allow people to face their own death and the deaths of friends and relatives with a feeling of peace and acceptance. (Adapted from Douglas A. Bernstein et al., *Psychology*. Boston: Houghton Mifflin, 1997, p. 425.)

   a. definition
   b. time order
   c. simple listing
   d. comparison and contrast
   e. cause and effect
   f. classification

5. According to Maslow's theory of needs, human beings have five different kinds of needs that can be ranked in order of importance. First, humans have physiological needs such as the needs for food, air, and water. Next comes security needs, which reflect the desire for physical and emotional safety from harm. Third in rank are needs for belonging. These include the desire for love and affection. Next comes esteem needs, which include the need for recognition and respect. Finally, at the top of the list are self-actualization needs like the need to grow, develop, and expand one's abilities.

   a. definition
   b. time order
   c. simple listing
   d. comparison and contrast
   e. cause and effect
   f. classification

6. In the 1960s, Rubin "Hurricane" Carter was a top contender for the middleweight boxing championship. In 1966, however, he and a friend were arrested for shooting to death three white people in a tavern. Though he maintained his innocence, Carter was convicted of the crime by an all-white jury and imprisoned. In 1974, he published his autobiography, claiming that he was a falsely accused victim of racism. In 1975, his story inspired singer/songwriter Bob Dylan to write a song about the injustice of the case. This song, entitled "Hurricane," elevated Carter to the status of a folk hero. About the same time, witnesses who helped convict Carter recanted their testimony. In 1976, Carter was granted a new trial and released for six months. However, he was convicted a second time and sent back to prison, where he spent another nine years. During that time, a group of Canadians worked to free him, and in 1985, a federal judge affirmed Carter's charge of racism and released him.

   a. definition
   b. time order
   c. simple listing
   d. comparison and contrast
   e. cause and effect
   f. classification

7. El Niño, which is Spanish for "boy child" or baby Jesus, was named by a fisherman who noticed a warm ocean current around Christmas. This abnormal warming of a huge area of the tropic Pacific Ocean occurs every few years as part of the "Southern Oscillation," the varying pattern of air pressure in different parts of the Pacific, and lasts about eighteen months. El Niño creates changes in rainfall patterns, ocean currents, and water temperatures, which affect weather all over the world. It produces more hurricanes in the Pacific Ocean and decreases hurricane activity in the Atlantic Ocean and Gulf of Mexico. Also, it's been blamed for increased flooding in North America as well as droughts in Australia, Africa, and South America. The El Niño of 1982–1983 was responsible for weather that damaged hundreds of thousands of homes and killed 2,000 people. The 1997–1998 El Niño contributed to a shipwreck and an airplane crash.

    a. definition
    b. time order
    c. simple listing
    d. comparison and contrast
    e. cause and effect
    f. classification

8. To decide what type of fire extinguisher to purchase, a homeowner needs to understand the three basic classes of fires. Class A fires are those caused by ordinary combustibles such as wood, paper, cloth, and plastic. This type of fire can be extinguished with water or foam. Class B fires are caused by flammable liquids, greases, or gases. These fires are extinguished by depriving them of oxygen or inhibiting their chemical chain reaction. Therefore, foam, carbon dioxide, or dry chemicals are the most effective extinguishers. Class C fires are electrical fires. They only can be snuffed out with a substance that does not conduct electricity. Therefore, they should never be doused with water. Instead, they must be extinguished with carbon dioxide or dry chemicals.

    a. definition
    b. time order
    c. simple listing
    d. comparison and contrast
    e. cause and effect
    f. classification

9. Prompt treatment of a snakebite can prevent serious or long-term medical problems. First, the victim should wrap a bandage tightly two to four inches above the bite, applying pressure but not cutting off the blood flow to the area. Second, he or she should immobilize the bitten area to avoid increasing circulation. If possible, a splint should be applied by wrapping a rigid object in place with a bandage or gauze. Third, the victim should lower the bitten area so that it's below his or her heart. Fourth, the victim should immediately report to a hospital or urgent care facility so that a medical professional can determine whether an injection of anti-venom is necessary.

    a. definition
    b. time order
    c. simple listing
    d. comparison and contrast
    e. cause and effect
    f. classification

10. "Junk" mail delivered by the United States Postal Service and computer "spam" are both legal, unsolicited forms of commercial advertising; however, they differ in their format, the ethics of the advertisers, and their cost to the recipient. While junk mail is almost always printed on paper and sent to an individual's U.S. postal address, spam is an electronic message sent to a computer user's

e-mail address. Advertisers who send out junk mail or spam can obtain lists of recipients' addresses from either legitimate or unethical sources, but those who generate spam are more likely to resort to unscrupulous practices, such as stealing mailing lists, to gather the contact information of potential customers. Also, many spam messages are often deceptive or fraudulent. For example, they frequently advertise get-rich-quick schemes or questionable products. In contrast, junk mail tends to offer more legitimate goods and services. The most significant difference, though, is in the cost of junk mail and spam. An advertiser pays for the printing and distribution of junk mail, and the recipient pays nothing to receive it. Spam, however, costs the recipient money. Computer users who pay for the amount of time they spend online are forced to use up some of that time to receive, read, and discard spam messages. Those who dial a long-distance telephone number to connect to the Internet must pay additional charges to deal with the spam they receive. Even users with unlimited local access to the Internet must absorb the cost of spam when Internet service providers pass the cost of transmitting it on to their subscribers. As a result, many people are working to limit and control the distribution of spam.

a. definition
b. time order
c. simple listing
d. comparison and contrast
e. cause and effect
f. classification

9.2 IDENTIFYING PRIMARY PATTERNS OF ORGANIZATION

Directions: Circle the letter of the primary pattern that organizes details in each of the following readings.

1. When it is young, a star is composed mostly of hydrogen. As the star ages, gravity pulls all of the hydrogen toward the star's center and compresses it. As it compresses, the hydrogen heats up, and the center of the star becomes very hot indeed. When the temperature passes a certain point, the hydrogen atoms smash into each other with enough force to cause *fusion*. In fusion, two hydrogen atoms collide and form one helium atom. As the temperature continues to rise, the helium atoms fuse into heavier elements, which in turn fuse into still heavier elements. Finally, when the star has formed iron, it can extract no further energy from fusion. Without this energy, the star begins to collapse. If it is large enough, the star will explode violently in a *supernova*. It is in these brief, spectacular supernovas that all elements heavier than iron (such as lead and gold) are formed. The explosion scatters these heavy elements into space, where they may gather once more to form new stars or planets.

    a. definition
    b. time order
    c. simple listing
    d. comparison and contrast
    e. cause and effect
    f. classification

2. Because of worries about chemicals leeching into the water from plastic containers, Americans have begun to cut back on their consumption of bottled water. However, many people still consume bottled water, sometimes several bottles a day, because they have fallen for the myths perpetuated, to a large degree, by companies who bottle and distribute water. One of those myths is that bottled water is always better for you than water from the tap. But, in fact, between 25 and 40 percent of bottled water comes from city water supplies. Bottling companies just buy the water and filter it. Another myth is that drinking eight glasses of water per day is a must. While getting a substantial amount of fluid on a daily basis is good for the body, it's also true that the coffee you drink and fruits you eat are all part of your fluid intake. Thus there is no medical reason for you to consume eight classes of water. Coffee, soda, and fruit can also replenish your fluid supply. Yet another myth is that bottled water with added vitamins and minerals is better for you than tap water. Bottled water with added minerals and vitamins has so little of each that it doesn't really qualify as a source of either.

    a. definition
    b. time order
    c. simple listing
    d. comparison and contrast
    e. cause and effect
    f. classification

3. While Alexander the Great is normally viewed as a hero of Greek civilization, some modern historians consider him to be in the same category with Adolf Hitler. But this comparison is somewhat extreme, given the fundamental differences between the two leaders. Alexander desired to explore the world, and while he fought to assert his dominance over other cultures, he never attempted genocide,* as Hitler did. Alexander was also content to leave a city or town essentially untouched as long as residents acknowledged him to be king. Hitler was incapable of such political flexibility. Whereas Hitler's lust for conquest and discovery matched Alexander's, his energies were

---

* genocide: the planned murder of an entire race or group.

turned toward a horrifying dream of "racial purification." Although both men sought to bring the known world under a single rule, Alexander maintained a moral standard—even in pitched battle—that Adolf Hitler refused to acknowledge.

a. definition
b. time order
c. simple listing
d. comparison and contrast
e. cause and effect
f. classification

4. After a bone fracture has been x-rayed, it can be identified as one of several different types. In a *transverse fracture,* the break is straight across the shaft of the bone. In an *oblique fracture,* the break is at an angle with the shaft. A *spiral fracture* has the appearance of a spring, and is often associated with twisting injuries. When the ends of the broken bones are pressed into each other, the fracture is said to be *impacted. Comminuted fractures* often occur with severe crush injuries that break the bone into several pieces. Lastly, a *greenstick fracture* occurs almost exclusively in children, whose bones are more flexible than an adult's. In this fracture, the break does not completely cross the bone, and is so called because the bone appears like a green stick or twig that has been bent but not fully broken.

a. definition
b. time order
c. simple listing
d. comparison and contrast
e. cause and effect
f. classification

5. Like so many true geniuses, Albert Einstein made his mark upon the world while still quite young. In 1905, at the age of twenty-six, Einstein published a scientific paper while working as a technical expert (third class) in a Swiss patent office. The paper, which described Einstein's special theory of relativity, radically changed the way in which people viewed the physical world, and Einstein became a world-famous figure. By 1907, Einstein had formulated a new fundamental principle—the *equivalence principle*—which asserted that gravity and acceleration were equivalent. Formulation of this principle paved the way for Einstein to work on a general theory of relativity, a theory that was free of problems which afflicted his special theory of relativity and that took into account the phenomenon of gravity. In 1909, Einstein resigned from the patent office to take up a faculty appointment at the University of Zürich. Although Einstein did not publish any papers concerned with gravity during this period, he was devoting considerable thought to it. Formulation of the general theory was not easy for Einstein, and it was not until 1916 that he was ready to publish it. The general theory forced physicists to further revise their concepts of time, space, and light. Unfortunately, Einstein's contributions to physics in the latter half of his life did not approach those made in the years 1905–1916. This was partly due to Einstein's inability to accept a new branch of physics called *quantum physics,* which postulates uncertainty at a fundamental level. Einstein could not believe that God, as he put it, would "play dice."

a. definition
b. time order
c. simple listing
d. comparison and contrast
e. cause and effect
f. classification

6. The sherry producers of Spain draw upon the chalky soil of the Jerez (Spanish for "sherry") region in southern Spain to grow the unique palomino grape, which provides the basis for four different sherries. *Oloroso,* a full-bodied Spanish sherry, is the basis for the best sweet sherries. True to its nature, the oloroso sherry is a fragrant beverage. The more delicate *fino* or dry sherry is a light gold wine in which a yeast is allowed to develop during production. This yeast gives a distinct character to the fino variety of sherries, which are not allowed to age much. *Amontillado* is a sherry made famous to teetotalers by Edgar Allen Poe in his short story "The Cask of Amontillado." The best amontillados are aged to produce a nutty, powerful flavor. *Cream sherries* are created by blending together dry and sweet sherries to create a dark rich wine with a high alcohol content. While sherry is produced elsewhere in the world, these four sherries are considered to be the finest.

   a. definition
   b. time order
   c. simple listing
   d. comparison and contrast
   e. cause and effect
   f. classification

7. World War II (1939–1945) stimulated renewed interest in propaganda research. Yale scholars studied orientation films used by the U.S. Army to indoctrinate new recruits. The research focused on measuring attitude change, which lent itself readily to "before/after" laboratory tests. These studies initiated a new phase of effects research, laying the groundwork for an attempt to set forth principles of communication effects backed by scientific evidence (Sydney W. Head, Christopher H. Sterling, and Lemuel B. Schofield, *Broadcasting in America.* Boston: Houghton Mifflin, 1994, p. 421.)

   a. definition
   b. time order
   c. simple listing
   d. comparison and contrast
   e. cause and effect
   f. classification

8. The golden age of the Roman Empire was defined by the reigns of what came to be called the "five good emperors." The first of the five was the Emperor Nerva, whose reign lasted only from A.D. 96 to 98. Possibly the most important act on Nerva's part was the adoption of one Marcus Ulpius Trajanus as his heir and successor. When Nerva died, Trajanus took his place on the throne. Known as the Emperor Trajan, his reign lasted until his death in 117 and was marked by extensive building programs, as well as social and economic reform throughout the empire. Succeeding Trajan was his younger cousin Hadrian, who had fought with the Roman army. As emperor, Hadrian reformed the Roman government while protecting the empire's frontiers from outside attacks. After Hadrian followed Antoninus Pius in 138. Antoninus, who ruled until his death in 161, was a just and gentle ruler, and his reign was probably the most peaceful in Roman history. Just as Nerva had adopted Trajan, so did Antoninus adopt Marcus Aurelius, who succeeded Antoninus and defended the empire against the first heavy barbarian attacks. Marcus died in 180, and with his death ended Rome's golden age.

   a. definition
   b. time order
   c. simple listing
   d. comparison and contrast
   e. cause and effect
   f. classification

9. **Competitive advantage** refers to the advantage or disadvantage a firm holds in relation to its competitors. For example, Microsoft's competitive advantages include its well-known name and its

dominance in the computer software market. As one might expect, holding on to a competitive advantage is a major goal of any firm. Microsoft, for example, has been highly criticized for some of the methods it uses to retain its competitive advantages.

a. definition
b. time order
c. simple listing
d. comparison and contrast
e. cause and effect
f. classification

10. CPR, or cardiopulmonary resuscitation, can save lives, but it must be performed properly to do so. If you suspect that someone is experiencing respiratory or heart failure, you need to assess the extent of his or her difficulties before beginning CPR. First, check the airway for signs of breathing. By looking for the rise and fall of the chest while listening and feeling for air movement, you can quickly determine whether the patient is breathing or not. If no signs of breathing are evident, then deliver two breaths into the patient's airway, allowing one to two seconds for each breath in an adult patient. After delivering the breaths, determine the presence or absence of a pulse by feeling one of the patient's carotid arteries, located on either side of the windpipe. If you can't feel a pulse, begin CPR. The ratio of chest compressions—which force the heart to pump blood—to rescue breathing is fifteen to two. CPR may be performed by one or two persons on people of any age and should be continued until the patient has been brought to a hospital or revived independently.

a. definition
b. time order
c. simple listing
d. comparison and contrast
e. cause and effect
f. classification

CHAPTER 10
Combining Patterns in Paragraphs and Longer Readings

SUGGESTIONS FOR TEACHING CHAPTER 10

1. Students need to know that the main idea governs the pattern, not the other way around. As soon as readers can determine the main idea, they are on their way to recognizing the organizational pattern or patterns likely to be used in the passage. Thus if they think the main idea is something like "As a resource for serious research, Wikipedia was slow to win respect, but since its creator Jimmy Wales instituted some crucial editorial changes, the web site has dramatically improved its reputation," then they would be wise to start looking for the key elements in two patterns: dates and events and simple listing. If elements from neither pattern appear, then they might reconsider what they believe to be the main idea.

2. Tell students to look for defining characteristics. For example, if the author breaks a larger group down into a specific number of subgroups and, at the same time, emphasizes the differences among them, readers should immediately recognize the two intermingled patterns: classification with comparison and contrast.

3. Tell students that some patterns combine more readily than others. For example, if a paragraph or reading describes a process, it's quite likely that the author will define key terms (definition) and explain how one step leads to another (cause and effect).

4. Give students this brief list of common combinations and tell them that they are *likely* combinations. These patterns will not always appear together, but they do frequently enough for readers to check for one whenever they see the other:
   a. process with cause and effect and/or definition
   b. classification with comparison and contrast and/or cause and effect
   c. time order with cause and effect
   d. simple listing with all of the others

SUPPLEMENTARY MATERIAL
10.1 Identifying Mixed Patterns in Paragraphs

10.1 IDENTIFYING MIXED PATTERNS IN PARAGRAPHS

Directions: Circle the letter of the pattern or patterns used in each paragraph.

1. All rocks can be classified into three different categories. **Igneous rocks** are solidified *magma*, the hot liquid material expelled from volcanoes. This type of rock, which includes basalt and granite, forms the earth's outer crust, or surface. **Sedimentary rocks** are formed when sediment shakes loose from the crust. The debris then accumulates and becomes cemented together over time to form a sedimentary rock. Sandstone and shale are examples of sedimentary rocks. In the third category, **metamorphic rocks** are those that have changed form. When existing rocks are subjected to intense heat and pressure, their chemical composition is altered. Slate and marble are examples of metamorphic roc.
   a. definition
   b. time order
   c. simple listing
   d. comparison and contrast
   e. cause and effect
   f. classification

2. The American Kennel Club sorts 140 breeds of dogs into seven different groups. **Herding** dogs are bred to help herd livestock. This group includes the Collie, German Shepherd, and Old English Sheepdog. The **sporting** dogs, which include Pointers, Retrievers, Setters, and Spaniels, are those who were bred to hunt birds. The **hounds** are dogs that are bred to use vision and smell to hunt wild game. This group includes dogs such as Beagles, Bassets, Dachshunds, and Greyhounds. The **working** category includes dogs used for guarding property or conducting search-and-rescue missions. The breeds in this group include the Boxer, Doberman Pinscher, and St. Bernard. The **terriers** were bred to kill rodents. They include dogs such as the Airedale, Bull Terrier, and Scottish Terrier. The **toy** dogs, which were originally bred to be the lap dogs of royalty aren't raised to work. True to their heritage, their sole function is to be spoiled and petted. This group includes the Chihuahua, Maltese, Pomeranian, and Pug. The final category is the **nonsporting** group. It includes dogs who do not fit into the other categories. The Chow, Bulldog, and Dalmatian are in this class.
   a. definition
   b. time order
   c. simple listing
   d. comparison and contrast
   e. cause and effect
   f. classification

3. What do United States Presidents Thomas Jefferson and George W. Bush have in common? For one thing, the elections of both chief executives—one in 1800 and one exactly 200 years later in 2000— were strikingly similar. In both, questions arose about voting irregularities and possible fraud in key states: New York in 1800 and Florida in 2000. Following both elections, America endured a long, drawn-out battle between the opponents, which was stirred by ever-present journalists. In 1800, a close election between Jefferson and his own running mate* had to be decided in the U.S. House of Representatives, who argued for six days before finally choosing Jefferson. In 2000, the media followed every second of the tense and dramatic uncertainty for several weeks. Both elections finally ended with a slender victory for a candidate many believed to be unqualified. Jefferson was criticized for his character, his religious beliefs, and his political philosophies, and many feared he would dismantle the brand new federal government. At President Bush's

---

* running mate: The election of 1800 happened before a Constitutional amendment clarified that the president and vice president candidates ran as a team on the same ticket.

inauguration, large numbers of protesters marched with signs that proclaimed him to be a "thief" and denounced his intellect as inadequate.

a. definition
b. time order
c. simple listing
d. comparison and contrast
e. cause and effect
f. classification

4. The Cold War, a post-World War II struggle at its most intense between the 1940s and early 1960s, was not a direct military confrontation with battles and bloodshed. Instead, it was a period of economic and political estrangement, tension, rivalry, and conflict between the Communist Soviet Union and capitalist, democratic nations such as the United States and Great Britain. Each side perceived the other as harboring hostile intentions, which caused the accelerated buildup of military weapons, including the atomic bomb. The era of the Cold War was also constantly unsettled by sabre rattling, or threats of a war that never materialized. As a result, the treat of a nuclear war seemed to loom over the world almost unceasingly. Tensions eased during the mid-1960s and 1970s but flared again in the 1980s as a result of United States President Ronald Reagan's firm anti-Communist policies. The Cold War, however, officially ended in the early 1990s as the Soviet Union lost control over the countries it had once dominated through military might.

a. definition
b. time order
c. simple listing
d. comparison and contrast
e. cause and effect
f. classification

5. You can set up a beautiful freshwater fish aquarium in just five easy steps. In step one, purchase a short or long glass tank that holds at least ten gallons of water. Step two involves preparing and adding gravel to the tank. Wash your gravel and spread the clean gravel three inches deep over the bottom of the aquarium. In step three, fill the tank with cold tap water and add aquarium water conditioner according to the package instructions. Step four involves warming the water by installing a heater with enough wattage to raise your tank's temperature to suit the type of fish you intend to keep. In step five, you're ready to add your fish by transferring them with a net from the bag to the aquarium.

a. definition
b. time order
c. simple listing
d. comparison and contrast
e. cause and effect
f. classification

6. During a typical night, a person experiences two different kinds of sleep. **Quiet sleep** lasts about fifty to sixty minutes at a time and is characterized by deep breathing, a calm heartbeat, and slower brain waves. The last thirty to forty minutes is a period of very deep sleep from which it's difficult to awaken. The other type is **Rapid Eye Movement (REM), or active sleep**. During this phase, the eyes flutter rapidly, the face and hands twitch with spasms, and the heart rate, brain waves, and breathing resemble those of an awake person. Studies indicate that most dreams occur during REM sleep, which lasts just a few minutes at first and then lengthens as it recurs throughout the night. Sleepers cycle through both of these types several times in a night's sleep.

a. definition
b. time order
c. simple listing

    d. comparison and contrast

    e. cause and effect

    f. classification

7. When a problem is so complicated that all of its elements cannot be held in working memory at once, you can use a strategy called **decomposition** to divide it into smaller, more manageable subproblems. Thus, instead of being overwhelmed by the big problem of writing a major term paper, you can begin by writing just an outline. Next, you can select the library materials most relevant to each successive section of the outline. Then you can write summaries of those materials, then a rough draft of an introduction, and so on. (Douglas A. Bernstein et al., *Psychology*. Boston: Houghton Mifflin, 1997, p. 276.)

    a. definition

    b. time order

    c. simple listing

    d. comparison and contrast

    e. cause and effect

    f. classification

8. National attention was focused on poultry producers several years ago after an outbreak of the toxic plant-like microorganism *Pfiesteria* piscicida in parts of the Chesapeake Bay. The outbreak killed thousands of fish and posed a serious health risk to humans living close by. Because each year millions of broiler chickens are raised by factory poultry famers located on the Eastern Shore of Maryland and Virginia and all of Delaware, the finger was immediately pointed at pollution from poultry droppings and fertilizers, which had been dumped or found their way into nearby rivers. As it turns out, Pfiesteria thrives in waters enriched with precisely those nutrients found in manure Following the problems in the Chesapeake Bay, environmental groups called for more regulation of how large poultry farms get rid of bird waste. Not surprisingly, spokespeople for the poultry industry reject the idea that chicken waste is finding its way into river waters and causing Pfiesteria organisms to multiply. (Source of information: Virginia Shepherd, "Down on This Farm, the Times They Are A-changin'." *Smithsonian,* July 2000, p. 69.)

    a. definition

    b. time order

    c. simple listing

    d. comparison and contrast

    e. cause and effect

    f. classification

9. Many times supervisors and managers confuse control with structure, states Mardell Grothe, training program design consultant to the National Tooling Machining Association. He says, "Structure is good. It means laying out very clearly what you want and when you want it done and letting the persons react. Control is trying to dictate how it should be done from moment to moment." When structure is present, employees know what is to be done but realize that they have some latitude in how to complete the task. Today's better-educated and better-informed employees appreciate structure but usually react negatively to too much control. (Barry L. Reece and Rhonda Brandt, *Effective Human Relations in Organization.* Boston: Houghton Mifflin, 1999, p. 317.)

    a. definition

    b. time order

    c. simple listing

    d. comparison and contrast

    e. cause and effect

    f. classification

10. The Black Death was a fourteenth-century plague that spread quickly through Europe, killing millions. The bacteria that caused the disease originated in the Gobi Desert in the 1320s. It was

carried by rodents and transferred to humans through fleas that bit the rats, ingested their infected blood, and then bit people. Those infected would be overcome with high fever, swelling of the lymph nodes, blackening of the face, and terrible pain. Victims usually died within three or four days of exposure to the bacteria, but before they did, they spread the contagion to others. Travelers moving west along trade routes transported this terrible disease with them. By 1347, it had reached Italy. By 1348, the worst of the plague years, it had spread to France, Germany, and England. Within two years, it had killed one-third of Europe's population.

a. definition
b. time order
c. simple listing
d. comparison and contrast
e. cause and effect
f. classification

CHAPTER 11
More on Purpose, Tone, and Bias

SUGGESTIONS FOR TEACHING CHAPTER 11

1. Try giving students some articles about a controversial issue like surrogate mothers who change their minds after the baby is born, private security forces used to play the role of police or soldiers, or the growing numbers of employers who block employees from access to social networking sites. After they have read about the topic you've chosen, ask your students to define a problem associated with the topic and to put forth a solution.

    For example: *Problem:* Sometimes a surrogate mother changes her mind about giving her baby away after the child is born, and a legal battle ensues for custody of the child. *Solution:* Surrogate mothers should always have the right to change their minds, and the adoptive parents must accept that possibility as part of the risk involved in using a surrogate. Have students debate the solution in class, making it clear that they can express any opinion they choose as long as they are willing to defend it.

2. `Have students bring in, read, and discuss examples of different tones in writing. Tell them as well to bring in examples of what they think are good and bad arguments. I wouldn't restrict them to written arguments. They can use any source from television to social networking sites. All they have to do is jot down the point and paraphrase some of the reasons offered for the argument's central claim.

3. When you teach fact and opinion, emphasize that your real objective in distinguishing between the two is to make sure (1) students do not accept another person's opinions as proven facts, and (2) they notice when opinions are mixed into seemingly factual statements.

4. Keep pushing students to develop their own opinions on the subjects they read about. As often as you can, ask them to explain, in discussion or on paper, where they stand on a particular issue. Although students are often timid about expressing opinions in class, you can usually get them started if you offer a solution of your own, preferably an outrageous one, to some problem. For example: *Problem:* Kids today are far too concerned with name-brand clothing. *Solution:* From kindergarten to high school, all American schoolchildren should be made to wear uniforms.

    Most students hate this solution and are intent on finding another one, or else they insist there is no problem. But that claim leads them into defending their point of view, since much as been written about kids being obsessed, at a very young age, with expensive brand name labels. Either way, students are bound to do some critical thinking.

5.   Not every one is interested in teaching propaganda as part of critical reading, but for those who are, some exercises are here included.

SUPPLEMENTARY MATERIALS

11.1 Distinguishing Between Fact and Opinion

11.2 Recognizing Errors in Reasoning

11.3 Recognizing Propaganda (Explanation)

11.4 Recognizing Propaganda

11.5 Propaganda Techniques

11.1 DISTINGUISHING BETWEEN FACT AND OPINION

Directions: Label each item *F* (fact), *O* (opinion), or *B* (both).

1. Jules Styne wrote nineteen wonderful musicals during his lifetime. He died at the age of eighty-eight. _____

2. In December of 1997, 150 nations adopted a treaty, known as the Kyoto Protocol, which would limit emissions of carbon dioxide. _____

3. In the world of children's literature, the Harry Potter series has no equal. _____

4. As of 2001, 1999 was the fifth hottest year on record. _____

5. One of the greatest ancient healers was a Greek priest and doctor named Asclepias. He lived between 1000 and 1200 B.C. _____

6. The root of all human suffering is isolation. Throughout our lives all human beings struggle to overcome a sense of separation. _____

7. Laura Hillenbrand is the author of *Seabiscuit,* a best-selling biography about the great-hearted horse whom nobody believed could ever be a winner and who proved everyone wrong. _____

8. Aspirin was invented by a chemist named Felix Hoffman while he was working for the German chemical firm Bayer in 1893. _____

9. By using plastic rather than metal in transistors, the French have created computers the size of credit cards and video screens that roll up like window shades. _____

10. Mountain climbing is a wonderful way to forget your cares. _____

11.2 RECOGNIZING ERRORS IN REASONING

Directions: Read each passage and then circle the appropriate letter to indicate the type of error in reasoning, if any, in the passage.

1. A recent article on hearing loss claimed that loud noise is a serious threat to health. According to the article, anything around eighty-five decibels* could produce hearing loss. It's hard to take this statement seriously given the fact that I have attended rock concerts for many years. At many concerts, the decibel level is way over a hundred. Yet if anything, my hearing is too good. I hear what is said even when I don't want to. It's just not true that loud noise can produce hearing loss.

   a. circular reasoning
   b. hasty generalization
   c. attack on the person
   d. false alternatives
   e. careless comparison
   f. no error

2. A recent editorial by several faculty members criticized this university's athletic department. The editorial maintained that the department has no interest in the academic achievement of athletes but instead encourages faculty to "go easy" on star athletes, passing the athletes when they should, in fact, fail. This kind of comment is typical of intellectuals, who spend all their time with their heads in the clouds, thinking abstract thoughts that have no practical use for us ordinary human beings. These are people who have never played a sport in their life, and they don't know anything about what it means to be an athlete. They'd rather spend their time writing articles about references to the color green in the works of William Shakespeare or about the fertility rites of the Oklahoma snail darter.

   a. circular reasoning
   b. hasty generalization
   c. attack on the person
   d. false alternatives
   e. careless comparison
   f. no error

3. People who are critical of boom cars* are claiming that, over time, the noise will cause drivers to lose some of their hearing. This is like saying that people who jog with audio-cassette players and earphones are going to go deaf. It doesn't make any sense.

   a. circular reasoning
   b. hasty generalization
   c. attack on the person
   d. false alternatives
   e. careless comparison
   f. no error

4. There is talk again about introducing legislation that would increase the minimum wage. How can anyone in this country complain about the minimum wage while there are countries in which people work from dawn to dusk for the equivalent of only a few dollars? People in this country

---

* decibel: a unit of measure that expresses intensity of noise level.
* boom cars: cars rigged with high-powered stereo systems.

who work for a minimum wage have no reason to demand more money. They should consider themselves lucky.

a. circular reasoning
b. hasty generalization
c. attack on the person
d. false alternatives
e. careless comparison
f. no error

5. The newspapers have been filled with letters complaining that our government should not be giving money to Russia when our cities are beset by such terrible problems. Don't these people understand that we must help the Russians all we can? Helping the Russians in their hour of need must be a primary objective of U.S. foreign policy. If we don't help the Russians when they need us, we can expect the current and more liberal government to fail and fail badly.

a. circular reasoning
b. hasty generalization
c. attack on the person
d. false alternatives
e. careless comparison
f. no error

11.3 RECOGNIZING PROPAGANDA

Authors who use propaganda techniques don't pretend to use logical arguments. Instead, they rely on emotional appeals meant to hide their lack of a reasonable argument. Those who use propaganda will even disguise information if they think it interferes with their cause or position.

Although we commonly associate propaganda techniques with wartime, some politicians and advertisers use propaganda methods to manipulate the public's thinking. They want people to vote for their candidate, buy their car, or believe in their cause. Because you might be the target of propaganda efforts, it is important that you learn to identify some of the most frequently used techniques.

Bandwagon

The **bandwagon** technique is commonly used in advertising. It takes advantage of people's desire to be part of a larger group. In its crudest form, this method simply says, "Everybody's doing it; you should too!"

> In a coffee commercial, we see a family newly moved into a suburban neighborhood. The camera zooms in. We see everyone unpacking and Mom and Dad drinking brand X coffee. Soon the neighbors arrive to welcome the new family; the neighbors bring brand O coffee as a gift and cheerfully inform the family that everybody in their neighborhood drinks brand O coffee.

The message here is very direct. If you want to be part of the neighborhood, you'd better drink brand O coffee. Everybody drinks brand O coffee; you should too. The bandwagon technique is particularly effective because it plays on people's desires to be accepted and to fit in. In effect, it tells the audience to jump on the *bandwagon* and drink brand O coffee.

Testimonial

The testimonial technique is used when a respected and well-known figure recommends a product, position, or cause to the general public. The message in the testimonial technique is simple: Buy this product or believe in this political cause because you like and respect me. Unfortunately, the people who make testimonials don't necessarily have any particular knowledge or experience that makes their opinion especially well informed. In the following example, the person offering his testimonial is known more for his film portrayals than he is for his political expertise.

> A famous actor, well known for his portrayal of trusted father figures or religious and political leaders in films, attends a political rally. During the rally, the actor gives a brief speech. He tells the audience how much he believes in this political group and its cause. He tells the crowd what a wonderful experience he has had working with this organization and that he is planning to give it a large donation immediately after his speech. The political group running the event films the speech and then uses the film in all its advertising and fundraising work.

Notice that the political organization chose an actor who was respected largely because of his film roles. What the organization hopes is that the public will accept what the actor says without thinking about it. They hope that because of the actor's film image, the public will assume that what he says is accurate and informed.

Card Stacking

When people "stack the cards" in a discussion, they are very selective about the facts they mention. If they want you to favor a project or a person, they tell you only positive facts about that project or person. If they want to achieve the opposite effect, they tell you only bad things, leaving out the good. With the card-stacking technique, you never get all the facts; you hear only those that support the speaker's position.

> A contractor has decided to build a housing development on the shores of a scenic lake. In response to his plan, several different environmental experts have written to him warning that three already endangered birds make their nests close to the lake and the environmentalists are worried about the effects the development will have on the birds' existence. When the developer goes before the zoning board to get a building permit, he enthusiastically tells the board that his development will increase low-cost housing along with the local tax base. He does not mention the environmentalists' concerns about the endangered birds.

In response to the zoning board's questions, the developer gave the members only the information that focused on the benefits of his project. He conveniently left out any drawbacks. In short, he stacked the deck in his favor.

Red Herring

Originally, the red-herring technique was a method of testing hunting dogs. To be sure their dogs could follow a scent without being distracted, hunters would drag a red herring—a very smelly fish—across the trail and watch to see if the smell of the fish could distract the dogs from the hunt.

Today, when speakers or writers make use of the red-herring technique, they start by discussing one subject and then suddenly veer off to another, quite different topic. Here's a good example:

> The local mayor is running for reelection. He has a very good record and his opponent is finding it hard to come up with reasons why she should be elected instead. During the campaign, she gives a speech and tells voters that the current mayor hasn't been effective in his job. She then begins to talk about the harm that pornography has caused the city. She mentions a recent exhibit at a local gallery that was filled with sexual images. She says pornography harms everyone, not just children, and she calls on voters to speak out against pornography. She ends by saying that she hopes voters will elect her mayor because she is against pornography and, besides, the current mayor has not been effective, so it's time for a change.

In this example, the opponent uses the red-herring technique to distract her audience from the fact that she can't support her claim that the mayor is ineffective. So she states that he is ineffective and then presents a red herring—pornography—so the audience loses track of the original subject: why the mayor is ineffective. At the end, she says again that the mayor is ineffective and "it's time for a change." She hopes no one will notice that she hasn't given any reasons to support her opinion.

11.4 RECOGNIZING PROPAGANDA

Directions: Read the following examples of propaganda techniques. For each one, circle the letter of the method used.

Example: An actor famous for his soap opera portrayal of a caring doctor is featured in a commercial for a new brand of antacid. The commercial shows the actor standing in front of a hospital and saying, "Every time I get an upset stomach, I take Antacid Extra. I wouldn't trust any other brand."

a. bandwagon
b. testimonial
c. card stacking
d. red herring

Explanation: Notice how the makers of this commercial chose an actor whose television role presents him as a medical authority. However, the man is an actor. He has no real claim to medical knowledge. This is a perfect example of the testimonial technique used in the service of propaganda.

1. An important politician is interviewed by the press and asked about his political record. In response, he tells the reporters that he is a strong supporter of the crime bill and that he is heavily involved in efforts to promote universal health care. What he doesn't mention are his current problems with the IRS and his growing troubles with environmental groups, who claim his policies are destroying the planet.

   a. bandwagon
   b. testimonial
   c. card stacking
   d. red herring

2. In Washington, D.C., there is a huge rally against gun-control laws. The main speaker is a famous actress well known for her portrayals of saintly women who fight back only after the world has badly mistreated them. In a voice filled with emotion, she insists the proposed gun-control laws are completely worthless and tells the audience to write members of Congress and oppose their passage. The crowd doesn't seem to notice that she offers no evidence for her claims. Thrilled by the sound of her voice, they interrupt her to applaud after every sentence.

   a. bandwagon
   b. testimonial
   c. card stacking
   d. red herring

3. A real estate agent shows a newlywed couple a lovely old house. The couple is interested in buying but voices concerns about the state of the furnace. The real estate agent responds by telling them that the furnace is a top-of-the-line model that was installed only a short while ago. What she doesn't mention is that the furnace has not been functioning properly since it was first installed and that no one quite knows what the problem is.

   a. bandwagon
   b. testimonial
   c. card stacking
   d. red herring

4. A customer interested in a particular make and model goes to a car dealership to get more information. He likes the look of this particular car, but is it a good buy? He asks the salesperson a lot of questions, including one about gas mileage. How many miles does it get to the gallon? The salesperson responds by saying that it's a shame how expensive gas is these days. Oil companies seem to think people are made of money. And today people even have to pump their own gas. Did the customer notice that this model comes with a full-surround-sound stereo radio and cassette player? For a little extra, he can get a CD player, too.

   a. bandwagon
   b. testimonial
   c. card stacking
   d. red herring

5. A well-known athlete appears on television. He is famous for having won four gold medals in the most recent Olympic games, and his face appears everywhere, from cereal boxes to billboards. Standing before an American flag, wearing his medals, he tells his audience how important it is to reelect the current president. He strongly implies that all criticism of the president's first term in office is the result of ignorance or dishonesty. When he finishes speaking, the "Star-Spangled Banner" can be heard in the background.

   a. bandwagon
   b. testimonial
   c. card stacking
   d. red herring

11.5 PROPAGANDA TECHNIQUES

Directions: Identify the propaganda technique described in each paragraph by circling the letter of the correct answer.

1. When shoppers entered a well-known computer store, they were greeted by a stack of pamphlets describing the advantages of subscribing to CyberConnect. This company would, for a monthly fee, provide computer users with a link to the Internet and many other services. The colorful pamphlets described CyberConnect's wide variety of services, its low fee, its years of experience, and its friendly staff. However, the pamphlets neglected to explain that CyberConnect had gained so many customers recently that the company could not possibly keep up with the demand. CyberConnect had neither the equipment nor the employees to link all of its subscribers to the Internet—or do anything else it promised. Therefore, when they tried to hook up to CyberConnect via their telephone lines, most clients got a busy signal.

    a. bandwagon
    b. testimonial
    c. card stacking
    d. red herring

2. As newcomers cross the city limits of Carrville, a rapidly growing metropolis in North Carolina, they cannot fail to see a huge billboard that dominates the landscape. Targeted at people who are searching for homes and apartments in an unfamiliar city, the billboard depicts a luxury housing development and several smiling clusters of adults and children. It reads: "All the happy families in Carrville live at Pinewood Manor."

    a. bandwagon
    b. testimonial
    c. card stacking
    d. red herring

3. A small and little-known religious group, Astronomics decided it would try to recruit new followers with a short video explaining its rules and beliefs. To describe their faith, members hired a popular film actor, famous for his role as the dashing captain of a spaceship that zooms off to far-off worlds and spreads universal harmony. The night the video was screened, viewers watched the actor take them through a tour of the Astronomics headquarters, which resembled a high-tech planetarium. Throughout the tour, he flashed his famous toothy smile and repeatedly told the audience how Astronomics had improved and enriched his life. At the very end of the short film, he looked directly at the audience and said, "Astronomics. It'll help you find peace in this life—and adventure in the next one." The following day, phones at the Astronomics office rang off the hook with people wanting to know how they could become one of the faithful and attend services. The video had apparently done its work.

    a. bandwagon
    b. testimonial
    c. card stacking
    d. red herring

4. Last year, on the Fourth of July, my brother, Sam, injured his friend, Tom, while playing with firecrackers. Tom was just watching Sam and he had nothing to do with the firecrackers; in fact, Tom warned Sam that what he was doing was dangerous. Now Tom is suing Sam for his medical bills and loss of work time, claiming that Sam's carelessness did some real harm. This is terribly unfair of Tom. When Tom broke up with his girlfriend, Sam was there for him. When Tom was

failing history, Sam tutored him. And every time Tom's car was in the repair shop, Sam drove him to work and picked him up.

    a. bandwagon
    b. testimonial
    c. card stacking
    d. red herring

5. Want to get online and surf the Web? Then you need Web Watch, America's most popular Internet service provider. There's a reason why most Internet users are linked up to us. The reason is that we are simply the best. Don't be left out. Get online now and surf the Web with Web Watch. You won't be sorry.

    a. bandwagon
    b. testimonial
    c. card stacking
    d. red herring

6. In a commercial for a new breakfast cereal called Raisin Puffs, we see a stadium filled with enthusiastic children. Then the camera focuses on an interviewer who talks with a small group of children, all of whom claim to love the new cereal. As the commercial ends, the announcer asks, "How many of you are going to switch to Raisin Puffs?" In response, the whole stadium begins to cheer.

    a. bandwagon
    b. testimonial
    c. card stacking
    d. red herring

7. During a rally designed to protest the use of animals in scientific research, a well-known actress climbs onstage. She is famous for her portrayals of characters who appear hard as nails but are actually sensitive and caring, and the audience greets her with applause. In her speech, she argues that animals are no longer necessary for scientific research because computers can take their place. At the end of her speech, the applause is even louder than it was when she was introduced.

    a. bandwagon
    b. testimonial
    c. card stacking
    d. red herring

8. Our union simply asks that management restore our medical benefits. There are several reasons why this is a fair request. Just consider the terrible suffering of early union members, whose requests for an eight-hour day were flatly denied by employers. Employers even used armed thugs to break up rallies and protests.

   a. bandwagon
   b. testimonial
   c. card stacking
   d. red herring

9. When representatives of Datron drugs appeared before the panel for the Food and Drug Administration, they described the benefits of their new arthritis drug. They explained that the drug could reduce the inflammation caused by arthritis and considerably diminish the pain caused by the disease. They failed, however, to mention the unpleasant side effects, such as weight gain, hair loss, and muscle fatigue.

   a. bandwagon
   b. testimonial
   c. card stacking
   d. red herring

10. My opponents have asked about my proposed plan for tax cuts. They have claimed that the majority of those cuts will benefit the rich. This is pure prevarication* on their part. Consider, if you will, the staunch union support I have received from the very beginning of my campaign. This in itself should prove that I am a true friend to working people.

    a. bandwagon
    b. testimonial
    c. card stacking
    d. red herring

---

* prevarication: lying, dishonesty.

PART II

Answer Keys for
Supplementary Materials

CHAPTER 1: Strategies for Mastering Your Textbooks

An answer key is not applicable to these materials.

CHAPTER 2: Building Word Power

2.2 Using Context (p. 14)

The following are possible answers.

1. What <u>form</u> does the disease take?
    The card had a heart-shaped <u>form</u>.
    <u>Form</u> a line to the left.

2. He tried to <u>block</u> the kick.
    They delivered a huge <u>block</u> of ice.
    The child was playing with <u>blocks</u>.

3. Don't take that <u>flip</u> tone with me.
    He did a back <u>flip</u>.
    Everyone ordered a chocolate <u>flip</u>.

4. I enjoyed reading that <u>book</u>.
    He runs his business by the <u>book</u>.
    The lawyer threw the <u>book</u> at the offender.

5. There were large blue tulips in the <u>border</u> of the garden.
    The <u>border</u> of the dress was bright red.
    That <u>borders</u> on heroism.

2.3 Using the Dictionary (pp. 15-16)

1. to attack
2. no
3. hə-'răng
4. The word means "under the rose," and it came from the practice of using the rose as a symbol of secrecy. Legend has it that Cupid gave a rose to the god of silence.
5. four
6. hay
7. noun
8. The word is archaic and not in current use.
9. the first syllable
10. lessened, lessening, lessens

2.4 Borrowed Words and Phrases (pp. 18-19)

1. déjà vu
2. prima facie
3. ad hoc
4. fin de siècle
5. raison d'être
6. nom de plume
7. Noblesse oblige
8. entrée
9. idée fixe
10. ad infinitum
11. non sequitur
12. quid pro quo
13. double-entendre
14. bona fide
15. a posteriori
16. in loco parentis
17. carte blanche
18. in toto
19. a priori
20. Vis-à-vis

2.5 Handout: No Answer Key Necessary

2.6 Idioms (pp. 23-25)

1. steal my thunder
2. whitewash
3. tenterhooks
4. jumped on the bandwagon
5. ivory tower
6. writing on the wall
7. brought down the house
8. white elephant
9. blowing hot and cold
10. tilting at windmills
11. show her hand
12. in the doldrums
13. gild the lily
14. lion's share
15. splitting hairs
16. off the beaten track
17. raise Cain
18. turned thumbs down
19. rule with an iron hand
20. take the bull by the horns

2.7 Vocabulary Practice: Some Commonly Confused Words (p. 26)

1. flaunt
2. flout

a. illusion
b. allusion

a. discreet
b. discrete

2.8 Considering Clichés (p. 27)
Answers will vary.

2.9 Analyzing Acronyms (p. 28)

1. laser: Light Amplification by Stimulated Emission of Radition
2. NATO: North Atlantic Treaty Organization
3. scuba: Self-contained Underwater Breathing Apparatus
4. JPEG: Joint Photograph Experts Group
5. SMS: Answers vary a lot, but Short Message Server is the most common.

2.10 Understanding Allusions (pp. 29-30)

1. b
2. a
3. c
4. c

2.11 Borrowing From the French (p. 31)

1. déjà vu
2. entrepreneur
3. carte blanche
4. coup de grâce

2.12 Context Clues and Word Analysis (pp. 32-35)

Part A: Using Context
1. unwise, silly, mistaken; *Context Clue:* G
2. sloppy, uninteresting, careless; *Context Clue:* R
3. faker, phony, liar; *Context Clue:* C
4. fatigue, tiredness, exhaustion; *Context Clue:* E
5. effectiveness, usefulness; *Context Clue:* R
6. loud, angry, aggressive; *Context Clue:* R
7. dangerous, bad, awful, hurtful; *Context Clue:* E
8. abnormality, unusual event; *Context Clue:* C
9. overweight, heavy, fat; *Context Clue:* G
10. hiring of relatives; *Context Clue:* R

Part B: Context Clues and Word Analysis
11. idea about the future, premonition
12. energy, liveliness
13. determination
14. overcome, survive, get beyond
15. travel across, cross
16. feeling, attitude
17. acceptable, supportable
18. following, remaining
19. offered, gave
20. conscious, feeling

CHAPTER 3: Connecting the General to the Specific in Reading and Writing

3.2   General and Specific Words (pp. 39-40)

Answers will vary.

1. feelings
   - **happiness**
   - **anger**
   - **sadness**

2. music
   - **jazz**
   - **rap**
   - **classical**

3. machinery
   - **chain saw**
   - **lawn mower**
   - **jackhammer**
   - **leaf blower**

4. illness
   - **cold**
   - **flu**
   - **pneumonia**
   - **ear infection**

5. fruit
   - **apple**
   - **orange**
   - **banana**
   - **pineapple**

3.3   General and Specific Words (p. 41)

1. books, novels, reading material
2. wood, kinds of wood, kinds of trees
3. computer parts
4. cartoon characters
5. magazines

3.4 Levels of Specificity (p. 42)

1. a. Children's Hospital   **b**
    b. building   **c**
    c. hospital   **a**

2. a. flu   **b**
    b. disease   **a**
    c. swine flu   **c**

3. a. water   **a**
    b. Indian Ocean   **c**
    c. ocean   **b**

4. a. detergent   **b**
    b. product   **a**
    c. Tide   **c**

5. a. continent   **b**
    b. land mass   **a**
    c. South America   **c**

3.5 Levels of Specificity (pp. 43-44)

1. object _____
    knife ___S___
    weapon _____
    gun ___S___

2. clothing _____
    dress ___S___
    coat ___S___
    wedding dress _____

3. product _____
    soap _____
    Ivory ___S___
    Dove ___S___

4. machine _____
   automobile   **S**

   For
   d   _____
   motorcycle   **S**

5. insect _____
   butterfly   **S**
   animal _____
   bumblebee   **S**

3.6 From General to Specific (p. 45)

1. activities
       occupations
           white-collar workers
               managers
                   sales managers
                       sales managers for a wholesale company

2. entertainers
       musicians
           singers
               country-western singers
                   well-known country-western singers
                   Faith Hill

3. things powered by electricity
       appliances
           household appliances
               vacuums
                   Hoover vacuums
                     Hoover upright vacuums

3.7 General and Specific Sentences (p. 46)

1. b
2. a
3. a
4. b
5. a
6. a
7. a
8. b
9. b
10. a

3.8 General and Specific Sentences (p. 47)

1.   c
       a
         b

2.   b
       c
         a

3.   c
       a
         b

4.   a
       c
         b

5.   b
       c
         a

3.9 General and Specific Sentences (pp. 48-49)

1. 1 ✓
2. 1 ✓
3. 3 ✓
4. 2 ✓
5. 3 ✓

3.10 General and Specific Sentences (p. 50)

1. **a.** G
    b. S
2. **a.** S
    b. G
3. **a.** G
    b. S
4. **a.** S
    b. G
5. **a.** G
    b. S

3.11 General and Specific Sentences (pp. 51-52)

1. b, c, e
2. a, d, e   Answer *c* is possible, but it's not as good as *a*, *d*, and *e*, because it does not support the idea of a growing interest among Americans.
3. a, c, f
4. a, b, c
5. c, d, e

CHAPTER 4: From Topics to Topic Sentences

4.1 Identifying Topics (pp. 55-56)

1. b
2. b
3. a
4. a
5. c

4.2 Identifying Topics (pp. 57-58)

1. c
2. b
3. a
4. a
5. c

4.3 Identifying Topics and Topic Sentences (pp. 59-61)

1. *Topic:* a
   Topic Sentence: 2
2. *Topic:* a
   Topic Sentence: 2
3. *Topic:* b
   Topic Sentence: 3
4. *Topic:* c
   Topic Sentence: 3
5. *Topic:* c
   Topic Sentence: 1

4.4 Identifying Topics and Main Ideas (pp. 62-66)

1. b, a
2. a, b
3. a, b
4. b, a
5. c, a
6. a, b

7. b, b
8. b, a
9. c, b
10. c, a

4.5 Paraphrasing (pp. 67-69)

1. a
2. b
3. b
4. b
5. a
6. b
7. a
8. b
9. a
10. a

4.6 Recognizing an Accurate Paraphrase (pp. 70-72)

1. *Topic Sentence:* 1
   Paraphrase: b
2. *Topic Sentence:* 4
   Paraphrase: b
3. *Topic Sentence:* 1
   Paraphrase: c
4. *Topic Sentence:* 7
   Paraphrase: a
5. *Topic Sentence:* 3
   Paraphrase: c

CHAPTER 5: Focus on Supporting Details

5.1 Recognizing Supporting Details (pp. 74-75)

1. b
   c
   e

2. a
   c
   e

3. a
   b
   d

4. c
   d
   e

5.a
  c
  d

5.2 Recognizing Supporting Details (pp. 76-79)

 1. a, c, d
 2. a, d, e
 3. a, c, d
 4. b, d, f
 5. b, c, e
 6. a, b, e
 7. b, c, d
 8. c, e, f
 9. a, e, f
10. a, c, e

CHAPTER 6: More About Inferences

6.1 Drawing Inferences (pp. 82-83)

1. 2
2. 3
3. 3
4. 1
5. 1

6.2 Logical and Illogical Inferences (pp. 84-85)

1. a
2. b
3. b
4. a
5. a

CHAPTER 7: Drawing Inferences From Visual Aids

No additional exercises included. See website suggestions under Supplementary Materials: Suggestions for Teaching.

CHAPTER 8: Beyond the Paragraph: Reading Longer Selections

8.1 Recognizing Thesis Statements (pp. 89-91)

1. Statistics show that athletic activities requiring a lean physical body predispose serious, competitive female participants to eating disorders.
2. Similarities are what bring people together into romantic or sexual relationships.

3. An affirmative action program is a plan designed to increase the number of minority employees at all levels within an organization.

4. Grigori Rasputin, the Russian monk, was an influential member of Czar Nicholas's court from 1907 until 1916. During that time, he managed to discredit not only himself but the czar's authority as well.

8.4 Summarizing Exercise (pp.)

Although at one time Christian music was limited to being played on Christian radio stations

And sold through religious bookstores, it has now become very mainstream—so much so that

albums of Christian music can be found almost anyplace where records are sold. According to

recent figures, Christian music is now a $750 million a year industry. With profits like these at

Stake, Christian artists are understandably worried that record companies now selling

Christian music care more about the money than the message.

CHAPTER 9: Recognizing Patterns of Organization in Paragraphs

9.1 Identifying Patterns of Organization (pp. 98-101)

1. b
2. c
3. b
4. d
5. e
6. b
7. d *Note:* Answer *a* is also possible although it's not the primary pattern.
8. e *Note:* Although the primary pattern is classification, students who choose *d* should get partial credit because the defining characteristic of each category is a cause and effect relationship.
9. b *Note:* Yes, there are elements of cause and effect, so a student who argues for *b* and *d* should get partial credit.
10. c

9.2 Identifying Patterns of Organization (pp. 102-105)

1. b
2. b *Note:* As is so often the case, the time order pattern contains cause and effect elements, so students who choose *d* should get partial credit.
3. c
4. e
5. b
6. e
7. d
8. b *Note:* Some students might opt for classification, but the passage does not break all emperors into five types, which is what it would need to do to qualify as a classification paragraph.
9. a
10. b

CHAPTER 10: Combining Patterns in Paragraphs and Longer Readings

10.1 Identifying Mixed Patterns in Paragraphs (pp. 107-110)

1. a, d, e
2. e
3. c
4. a, b, d
5. b
6. a, e
7. a, b
8. d
9. a, c, d
10. a, b, d

CHAPTER 11: More on Purpose, Tone, and Bias

11.1 Distinguishing Between Fact and Opinion (p. 113)

1. B
2. F
3. O
4. F
5. B
6. O
7. B
8. F
9. F
10. O

11.2 Recognizing Errors in Reasoning (pp. 114-115)

1. b; hasty generalization
2. c; attack on the person
3. e; careless comparison
4. a; circular reasoning
5. d; false alternatives

11.4 Recognizing Propaganda (pp. 118-119)

1. c
2. b
3. c
4. d
5. b

11.5 Propaganda Techniques (pp. 120-122)

1. c
2. a
3. b
4. d
5. a
6. a
7. b
8. d
9. c
10. d

PART III
Reading Tips from Chapters 1-11

The reading tips are collected here so that you can, if you wish, copy the list and hand it out to students for review before and/or after they cover a specific chapter.

Chapter 1: Strategies for Textbook Learning

⮑ Be a flexible reader who consciously adapts your reading strategies to the text in front of you. If, for instance, reading your history text at the same pace you were reading your health text leaves you confused, be ready to adapt to the more difficult material by slowing down your reading rate.

⮑ Serious learners use trial and error to figure out what works for them and for the material they want to master. When one strategy doesn't work, they try another.

⮑ Using a variety of page-marking techniques will keep you focused and sharp. It will also help your remember what you read.

Chapter 2: Building Word Power

⮑ If you are an ESL student, pronunciation of new words is especially important to you. Anytime you can get access to an online dictionary, you should use it. Hit the audio link (◀ᴖ) that will allow you to hear the words pronounced, over and over again if need be.

⮑ Next time you turn to a dictionary to look up an unfamiliar word, and find several definitions, quickly eliminate any meanings that have no bearing on the word's context. Then look for the meaning that makes the most sense within the original sentence or passage.[†]

Chapter 3: Connecting the General to the Specific in Reading and Writing

⮑ As soon as you spot a general sentence, check to see how the sentences that follow clarify or explain it.[†]

⮑ If the second sentence in a paragraph explains the first, the chances are good that the opening general sentence expresses the main idea.

Chapter 4: From Topics to Topic Sentences

⮑ If a text is particularly difficult to read, pronouns are often the source of the confusion. If you are struggling with a passage, re-read it to nail down the *antecedent*, or reference, for every pronoun.

⮑ To test whether a sentence is a topic sentence, turn it into a question. If the remaining sentences answer the question, you've found the topic sentence.

[†] For more on dictionary labels that will help you in the process of elimination, see pages 000-000 of the Appendix.
[†] This advice will become crucial in Chapter 4, when you look for the main idea or message of a paragraph.

⊃ When taking notes, think of the main idea as the headline you would write if the paragraph were a newspaper article, e.g., "Citizens Blow Off Jury Duty" or "Excessive Self-esteem More Common than Low."

⊃ If the second sentence of a paragraph functions as a transition, then the third sentence is likely to be the topic sentence.

⊃ If a paragraph maintains a consistent level of specific detail and suddenly branches out into the general statement at the end, that last sentence is probably the topic sentence.

⊃ If a paragraph opens with a general statement, becomes more specific, and then turns more general again at the end, check to see if the opening and closing sentences say much the same thing. If they do, you are reading a paragraph with a double topic sentence.

Chapter 5: Focusing on Supporting Details

⊃ Once you think you have identified the topic sentence, ask yourself which of the remaining sentences provide clarification or evidence for that sentence. If the remaining sentences don't do either, you need to rethink your choice of topic sentences.

⊃ If you eliminate a minor detail from a paragraph, the main idea expressed by the topic sentence should remain clear and convincing. If it doesn't, the detail you eliminated is probably more major than minor.

⊃ Evaluate minor details very carefully. If the minor details are essential to explaining a major detail, they belong in your notes.

⊃ To decide what major or minor details are essential to the main idea, ask yourself, How would I explain the content of this paragraph to someone who has never read it? The answer to that question will also identify essential details.

⊃ Never assume the writers provide you with every single word or phrase you need to construct their intended meaning. Be ready to fill in the gaps with the right inferences.

Chapter 6: More About Inferences

⊃ Inferring implied main ideas is a two-step process. First, you need to understand what each sentence contributes to your knowledge of the topic. Next, you need to ask yourself what all the sentences combine to imply as a group. The answer to that question is the implied main idea of the paragraph.

⮑ The main idea you infer from the specific details should sum up the paragraph in the same way a topic sentence does.

⮑ When a writer describes an event or experience by piling up specific details without including a topic sentence that interprets or evaluates them, you need to infer the main idea implied by the author.

⮑ When the opening question of a paragraph is *not* followed by an immediate answer, it's usually the reader's job to infer an answer that is also the implied main idea.

⮑ When the author offers several competing points of view without evaluating them, you need to infer a main idea that expresses the variety of opinions concerning the issue, or event under discussion.

⮑ If a paragraph lists similarities and differences between two topics but doesn't tell you what those similarities and differences *mean* or how to evaluate them, you need to infer a main idea which makes a general point that can include all or most of them.

⮑ If the author cites research but doesn't interpret the results, you need to infer what the research results suggest about the problem or issue under study.

Chapter 7: Drawing Inferences from Visual Aids

⮑ Look at pie charts both before and after reading. Look the first time to make predictions about the reading, the second to make sure you understand what the pie chart adds to the author's point.

Chapter 8: Beyond the Paragraph: Reading Longer Selections

⮑ When you spot a concluding paragraph in a chapter section, check to see if it contains a prediction, consequence, or solution you should record in your notes. If the paragraph functions as a transition, use that information to make some predictions about what the upcoming chapter section will accomplish.

⮑ As soon as you see a title or heading, consider what it reveals about the material. Some titles do not reveal main ideas or the author's purpose—for example, "Shadow Juries."* Others all but announce both—for example, "We Need to Question the Ethics of Shadow Juries."

⮑ If the author maintains a formal, impersonal style and does not offer a judgment or call for change, the primary purpose is probably informative, rather than persuasive.

---

* Shadow juries mimic real juries as closely as possible. Lawyers assemble shadow juries to decide how jury verdicts might turn out.

⊃ Look at the beginning of paragraphs for the answer to two questions that should *always* be on a reader's mind: Why does this paragraph follow the previous one? What connects them to one another?

⊃ Any time you read descriptions of physical characteristics or chains of events, try to visualize the characteristics, the events or both while you read.

Chapter 9: Recognizing Patterns of Organization in Paragraphs

⊃ In the listing pattern, it's unlikely that the topic sentence would be in the middle of the paragraph. In this pattern, the topic sentence appears at the very beginning or the very end.

⊃ Make sure you know what main idea is developed by the description of differences and similarities.

Chapter 10: Combining Patterns in Paragraphs and Longer Readings

⊃ In a reading that combines several patterns, one pattern might well dominate, or be primary, but you still need to find and evaluate the key elements in the less important patterns. Then you can decide which of those elements are important enough to appear in your notes.

Chapter 11: More on Purpose, Tone, and Bias

⊃ Sometimes what writers leave out of an explanation is as important as what they put in.

⊃ Any time a writer decides to do your thinking for you by saying that a particular point of view is "undeniable" or evidence is "overwhelming," it probably means that the person writing hasn't built a convincing case.

PART IV

Word Check Vocabulary with Definitions

Words and Definitions for Review

For ease of oral review in class, the list contains all the footnoted words defined in the chapters.

CHAPTER 1: STRATEGIES FOR TEXTBOOK LEARNING

acoustic:	related to sound
acquisition:	the act of acquiring or obtaining something
acronym:	word created out of initials from several words; NATO (North Atlantic Treaty Organization) and SCUBA (Self-Contained Underwater Breathing Apparatus) are both acronyms
adaptive:	capable of responding effectively to new situations
ambiguous:	uncertain, open to interpretation
chromosomal:	related to chromosomes, the microscopically visible carriers of genetic inheritance
cognitive:	related to thinking
congenital:	present at birth
contemplate:	consider; think about
convert:	transform, change
determinants:	causes
deviance:	the failure to follow established social rules
fetal:	related to unborn offspring still in the womb
hypotheticals:	things existing only as theories, not yet realities
icons:	1. visual symbols or representations, which, in textbooks, signal significance 2. a person who is the object of much attention, as in "a pop *icon*"
incurs:	produces, brings about
landmark:	having important consequences on future studies or events; also a decisive turning point
mnemonic:	memory aid; a famous and common mnemonic used for spelling is "*i* before *e* except after *c*"
molten:	heated to the point of becoming liquid
oblivion:	condition of being completely forgotten
personified:	offering the perfect illustration
prenatal:	before birth; related to unborn offspring still in the womb
projection:	prediction of future sales
regress:	move backward
repulsed:	disgusted

CHAPTER 3: CONNECTING THE GENERAL TO THE SPECIFIC IN READING AND WRITING

anecdotal: not scientific; based on personal stories

asteroid: small or minor planet

commitment: the state of being bonded emotionally or intellectually to another person

conformity: obedience; willingness to follow rules

creed: belief, religion

denomination: a group of units having specific values

discrimination: the act of showing prejudice in favor of or against a particular group

fidelity: faithfulness, loyalty

obscurity: the state of being unknown

sage: wise person; also, wise

CHAPTER 4: FROM TOPICS TO TOPIC SENTENCES

analogies: comparisons between two unlike things that share a similar function or process, suggesting that two things alike in some respects are alike in others, e.g., "The heart is like a pump. The heart pumps blood from one part of the body to another like a pump pumps water from a reservoir that is fed by a stream" (from www.altoonafp.org/how_to_use_ analogies.htm)

anthropological: related to the study of human cultures

charisma: personal magnetism or charm

comprehensive: wide-ranging or complete in coverage

conclusive: final; putting an end to doubt

consolidate: combine

cultivated: cared for

dementia: loss of the normal ability to think, concentrate, and remember

devotees: followers, believers

dignitaries: people in high positions

disorienting: causing mental confusion

electors: people chosen to cast their vote for president

etching: art made by imprinting an image on a metal plate

flouting: showing contempt for or disregarding; commonly confused with *flaunting*, or showing off

genetic: having to do with biological inheritance

geriatric: related to the elderly

graphic:	obvious and vivid, often associated with sex and violence
habitats:	living spaces for specific species
homage:	a show of respect
innovative:	original, inventive
instigated:	caused, motivated
liberate:	set free
mutilation:	the crippling or deforming of a body part
nocturnal:	nighttime
paradoxically:	ideas or events seemingly in contradiction, but actually making sense or fitting together, e.g., "Some day you will be old enough to start reading fairy tales again" (C. S. Lewis)
placebos:	substances that have no healing effect on the body but are believed by the people taking them to have medical value
pollutants:	substances that are harmful
precedent:	an example that becomes a pattern for future actions
predators:	animals that kill to survive
productivity:	ability to produce goods
quarantine:	period of isolation to prevent the spread of disease
random:	not occurring according to a set pattern; inconsistent
renovated:	repaired
reproductive:	related to birth
sociopathic:	lacking all moral or ethical sense
speculators:	people who buy something with the expectation of a quick sale and a quick profit
staple:	a basic or essential part of something (especially in reference to diet)
subsequent:	following in time
toxic:	poisonous
traumatic:	causing serious injury

CHAPTER 5: FOCUS ON SUPPORTING DETAILS

amphibians: animals that can live in water and on land

barren: unable to reproduce; dry; lacking in vegetation

cardiovascular: related to the heart and vessels

commodity: something that is bought or sold in the market

compound: building or buildings used as housing and surrounded by walls

disreputable: lacking in respectability

edict: ruling, law

fray: battle, contest, test

imperial: royal

inherently: at the core, by nature

maim: injure severely, usually with scarring or loss of limbs

mediums: people who claim they can communicate with the dead

notorious: famous for bad reasons

orbits: paths of movement

psychosis: a mental disturbance that causes severe reality distortion

purge: remove waste from the bowels or stomach; also, to eliminate or get rid of

respiratory: related to breathing

satellite: an object propelled into space to circle Earth or other planets

supernatural: relating to the miraculous or things not of the ordinary world.

thrive: grow

CHAPTER 6: MORE ABOUT INFERENCES

adverse: negative

catapult: launch

chortles: laughs, chuckles

confidante: friend

dissembled: pretended

distillation: the process of heating a liquid until it boils and then collecting what's left after boiling; also, reducing something to its essence, or most basic elements

gravitas: dignity or seriousness

heresy: challenging church law

hypothermia: abnormally low body temperature

indulgent: lenient; inclined to spoil

innovation: introduction of something new

ludicrous:	absurd, ridiculous
logos:	symbols representing institutions or companies, e.g., Apple Computer's apple or the Hartford Insurance Company elk
martyrs:	people willing to die for their faith or to save the lives of others
palpitations:	unusually fast heartbeat
progressive:	supporting social or political change
quips:	quick one-liners
stamina:	ability to stay strong over time
suffrage:	the right to vote
terrain:	an area of ground or land

CHAPTER 8: BEYOND THE PARAGRAPH: READING LONGER SELECTIONS

abolitionist:	a person who wanted to end slavery
abstract:	describes ideas that cannot be understood or felt by the physical senses, e.g., justice, honesty
altruistic:	unselfish
ambiguous:	having more than one meaning
apathy:	lack of feeling or energy
aspirations:	hopes, desires
aura	feeling, atmosphere; area surrounding
authoritarian:	demanding strict obedience
candidly:	openly, directly
certifies:	formally confirms as accurate
concrete:	describes ideas that can be comprehended by one or more physical senses
consensus:	form of group agreement
credence:	belief
dubbed:	named
electoral:	related to voting
exorbitant:	excessive, especially in the sense of price or demands
extroverted:	outgoing
incarnate:	in the flesh; representing a perfect example of something
ingenuity:	imagination, originality
integrated:	connected to or made part of something else
invigorating:	energizing
jubilation:	joy, celebration

judicial:	related to the courts and judges
litigation:	lawsuits
momentum:	force or speed of movement
munificent:	generous
neural:	related to the nerves
perceived:	recognized and understood
physiology:	the study of how the body functions
plaintiffs:	people who bring the suit to court wanting damages
predisposition:	leaning
prodigy:	a person of unusual gifts
prognosis:	indication of how the injury or disease will respond to treatment. *Note:* In reading on privately run prisons, the context required a different definition. See p. 000.
rehabilitation:	being restored to good health
scrutiny:	careful study or observation
specifications:	requirements, desires
sumptuous:	delicious, rich, fancy
therapeutic:	related to healing
verify:	prove true
wake:	the course or track left behind by someone or something that has passed

CHAPTER 9: RECOGNIZING PATTERNS OF ORGANIZATION IN PARAGRAPHS

activists:	people devoted to fighting for a cause
adversarial:	challenging; ready to criticize
alluding:	referring, mentioning
ascent:	climb
chromosomes:	bodies within a cell that consist of hundreds of clear, jellylike particles strung together like beads. They carry the genes.
civic:	relating to the city or citizenship
coercive:	forcing someone to do something against his or her will
commerce:	trade
compassionate:	caring of others
dubious:	questionable, suspicious
extensive:	large, wide-ranging
genes:	the elements responsible for hereditary characteristics, such as hair and eye color

graphics:	visual images
hindrance:	obstacle
illumination:	understanding
inbreeding:	reproducing by mating with a closely related individual
literacy:	ability to read and write
ousted:	removed
province:	area governed as a unit of a country or an empire; area of knowledge or interest
provocation:	stimulus to anger or punishment
range:	move about, travel
socialist:	a person who believes that the means of production in a society should be owned by a large group rather than an individual
stench:	smell, stink
synthesizing:	the combining of separate thoughts to create a new idea
utterances:	verbal statements

CHAPTER 10: COMBINING PATTERNS IN PARAGRAPHS AND LONGER READINGS

biographical:	related to a person's life
convulsions:	uncontrolled fits in which the muscles contract wildly
diluted:	weakened
diversion:	pleasant activity
giddiness:	silliness
incomparable:	having no equal
lax:	careless
posh:	fancy
propaganda:	a method of persuasion that relies on emotional appeal and discourages logical thinking
synthetic:	artificial, made by people rather than nature

CHAPTER 11: MORE ON PURPOSE, TONE, AND BIAS

alarmist:	given to exaggerating real or potential danger
bureaucratic:	typical of institutions with many departments and numerous regulations
crustacean:	shellfish
equitable:	fair, balanced
forensic:	related to courts of law and criminal investigations

imperiled: endangered

indigenous: native to the region

oratory: speech making

segregationist: someone who believes in strict separation of races

zealous: excessively enthusiastic

PART V

Syllabus, Mid-Term, and Final

Note to Instructors

Here's a syllabus that covers a sixteen-week course in which students meet twice a week. The syllabus moves the class along at a pretty fast clip, largely because I believe that many of the exercises should be done as homework or in a lab setting. From my perspective (and that doesn't have to be yours), the terminology and skills are introduced in class with at least one follow-up exercise being done as a group. While you might not be able to finish an entire exercise in class, I think modeling how the paragraphs should be analyzed and encouraging students to explain their thought process for arriving at answers is the best way to introduce specific skills. Then you can individualize the number of exercises a student actually completes from beginning to end.

Laraine Flemming

SYLLABUS

Week 1:   **Chapter 1   Strategies for Mastering Your Textbooks**

          Monday   Introducing SQ3R
          The Role of Informal Outlining; Equality and Subordination

          Wednesday   Mining the Web for Background Knowledge; Search Terms are
          Critical; The Role of Flexibility in Reading

          Friday   Vocabulary Check; "Memories are Made of This"

Week 2:   **Chapter 2   Building Word Power**

          Monday   Using Context Clues; Using Word Parts; The Importance of Review
          and Recall

          Wednesday   Connotation and Denotation; Mnemonic Devices; Thinking About
          Reading Rate

          Friday   Context Clues and Word Parts; Diagrams vs. Outlines (Criteria for
          Using); "Beyond Time Management"

Week 3:   **Chapter 3   Relating the General to the Specific in Reading and
          Writing**

          Monday   General and Specific Words and Sentences; Applying the
Concept   to Writing

          Wednesday   Diagramming Levels of Generality; Test 2: Distinguishing Between
          General and Specific Sentences

          Friday   Clarifying General Sentences; Connecting General and Specific
          Sentences in Paragraphs; "Going Global"

Week 4:   **Chapter 4   From Topics to Topic Sentences**

          Monday   The Role of Repetition and Reference in Identifying the Topic
and   Main Idea; Vocabulary Check

          Wednesday   Practice Using the Topic to Get to the Main Idea

          Friday   Topic Sentences and Main Ideas; Vocabulary Review

<u>Week 5</u>:	**Chapter 4**	**From Topics to Topic Sentences**

Monday   Main Ideas and Topic Sentences; Paraphrasing

Wednesday   Recognizing an Accurate Paraphrase; Vocabulary Check

Friday   Identifying and Paraphrasing Topic Sentences; "Jury Dodgers Beware!"

<u>Week 6</u>:	**Chapter 5:**	**Focusing on Supporting Details**

Monday   Function of Supporting Details; Major and Minor Details; Using Clues to Identify Major Details; Test 5: Recognizing Topics and Topic Sentences from Chapter 4

Wednesday   Diagramming Details; Spotting Irrelevant Details

Friday   Inferring Supporting Details; "Debating Private Prisons"

<u>Week 7</u>:	**Chapter 6**	**More on Inferences**

Monday   Inferences in Everyday Life, Quips, Quotes, Jokes, and Constructing Topic Sentences; Vocabulary Review

Wednesday   Evaluating Inferences; Recognizing the Implied Main Idea; Five Types of Paragraphs that Imply the Main Idea

Friday   Inferring the Implied Main Idea; Evaluating Inferences; "Black Baseball"

<u>Week 8</u>:	**Chapter 6**	**More on Inferences**

Monday   Logical and Illogical Inferences; Test 3: Recognizing the Implied Main Idea

Wednesday   Test 6: Recognizing the Implied Main Idea

                 Chapter 7: Drawing Inferences from Visual Aids: How Inferences and Visual Aids Need One Another

Friday   The Function of Pie Charts and Bar Graphs

<u>Week 9</u>:	**Chapter 7**	**Drawing Inferences from Visual Aids**

Monday   Line Graphs and Drawings; Paragraph Elements Review

Wednesday   Paragraphs Elements and Vocabulary Review

Friday   Paragraph Elements and Vocabulary Review

<u>Week 10</u>:	**Chapter 8**	**Beyond the Paragraph: Reading Longer Selections**

Monday   Differences Between Paragraphs and Longer Readings; Recognizing Main Ideas in Longer Readings; "Voting Goes High Tech"

Wednesday   Recognizing Main Ideas in Longer Readings; Implying Main Ideas in Longer Readings; Vocabulary Check

Friday   Recognizing Implied Main Ideas; Inferring Main Ideas; Monitoring Comprehension with Informal Outlines and Diagrams; "Legal Rights for Animals"

<u>Week 11</u>:	**Chapter 8**	**Beyond the Paragraph: Reading Longer Selections**

Monday   Taking Notes with Informal Outlines; Introducing Graphic Organizers

Wednesday   Test 4: Recognizing Controlling Main Ideas and Supporting Details; Vocabulary Review

Friday   Test 5: Recognizing the Main Idea, Supporting Details, and Author's Purpose

<u>Week 12</u>:	**Chapter 9**	**Recognizing Patterns of Organization in Paragraphs**

Monday   Definition and Time Order: Process

Wednesday   Sequence of Dates and Events; Simple Listing

Friday   Comparison and Contrast; Cause and Effect

<u>Week 13</u>:	**Chapter 9**	**Recognizing Patterns of Organization in Paragraphs**

Monday   Classification; "Types of Love"

Wednesday   Vocabulary Check; Test 3: Recognizing Primary Patterns

Friday   Tests 4 and 5: Recognizing Primary Patterns

Week 14:   **Chapter 10**   **Combining Patterns in Paragraphs and Longer Readings**

Monday   Combining Patterns in Paragraphs; Recognizing Combined Patterns; Seeing Patterns in Longer Readings

Wednesday   Identifying the Primary Patterns in Longer Readings; Vocabulary Check

Friday   Using Organizational Patterns to Take Notes; "The Development of Self in Childhood"

Week 15:   **Chapter 11**   **More on Purpose, Tone, and Bias**

Monday   More on the Role of Purpose in Reading and Writing; The Characteristics of Informative and Persuasive Writing

Wednesday   Facts and Opinions; Combining Opinions with Facts

Friday   Bias and Tone in Persuasive Writing

Week 16:   **Chapter 11**   **More on Purpose, Tone, and Bias**

Monday   Evaluating Bias; "Marla Ruzicka: Activist Angel"

Wednesday   Review for Final; "Arriving at a Crossroads"

Friday   Review for Final; "The Altruistic Personality"

MID-TERM EXAM

Part 1: Using SQ3R

Directions: Answer the question by writing your responses on the blanks.

1. Name and describe each of the steps in the study system known as *SQ3R*.

    S: _____

    Q: _____

    R: _____

    R: _____

    R: _____

Part 2: Recognizing General and Specific Sentences

Directions: In each group of sentences, one is more general than the others. Circle the letter of the most general sentence.

2. a. Research shows that we eat more when we're in groups and with friends than we do when we eat alone.
    b. When we eat dinner with one other person, we eat an average of 44 percent more food.
    c. Meals eaten with large groups of friends can be as much as 75 percent larger than meals eaten alone.

3. a. Crews in California pick up roadside litter and pile it in mounds underneath signs that read "Don't Trash California."
    b. In the state of Washington, where an ad campaign warns citizens "Litter and It Will Hurt," litterbugs are slapped with fines of up to $950.
    c. States are using aggressive tactics to try to reduce their litter problems.

Directions: In each group of sentences, one is more specific than the others. Circle the letter of the most specific sentence.

4   a. People enjoy spending their leisure time at amusement parks.
    b. In 2003, 90 million visitors went to Walt Disney's ten parks.
    c. The Walt Disney amusement parks are among the world's most popular.

5. a. An ounce and a half of peanuts, for example, contains not only a healthy dose of unsaturated fat but also magnesium, a mineral that may lower blood pressure, and a B vitamin that helps prevent the buildup of plaque in the arteries.
    b. Nutritionists say that the regular consumption of nuts can help reduce cardiovascular disease.
    c. Nuts like almonds, peanuts, pecans, pistachios, and walnuts are full of healthy unsaturated fat and vitamins and minerals that are good for the heart.

Part 3: Topics, Topic Sentences, and Context Clues

Directions: Circle the letter of the correct topic. Then circle the letter of the topic sentence that best fits in the blank.

6. _____. According to food industry researchers, in the last 10 years, the amount of dinners sold in American grocery store freezers or takeout counters increased by 24 percent. In 2002, supermarkets sold $1.57 billion of hot entrees, a 38 percent increase just since 1997. Restaurants, too, have seen a steady increase in their takeout sales. As a matter of fact, almost all of the growth in the restaurant business over the past 15 years has been in takeout. Not surprisingly, one in every four meals served at home takes the form of frozen or prepared food from a supermarket or restaurant, in other words what's commonly known as "fast food." Only 53 percent of dinners eaten at home require turning on the stove; that proportion has dropped from 67 percent in 1985. (Source of statistics: Jerry Adler, "Takeout Nation," *Newsweek,* February 9, 2004, pp. 52–53.)

Topic
a. fast food
b. pre-prepared foods
c. frozen foods

a. Many Americans do not know how to cook.
b. These days, takeout food is just as good as home-cooked meals.
c. Americans aren't cooking as much as they used to.

7. Many people argue that the money used to fund the space-exploration projects of the National Aeronautics and Space Administration (NASA) could be better used to improve human lives here on Earth. _____. It was NASA that made our current cell phone technology possible. Thanks to NASA scientists, we have MRI machines that help doctors diagnose what ails us. Other NASA experiments have led to the development of implants that help deaf people hear again, as well as instruments now used to diagnose cataracts and other eye diseases. The space agency's research has given us DVDs and smoke detectors. It has provided our law enforcement personnel with bullet-proof Kevlar vests and our rescue personnel the Lifeshears, a tool that quickly cuts away debris to free accident victims. NASA's innovations have also reduced accidents on highways and made flying safer. Over the last 40 years, NASA has been responsible for advances in computers, robotics, human biology, biotechnology, ecology, and many other fields that directly affect us all.

Topic
a. space exploration
b. NASA's innovations
c. NASA's failure to improve human life on Earth

a. Indeed, NASA's work is a waste of taxpayers' money.
b. However, NASA's innovations have always benefited everyday life on Earth.
c. However, NASA's projects have resulted in improvements in communication.

8. _____. As a teenager, Snoop Dog, born Cordazar Calvin Broadus, was a member of the Crips, a gang in Long Beach, California. He made up to $1,000 a day selling crack cocaine and served eight months in prison after being convicted of

felony drug charges. Following his release from prison, Broadus found himself in trouble again when he was implicated in the murder of a rival gang member. Things turned around for Broadus in 1993 when Death Row records, released his debut rap music album *Doggystyle,* under the name of Snoop Dog. The album was a huge and immediate success, going quadruple platinum. In addition to continuing a musical career that won him several Grammy Award nominations, Snoop began to pursue an acting career. He won kudos for his good performances in films such as *Bones, Training Day,* and *Starsky & Hutch* and starred in several commercials for major companies. He established the Save a Life Foundation to raise money for children's hospitals, inner-city youth centers, and other charitable causes. He has three children to whom he is devoted, and he even coaches his oldest son's football team. In February of 2009, Snoop Dog left Geffen records to develop a more international market for his music and his stage persona.

Topic
a. Snoop Dog's teenage years
b. Snoop Dog's movie career
c. Snoop Dog's life

a. Snoop Dog was a drug dealer when he was a young man, and he has never quite escaped his early image as a gangster.
b. Snoop Dog rose from humble beginnings to become a successful movie star.
c. Snoop Dog is rap music's most successful performer.
d. The popular performer known as Snoop Dog left behind a life of crime to become successful both personally and professionally.

9. Computer users are tired of dealing with spam e-mail messages and pop-up advertisements in web sites, and some have demanded that the federal government do something to eradicate these annoyances. _____. For one thing, the Internet community can solve these problems much faster than the government can. The creation of new laws that could put a stop to unwanted ads in cyberspace is always a very slow process. Internet service providers, search engine companies, computer manufacturers, and the rest of the marketplace can respond much faster, especially when their profits are threatened. For example, when computer users complained about pop-up ads cluttering their screens, Google and Earthlink were quick to supply free "pop-up stopper" software, which blocks the appearance of almost all of these ads. The Internet community's solutions are also more effective than the government's solutions. A federal law that took effect in 2004, for instance, outlawed using false e-mail addresses to generate spam. However, if the e-mail address is false, then the person who sent it is impossible to trace, and the law cannot be enforced. On contrast, the Internet experts are have developed technology that can verify e-mail addresses and prevent mail sent from false addresses from ever reaching computers. (Source of information: Larry Downes, "Internet Cleans Its Own House," *USA Today,* January 8, 2004, p. 13A.)

a. The government has responded with legislation that will put a stop to the problem of unwanted e-mail.
b. The government and the Internet community are working together to solve the problem of Spam.
c. Government involvement, however, is unnecessary; the Internet community can take care of the problem.
d. The problem of seemingly ever present e-mail spam will not be easy to solve.

Directions: Circle the letter of the correct definition.

10. Based on the context, the word *kudos* in paragraph 8 must means
a. praise.

b. criticism.

c. medals.

d. money.

11. Based on the context, the word *eradicate* in paragraph 9 must means

a. increase.

b. punish.

c. explain.

d. get rid of.

Part 4: Topics and Main Ideas (Stated and Implied)

Directions: Read each passage. Then answer the questions by circling the letter of the correct response or writing the answer on the blank.

12. [1]Sixty-two percent of pet owners celebrate their pet's birthday, and half of pet owners sing the "Happy Birthday" song to their pets. [2]Sixty-seven percent of pet owners include their pet in their celebration of holidays like Christmas. [3]Forty-nine percent of pet owners consider their pets to be family members, and 73 percent would go into debt to provide for their pet's food, medical care, and other necessities. [4]Sixty-seven percent of pet owners admit to experiencing feelings of sad remorse when they leave their pet home alone. [5]As a result, 39 percent even talk to their pet on the phone when they're away on trips so that the animals can hear their voice. (Source of information: Diana McCabe, "Can Animal Communicator Really Know What Your Pet Thinks?" *The Charlotte Observer,* February 15, 2004, p. 10G.)

(a) What is the topic of the reading?

a. pets

b. the benefits of pet ownership

c. pet owners' feelings about their pets

d. how to take care of a pet

(b) If there is a topic sentence, please paraphrase it on the blank below. If the main idea is implied, please write the implied main idea on the blank below.

---

13. [1]According to the American Association for Single People (AASP), this nation's unmarried citizens are regularly subjected to discrimination. [2]For one thing, says AASP, single people get a lot fewer employee benefits than married people get. [3]Married people, for example, get hundreds or even thousands of dollars more in medical and dental benefits for their spouses and children. [4]Single people, however, rarely receive comparable compensation. [5]Furthermore, single people often pay higher taxes than married people do, especially when compared to a married couple with only one wage earner. [6]And single people usually pay higher insurance rates than married people pay. [7]In California, for example, an unemployed, 20-year-old married male driver who drinks pays less for his auto insurance than a 20-year-old single student who is a member of the honor society and does not drink pays for his. [8]In addition, a landlord can discriminate against a single person by refusing to rent to him or her. [9]If the unmarried person wants to fight this unfair treatment, his or her only recourse is to file a lawsuit and spend thousands of dollars in legal fees. (Source of information: Thomas F. Coleman, "The High Cost of Being Single in America," American Association for Single People, http://www.unmarriedamerica.org/cost-discrimination.htm)

(a) What is the topic of the reading?
   a. the American Association for Single People
   b. discrimination against single people
   c. married life vs. single life
   d. the effect of marital status on employee benefits

(b) If there is a topic sentence, please paraphrase it on the blank below. If the main idea is implied, please write the implied main idea on the blank below.

_____

14. [1]A recent study conducted by the National Institute for Occupational Safety and Health, which examined about 7,000 former National Football League (NFL) football players, showed that NFL linemen are three times more likely than other football players and six times more likely than the general population to get heart disease. [2]Linemen also have a 52 percent higher chance of dying of heart disease. [3]Half of all retired linemen, the players who take the most pounding out on the football field, suffer from arthritis and skeletal maladies such as bad backs. [4]And almost all linemen, who have to ingest 6,000 to 10,000 calories a day to maintain their huge bulk, can also be classified as obese. [5]But linemen aren't the only ones who suffer health problems after playing in the NFL. [6]Yet another study of about 2,500 retired NFL players revealed that more than one in every ten had been diagnosed with clinical depression, a condition that is thought to be caused by repeated head concussions. [7]Other research published in *The New England Journal of Medicine* found that 14 percent of all football players suffer from sleep apnea, a condition that causes them to stop breathing while they're sleeping. [8]Experts say that the life expectancy of a typical pro football player is in the low to mid-60s, which is about 10 years shorter than the life expectancy of the average male. [9]Clearly, playing in the NFL is hazardous to players' health. (Sources of statistics Stan Grossfeld, "Not Much Headway," *The Boston Globe,* December 26, 2003, http://www.boston.com/sports/articles/ 2003/12/26/not_much_ headway/; Art Carey, "Big Men of the NFL Pay for Their Play Later in Life," *Philadelphia Inquirer,* January 27, 2003, http://www.philly.com/mld/philly/living/ columnists/art_ carey/5038288.htm)

(a) What is the topic of the reading?
   a. the National Football League
   b. NFL linemen
   c. health problems
   d. NFL players' health problems

(b) If there is a topic sentence, please paraphrase it on the blank below. If the main idea is implied, please write the implied main idea on the blank below.

_____

15. [1]Americans throw away 100 billion thin plastic grocery bags every year. [2]Most of these bags are carted off to overflowing landfills, where they make up 4 percent of our garbage. [3]However, about one to three percent of the bags escape and become litter. [4]Consequently, discarded bags are everywhere, blowing down streets, getting caught in trees and bushes, washing up on beaches. [5]They clog drains and eventually wash out into the ocean, where thousands of marine animals, such as sea turtles, choke on the bags or get tangled in them. [6]If the bags do make it into a landfill, they will stay there for 100 to 1,000 years before they finally decompose. [7]Wherever they end up, though, the ink used to print stores' logos on the bags degrades and becomes a toxic poison released into the soil or water. (Sources of information: L. J. Williamson, "It's in the Bag," *Utne,* January–February 2004, p. 32; John Roach, "Are Plastic Bags Sacking the Environment?" *National Geographic News,*

September 2, 2003, http//news.nationalgeographic.com/news/2003/09/0902_030902_plasticbags.html)

(a) What is the topic of the reading?
    a.   trash in America
    b.   plastic grocery bags
    c.   discarded plastic grocery bags
    d.   discarded plastic grocery bags in landfills

(b) If there is a topic sentence, please paraphrase it on the blank below. If the main idea is implied, please write the implied main idea on the blank below.

_____

16. [1]In the 1920s, Mohandas Gandhi showed the people of India how to use Henry David Thoreau's ideas about "civil disobedience," the nonviolent resistance of unjust laws and policies, to win their country's independence from the British Empire. [2]In 1955, the Reverend Martin Luther King Jr. led a bus boycott in Alabama founded on the principles of civil disobedience, which led to the civil rights movement of the 1960s. [3]During that same decade, people who opposed the Vietnam War engaged in nonviolent demonstrations modeled on Thoreau's ideas. [4]Since the 1970s, adversaries of nuclear weapons and nuclear power have used civil disobedience tactics for their protests at test sites, storage facilities, government offices, and power plants. [5]Thoreau's concept of civil disobedience has also influenced how activists have battled since the 1980s against the racial segregation that has divided blacks and whites in South Africa.

(a) What is the topic of the reading?
    a.   Mohandas Gandhi and Henry David Thoreau
    b.   Henry David Thoreau
    c.   Thoreau's influence on acts of civil disobedience
    d.   the civil rights movement of the 1960s

(b) If there is a topic sentence, please paraphrase it on the blank below. If the main idea is implied, please write the implied main idea on the blank below.

_____

Part 5: Topics, Main Ideas, and Supporting Details

Directions: Read each passage. Then answer the questions by circling the letter of the correct response or writing the answer on the blank.

17. [1]All material on Earth exists in one of three states. [2]In **solid** materials, the particles that constitute the material are tightly packed and locked together in place, usually in a regular pattern, so they form a fixed shape. [3]Wood, peanut butter, and ice are all examples of solids. [4]The second type of physical state is **liquid**. [5]In a liquid, the particles are close together, but they have no regular arrangement. [6]The particles of a liquid move about and slide past one another, allowing the material to flow and assume the shape of the container that holds it. [7]Examples of liquids include water, oil, and milk. [8]**Gas** is the third and final form that matter can take. [9]In gases, the particles

have no regular arrangement, and they are separated from one another, with space in between, so they can move around freely and flow easily. [10]The air we breathe is a good example of a gas.

(a) What is the topic of the reading?
   a. solids
   b. particles
   c. states of matter
   d. the differences between liquids and gases

(b) If there is a topic sentence, please paraphrase it on the blank below. If the main idea is implied, please write the implied main idea on the blank below.

_____

(c) Sentence 3 is a
   a. major detail.
   b. minor detail.

(d) Sentence 4 is a
   a. major detail.
   b. minor detail.

(e) Sentence 7 is a
   a. major detail.
   b. minor detail.

18. [1]After conducting eight years of research about luck and concluding that luck actually has very little to do with chance, psychologist Richard Wiseman claimed that the real difference between "lucky" people and "unlucky" people has to do with their personalities and behaviors. [2]People who are considered lucky are really just outgoing and curious people who remain optimistic and open to new experiences. [3]They are constantly expanding their social networks, so they increase their odds of getting lucky by finding the right job, the right companion, the right house, and so on. [4]"Lucky" people tend to pay attention to their instincts when opportunities arise, which often leads to lucky outcomes. [5]"Unlucky people," on the other hand, tend to be introverted and preoccupied with their own problems and responsibilities. [6]They are also more pessimistic, and they are reluctant to try new things. [7]Consequently, unlucky people don't notice the possibilities around them. [8]They focus only on the obstacles, failing to take advantage of new opportunities and end up limiting the number of good things that happen to them. (Source of study: Anne Underwood, "Want to Improve Your Luck?" *Newsweek,* May 5, 2003, www.msnbc.com)

(a) What is the topic of the reading?
   a. research about luck
   b. the personality traits of lucky people
   c. characteristics of unlucky people
   d. the differences between lucky and unlucky people

(b) If there is a topic sentence, please paraphrase it on the blank below. If the main idea is implied, please write the implied main idea on the blank below.

_____

(c) Sentence 2 is a
   a. major detail.
   b. minor detail.

(d) Sentence 5 is a
   a. major detail.
   b. minor detail.

(e) To correctly understand the author's meaning, readers need to supply what connection between sentences 1 and 2.

---

19. [1]According to research conducted at the University of Washington, wives view their husbands as more loving and supportive when the men help with the housework. [2]Working wives who get help with chores are also less stressed and less tired. [3]As a result, when husbands take on tasks such as the mopping, the laundry, and the dirty dishes, wives tend to find them more attractive and feel more affectionate and amorous than they do if the men do not help. [4]What's more, studies at the University of California have found that witnessing their dads pitching in on household chores has a significant impact on children. [5]Researchers concluded that when men perform domestic duties, they are modeling cooperative relationships, so their children are more likely to learn positive family values and become well adjusted. [6]Surveys show that children with fathers who help with housework tend to have more friends, get into less trouble at school, and are less depressed or withdrawn than kids whose fathers do not help with housework. (Sources of studies: "A Reason to Mop," no author credited, ABCNews.com,
October 3, 2003, http://abcnews.go.com/sections/GMA/WaterCooler/GMA031003House-keeping_study.html; "Dusting Dads 'More Attractive,'" no author credited, BBC News, June 11, 2003, http://news.bbc.co.uk/go/pr/fr/-/1/hi/health/2980642.stm)

(a) What is the topic of the reading?
   a. housework
   b. housework's effect on wives
   c. the effects of husbands doing housework
   d. the effects of household chores on children

(b) If there is a topic sentence, please paraphrase it on the blank below. If the main idea is implied, please write the implied main idea on the blank below.

(c) Sentence 4 is a
   a. major detail.
   b. minor detail.

(d) Sentence 6 is a
   a. major detail.
   b. minor detail.

(e) To correctly understand the author's meaning, readers need to make what connection between sentences 4 and ?

20. [1]Many Americans are far more apprehensive about flying than driving, and we usually don't worry that much at all about drowning. [2]However, according to the National Safety Council, we have a 1 in 1,028 chance of drowning and only a 1 in 4,608 chance of dying in an airplane crash. [3]The risk of dying in a car accident is far greater (1 in 242), but few of us worry about that when we get into our vehicles. [4]As this example illustrates, our worries often do not match actual levels of risk. [5]We fear being exposed to the new disease-of-the-year, such as the 2003's SARS respiratory virus or 2002's West Nile virus, or we worry about becoming a victim of bioterrorism. [6]Yet, such viruses usually take relatively few lives, and we have only a 1 in 56,424,800 chance of being attacked by a bioterrorist. [7]We have a much better chance (1 in 197) of dying from heart disease; few of us, though, worry about that. [8]We're also more concerned about getting cancer from exposure to radiation from nuclear power, cell phones, and power lines than we are about getting cancer from the sun. [9]In reality, though, the sun causes 1.3 million annual cases of skin cancer and claims almost 10,000 lives a year. [10]Since we don't seem to worry about the right things, it would probably be good if we just stopped worrying. (Source of study: Neil Osterweil, "Worry vs. Reality: The Real Risks You Face," *WebMD,* February 18, 2004, http://content.health.msn.com/content/article/82/97245.htm)

(a) What is the topic of the reading?
    a. things that frighten people
    b. fear of flying
    c. worries about risks
    d. modern health risks

(b) If there is a topic sentence, please paraphrase it on the blank below. If the main idea is implied, please write the implied main idea on the blank below.

_____

(c) Sentence 1 is a
    a. major detail.
    b. minor detail.

(d) Sentence 5 is a
    a. major detail.
    b. minor detail.

(e) The last sentence of the paragraph is a
    a. major supporting detail.
    b. minor supporting detail.
    c. concluding sentence.

Note. Although the sentence is not quite complete enough to fit the definition of a topic sentence—it doesn't mention risk taking—I'd accept as correct answers that called the last sentence the topic sentence.

FINAL EXAM

Reading 1

[1]Research on adolescents in junior and senior high school indicates five different levels of popularity. [2]At the first level are *admired* adolescents, young people who tend to be physically attractive, well-groomed, fashionable, social, self-confident, and able to command attention. [3]The individuals in this group receive mainly favorable ratings from other adolescents. [4]At the second level are the *controversial* adolescents. [5]They're the young people who receive very favorable or very unfavorable ratings from their peers and are strongly liked or disliked, sometimes for the same reason. [6]*Average* adolescents are at the third level and are generally accepted by their peers but don't arouse extreme positive or negative feelings. [7]At the next level are *rejected* adolescents. [8]Members of this group engage in antisocial and aggressive behaviors that cause them to be actively avoided by other teens. [9]*Neglected* adolescents aren't usually aggressive; however, they often have poor social skills. [10]Thus they engage in fewer positive interactions with their peers. [11]Many have hobbies and interests very different from their peers, so no one pays them much attention, and they are generally ignored. (Adapted from Paul S. Kaplan, *Adolescence*, Boston: Houghton Mifflin, 2004, p. 192.)

1. What's the topic of reading 1?

   _____

2. Which sentence is the topic sentence or stated main idea of the reading? _____

3. Please paraphrase, or re-word, the stated main idea.

   _____

   _____

4. Circle the letter of the **primary** pattern of organization. *Note:* The pattern of a paragraph cannot consist of one sentence.

   a. process   b. definition   c. classification   d. cause and effect

5. Read the description below. Based on your understanding of the reading, what group would Marisa belong to?

   _____

   Marisa is smart, funny, and opinionated. She has lots of friends and belongs to many different groups because of her various interests. Those students who are confident and opinionated themselves like being in her company and seek her out. Students who are shy, however, and less comfortable speaking their mind, avoid her. More than one has complained that no can get a word in the conversation when Marisa is present.

Reading 2

Tyrannosaurus Rex, Predator* or Scavenger

1   The dinosaur *Tyrannosaurus rex* has always had a reputation for being one of the fiercest predators that ever walked the earth. In school, every child learns that this vicious, six-ton killing machine ruled the dinosaur world. Typically in many museums, reconstructed *T. rex* skeletons reveal huge mouths filled with rows of teeth that seem perfect for ripping the flesh from prey.

2   However, some paleontologists* now convincingly argue that Tyrannosaurus rex was a scavenger who lived off the kills of other. Those huge teeth may have actually been perfect for crushing bone and tough cartilage rather than slicing meat. The *T. rex*'s teeth were cylinder-shaped and not as sharp and jagged as those of other known predators such as *Velociraptor*, a dinosaur that grew up to 10 feet in length and hunted in packs. The thinking now is that after dinosaurs like the *Velociraptor* had their fill, the *T. rex* may have moved in to scavenge what was left of the carcass. Further evidence fitting this new scenario is the fact that scientists have never come across any bones that have been scratched or otherwise damaged by *T. rex*'s teeth.

3   Many of the *T. rex*'s other body parts, also, seem inadequate for predatory behaviors but perfect for scavenging. Predators that walk on two legs usually have short thighs and long shins, a combination that allows them to run fast enough to catch fleeing prey. However, *T. rex*'s huge legs had longer thigh bones than shin bones, which means that is could have walked long distances in search of food. In fact, it could not have outrun most of the other dinosaurs. In addition, its arms were tiny and weak, so it would not have been able to grab and take hold of prey, and its eyes were too small for it to see prey at any great distance.

4   What the *T. rex* did have was an excellent sense of smell. Paleontologists who have studied *T. rex* skulls have determined that the beast had a huge olfactory lobe, the part of the brain used for smell. But here again, that evidence suggests that *T. rex* may have been not a killer but a scavenger. *T. rex* could not see well, but it could pick up a scent—such as that coming from a dead animal—at long distances. In fact, *T. rex*'s olfactory lobe was very similar to that of the greatest scavenger of them all—the vulture, who can smell decaying flesh from 25 miles away.

6.   What is the topic of the entire reading?

_____

7.   The main idea is
     a.   stated.
     b.   implied

8.   How would you express the main idea in your own words?

_____

_____

---

* Predators kill their food; scavengers live off the kills of other animals.

* paleontologists: scientists who study bones and fossils to learn about ancient cultures.

9. The second paragraph opens with what kind of transition?

    a. time order   b. reversal   c. addition

10. Identify four supporting details cited by paleontologists who challenge the traditional opinion on *T. rex.*

    1. _____

    2. _____

    3. _____

    4. _____

11. The author's purpose is to

    a. inform readers about a new theory concerning *T. rex.*
    b. persuade readers that a new theory about *T. rex* is more accurate than the old.

12. The author's tone is

    a. neutral.
    b. supportive.
    c. skeptical.
    d. argumentative.

Reading 3

To Sleep or Not to Sleep

1   Whenever you miss a few hours of sleep—or even more than a few—you probably muddle your way through the day without anything catastrophic occurring. Thus, you might well assume that getting six to eight hours of sleep is not essential. Yet given what numerous studies and statistics suggest about the effects of regular and ongoing sleep deprivation, this is an assumption that requires careful scrutiny.*

2   Several studies suggest, for instance, that sleep deprivation impairs both concentration and memory (Bowman, 200; Harrison and Horne, 2000; Stickgold, 2003, 2006). The more sleep you lose, the more

---

* scrutiny: close study.

difficult it is to master new information and store it away in long-term memory. As brain scans have repeatedly shown, the sleeping brain can be quite active, and sleep seems to be a time when the brain identifies, sorts, and stores new information. When sleep is cut short, the brain doesn't get as much time to do its work. As a result, an individual's mastery of new skills or concepts can take much longer than it would if the body and brain were getting eight hours of rest.

3   But losing sleep has wider implications as well. Sleep deprivation is among the most common causes of motor vehicle accidents. Not surprisingly, auto accidents have been shown to spike around two a.m. in the morning when drivers are at their sleepiest. Mistakenly thinking they can drive through the night and stay awake on coffee, drivers nod off at the wheel and end up causing a collision.

4   Then there are the medical consequences of sleep deprivation to consider. A 2005 study of 10,000 adults found that those between the ages of 32 and 49 who regularly slept less than seven hours a night are significantly more likely to be seriously obese. Lack of sleep makes people feel tired. Then, in response to feelings of fatigue, they reach for a snack. If sleep deprivation continues, they start piling on the pounds and serious obesity can be the result.

5   Even more disturbing consequences of sleep deprivation came out of a Harvard Medical School study involving 82,000 nurses. According to study leader Sanjay R. Patel, the Harvard study revealed an increased risk of death for those nurses who consistently slept less than six hours a night. The theory is that loss of sleep encourages the body to produce chemicals that cause a low-grade inflammation. The inflammation, in turn, produces cardiovascular* problems.

6   The results of the Harvard study are supported by similar studies showing that a prolonged sleep deficit puts the body into a constant state of high-alert, almost as if it were being continuously exposed to an external threat. This high-alert state stimulates the production of stress hormones like cortisol. It also drives up blood pressure. Elevated stress hormones and high blood pressure are major risk factors in heart attacks. As Virend Somers of the Mayo Clinic in Rochester, Minnesota, expresses it, "We've really only scratched the surface when it comes to understanding what's going on regarding sleep and heart disease." (Source of information: Jeffrey Nevid, *Psychology Concepts and Applications*, Boston: Houghton Mifflin, 2003, pp. 147-48, 150-51; "Scientists Find Out What Sleep Does to the Body," www.washingtonpost.com/ wp_dyn/content/article/2005/10/08.)

13. What is the topic of the entire reading?

_____

14. The main idea is

   a. stated.
   b. implied.

15. How would you express the main idea in your own words?

_____

_____

_____

* cardiovascular: related to the heart and blood vessels.

16. What is the topic of paragraph 4?

_____

17. The topic sentence in paragraph 5 is

    a. the first sentence.
    b. the second sentence.
    c. the third sentence.
    d. the last sentence.

18. The purpose of this reading is

    a. to inform.
    b. to persuade.

19. The author's tone is

    a. objective.
    b. outraged.
    c. relaxed.
    d. warning.

Reading 4

Let Barbaro be a Lesson

1   When Barbaro, the two-year-old winner of the Kentucky Derby, broke his leg right before the start of the Preakness Stakes horse race on May 19, 2006, there was a flood of sympathy and concern. Some well-wishers even volunteered their services as stable hands and caretakers. Hopes for the horse's survival rallied in the fall of 2006 as Barbaro's condition seemed to improve after his cast was removed in November. But in January of 2007, despite the best veterinary care available, Barbaro's condition declined still further. He was euthanized on January 29, leaving fans from all over the country stricken by his loss.

2   From the scrappy, come-from-behind Depression-era hero Seabiscuit[*] to the almost supernaturally fast Barbaro, racehorses have long won the hearts of Americans of all ages and classes. And why shouldn't they? Racehorses are heroic creatures. Running to exhaustion, often in pain, they race for the finish line, thrilling their fans and making their owners rich. No wonder people are horrified and shocked when they learn that some unscrupulous owners drug the horses to spur them on when they are injured or, even more despicably, kill them for the insurance money if the horses start losing.

---

[*] Seabiscuit: A champion thoroughbred racehorse, Seabiscuit (1933-1947) got off to a slow start but became one of the top racehorses of the century.

3   However, what people really need to think about is whether or not horseracing itself, even under the best conditions, isn't a cruel and inhumane sport. As many critics of horseracing pointed out after Barbaro's untimely death, horseracing, for all its thrilling beauty and excitement, poses a serious, even deadly, threat to a young horse's health. Thus, it might be time to take seriously an idea that animal rights activists have long proposed—the banning of horseracing.

4   Perhaps the most outspoken advocate of this position is Elliot Katz, the veterinarian-president of an organization called "In Defense of Animals." Katz bluntly calls horseracing a "killer sport" and argues that horseracing is by nature cruel and barbaric.* He points out that racehorses, bred for extreme speed, are highly vulnerable to fractures. Their thin bones help them break out of the gate fast. Unfortunately, those slender, fast-moving legs can also encourage the kind of painful bone fractures that left two-year-old Barbaro writhing in agony moments before the race began. If Katz had his way, horseracing would go the way of dog racing, which declined in popularity once people realized how the dogs involved, usually greyhounds, suffered from the sport.

5   The Humane Society, for its part, is much more muted in its criticism. If anything, it tried hard to seem supportive of horseracing. According to a staff veterinarian, the Humane Society of the United States does not oppose horseracing as long as it's done "correctly." However, in its list of policy statements, the Society explicitly opposes the racing of "young animals whose bones and bodies have not matured sufficiently." Thus, it's hard to see how horse races can be "correctly" done, since it is precisely those young animals the Humane Society wants to protect who participate in horse races. The Triple Crown winner Affirmed ran his first race at the age of two, so did Hall-of-Famer Dr. Faber, considered one of the great racing thoroughbreds. Horse races aren't run by mature animals. Two years old is the average age.

6   Fans of and participants in horse races insist that criticism of the sport is unfair because the horses themselves love to run. Still, they would be hard-pressed to disprove the words of Jim Orsini, a horse surgeon at the University of Pennsylvania's New Bolton Center, where Barbaro was sent to recover: ". . . at high speed, a horse's leg bones can actually deform, and keep deforming until they or their ligaments or tendons eventually fail. The stress to bones can be overwhelming."

7   Orsini's words seemed all too prophetic, when less than a year after Barbaro's death, the three-year-old filly Eight Belles finished the Kentucky Derby and collapsed at the finish line with two fractured legs. Because the horse couldn't even stand on one leg to be splinted, she was immediately euthanized. After her death, Eight Belles trainer Larry Jones fought back tears while maintaining that the filly came from a long line of equine* heroes: "We put everything into them that we have. They've given us everything they have. They put their life on the damn line, and she was glad to do it." Maybe so, but if Jones is right, then anyone watching a video of the Derby has to wonder why jockey Gabriel Saez, later cited for excessive use of his whip, had to whip Eight Belles so mercilessly as she struggled to catch the Derby's winner Big Brown. Perhaps, after all, she wasn't so "glad to do it," and fans of horseracing might keep that in mind the next time they think about buying a ticket or placing a bet. (Sources: http://www.usatoday.com/sports/horses/2008-05-04-eight-belles-cover_N.htm;   http://www.hsus.org/webfiles/PDF/HSUS_PolicyStatement_1_06.pdf; http:www.thoroughbredtimes.com/tc2000/history/winners/affirmed/default.asp.)

20. What is the topic of reading 3?

_____

_____

* barbaric: crude and cruel.
* equine: related to horses.

21. The main idea is

    a. stated.

    b. implied.

22. How would you express the main idea in your own words?

    _____

    _____

23. Circle the letter of the **primary** pattern of organization in paragraph 1.

    a. definition   b. classification   c. time order   d. comparison and contrast

24. Circle the letter of the **primary** pattern of organization for the entire reading.

    a. classification   b. comparison and contrast   c. time order   d. cause and effect

25. What claim does veterinarian Elliot Katz make in paragraph 4?

    _____

26. What support does he offer for that claim?

    _____

    _____

27. What is the topic of paragraph 5?

    _____

What's the main idea?

    _____

    _____

28. What is the implied main idea of paragraph 7?

    _____

    _____

29. What's the implied main idea of paragraph 6?

    _____

    _____

30. What would you say is the author's purpose?

    _____

    How would you describe the author's tone?

    _____

PART VI

Answer Keys for Mid-Term and Final

MID-TERM EXAM

Part 1

S: Survey or Preview to get a sense of the chapter's content and length.
Q: Pose questions to guide your reading.
R: Read the chapter, assigning yourself no more than fifteen to twenty pages per night.
R: Recall, or see how much you can remember of the chapter section you just completed.
R: Review see how much you remember about the chapter as a whole.

Part 2

2. a
3. c
4. b
5. a

Part 3

6. b; c
7. b; b
8. c; d
9. b; c
10. a
11. d

Part 4

12. (a) c
    (b) Implied: Many pet owners treat their pets as if they were beloved family members.

13. (a) b
    (b) T.S.: Single people are frequently discriminated against in comparison to married people.

14. (a) d
    (b) Implied Main Idea: NFL players end up with an unusual number of health problems.

15. (a) a
    (b) Implied Main Idea: In the United States. discarded trash is a major environmental
        problem.

16. (a) c
    (b) Implied Main Idea: Thoreau has had a powerful effect on civil rights movements around
        the world.

Part 5

17. (a) c
    (b) Matter can exist in three states.
    (c) b
    (d) a
    (e) b

18. (a) d
    (b) Personality and behavior may well determine how lucky or unlucky people are.
    (c) a
    (d) a
    (e) The claim about people being optimistic and therefore lucky is a result of the research mentioned previously.

19. (a) c
    (b) Implied Main Idea: There are some real benefits to husbands helping with housework.
    (c) a
    (d) b   *Note:* Sentence 6 provides more information about what it means to be "well-adjusted."
    (e) Readers need to recognize that sentence 5 introduces the "impact" mentioned in sentence 4.

20. (a) c
    (b) *Implied Main Idea:* The risks we worry about are often not the ones that may actually do us harm.
    (c) a
    (d) a
    (e) c

FINAL EXAM

1. levels of popularity, different levels of popularity
2. 1
3. Studies of kids in junior and senior high suggest that popularity can be divided into five different groups.
4. c
5. controversial
6. *T. rex*, Tyrannosaurus rex
7. a
8. Some paleontologists now think *T. rex* scavenged for food rather than hunting it down.
9. b
10. (1) The dinosaur's teeth seem better designed for eating than killing.
    (2) No bones have ever been found with *T. rex* teeth marks.
    (3) *T. rex* didn't have the right legs for running.
    (4) *T. rex* had weak arms, which could not have grabbed prey.
11. b
12. b
13. sleep deprivation, loss of sleep, consequences of sleep loss
14. b
15. Loss of sleep can have serious consequences
16. medical consequences of sleep deprivation
17. a
18. b
19. d
20. banning horseracing; the negative consequences of racing horses
21. a
22. Horseracing is torture for horses, and it should be outlawed.
23. c

24. d
25. Horseracing is deadly for horses.
26. Breeding horses for speed makes them vulnerable to fractures.
27. *Topic:* Humane Society's position on horseracing
Main Idea: The Humane Society takes a middle-of-the-road position toward horseracing.
28. The fact that horses love to run doesn't mean horseracing is good for them.
29. If fans of horseracing cared about horses, they would stop supporting it.
30. to inform

PART VII
Answer Keys for Chapters 1–11

ANSWER KEY FOR CHAPTERS 1–11

CHAPTER 1: STRATEGIES FOR TEXTBOOK LEARNI NG (pp. 1-67)

Exercise 1: Surveying for Advance Knowledge (pp. 5-9)

1. our sense of being male or female
2. c
3. trapped in the wrong body
4. the cultural expectations about being male or female
5. a

Check Your Understanding (p. 10)

1. A survey should (1) give you a general idea of what the chapter covers, (2) give you a feel for the writer's style and method of organization, (3) help you figure out what's important in the chapter, and (4) identify breaks in the chapter that will help you decide how many pages you want to read in each study session.
2. Reading flexibility is crucial to surveying and every other aspect of reading. Each new reading assignment calls for a different set of reading strategies that reflect the kind of material you are reading, the author's style, and your own purpose in reading.

Exercise 2: Using Questions to Focus Your Attention (pp. 14-16)

Answers will vary. How does food get changed so it can be digested? What does the alimentary canal do during digestion? Are the layers of the alimentary canal the same as the layers of the digestive system? What does the peritoneum do?

Check Your Understanding (p. 16)

1. It helps maintain concentration and improves the reader's ability to spot key passages.
2. They can use (1) introductory lists of questions or objectives, (2) major and minor headings, (3) key words that have been highlighted, and (4) summary sections.

Exercise 3: Making an Informal Outline (pp. 21-23)

Main Point: To effectively read a newspaper, look for three things.

Specifics
1. The kinds of stories that get covered
     crime, fraud, environment, or civil rights
        --What does the choice of topics say about the paper's biases?
2. The sources supplied
       --Ask, why does this source want me to know this?
           (1) source may be floating a trial balloon to test the waters
           (2) source may hope that leaking word of a new policy will kill it
           (3) source may want to take credit or shift blame
           (4) source may be trying to establish a fact that supports a specific point of view
3. Loaded language
       --recognizing loaded language can give you insight into writer's point of view

Check Your Understanding (p. 24)

1. Your eyes may still be moving across the page at the end of two hours, but more than likely your brain is not absorbing the meaning behind the words.
2. Vary your assignments.
3. Write, write, write.
4. It should identify the key point of each chapter section and explain it as much as memory allows. An informal outline should also indent to show relationships.

Exercise 4: Recalling After Reading (p. 27)

Delegation Process

Manager assigns employees a task.	Manager gives employees authority to complete task.	Manager makes employees accountable for completing the task.

Check Your Understanding (p. 28)

1. Recalling right after reading is a good way to monitor understanding. It also help slow down the rate of forgetting.
2. Readers can recall by (1) mental recitation, (2) writing out answers to the questions posed during the survey step of *SQ3R*, (3) covering up and recalling parts of an informal outline, and (4) drawing diagrams and pictures.

Exercise 5: Marking a Text (pp. 36-38)

b   Selection *b* is more selectively underlined. It also uses a variety of marking techniques so that different parts of the text get different kinds of highlighting, which makes it easier to spot relationships, key terms, and ideas.

Exercise 6: Using the Web for Background Knowledge (pp. 49-50)

1. an educational institution
2. No. It's too general and would call up sites about roses. The phrase would need to be modified to, say, "Germany's White Rose."
3. any words used in your search term
4. No. The description leans too heavily in favor of Roosevelt's presidency. The websites chosen for background knowledge need to be more neutral.

Check Your Understanding (p. 51)

1. It can provide the background knowledge that helps in the understanding of a textbook chapter.
2. A phrase will give more precise directions to the search engine you are using.
3. Blogs are inclined to express a personal bias. When a reader is trying to get background knowledge about a subject, he or she wants to get a sense of what is generally known or thought about a topic.

The reader's goal at this point is to understand what most informed people think rather than absorbing one individual's personal opinion.

Vocabulary Check (p. 52) Note: *Ambiguous* appears more than once in the chapter vocabulary checks. That's intentional. I wasn't sure if teachers would be using all the chapters, and I didn't want the word to be missed.

1. l
2. v/m
3. t
4. y
5. f
6. h
7. i
8. m/v
9. j
10. o
11. n
12. a
13. e
14. q
15. w
16. x
17. c
18. r
19. u
20. p
21. s
22. d
23. k
24. b
25. g

Digging Deeper: Memories Are Made of This (pp. 60-63)

Questions Based on Your Survey
1. T
2. F
3. T
4. c
5. b
6. F
7. c
8. F
9. T
10. T

Questions Based on Your Reading
1. b
2. a
3. b

4. b
5. blackboard
6. Miller discovered that the memory could absorb seven different chunks of information before it went into information overload and couldn't absorb anything else new.
7. Chunking is the process of breaking down a large amount of information into smaller, combined chunks, which then become easier to recall.
8. F
9. the phonological loop
10. the brain

Making Connections (p. 63)

Yes. *Answers will vary.* Robinson's emphasis on writing while reading and reciting or recalling what's been said after finishing each chapter strongly suggests that he was aware of how important it was to rehearse new information to retain it.

Drawing Your Own Conclusions (p. 63)

b   According to the author, elaborative rehearsal (paragraph 18), which focuses on the meaning is more effective than maintenance rehearsal (paragraph 13), which involves pure repetition. Paraphrasing forces the reader to keep the original meaning while changing the language.

Test 1: Vocabulary Review (pp. 64-65)

1. contemplating
2. adaptive
3. hypothetically
4. personified
5. prenatal
6. determinants
7. cognitive
8. repulsed
9. icons
10. chromosomes

Test 2: Vocabulary Review (pp. 66-67)

1. hot and liquid
2. sound
3. significant, decisive
4. the act of acquiring or obtaining something
5. not following accepted social standards
6. produced, taken, or assumed
7. transforming, changing
8. move backward
9. predictions of future goals, sales, or figures
10. condition of being completely forgotten

CHAPTER 2: BUILDING WORD POWER (pp. 68-121)

Exercise 1: Using Context Clues (pp. 74-75)

1. capable of being hurt; exposed to harm
2. beaten badly
3. jailing; imprisonment
4. denial of responsibility
5. symbol; perfect example
6. proved innocent, freed of guilt
7. able to see what others can't; insightful, capable of understanding
8. false and distorted beliefs
9. pleasure-loving, fond of good times
10. sad situation, misery

Exercise 2: Using Context Clues (pp. 75-76)

1. confusion, chaos, disturbance
2. punishing, harsh
3. hunting, searching
4. disgusting, uncared for
5. born that way; naturally; genetically
6. connection, relationship
7. sinking
8. profitable; financially successful
9. living longer; long life; advanced age
10. support; propose; are in favor of

Exercise 3: Using Context Clues (p. 77-78)

1. short accounts of colorful or humorous incidents
2. connected, clear
3. payment
4. traditional, usual
5. early, initial, trial, advance
6. produced, created
7. those in favor; supporters
8. new additions, inventions, clever changes, original ideas
9. persuasive, well-argued, forceful
10. following; coming after

Exercise 4: Using Context Clues (pp. 78-80)

1. laid at the door of; connected to
2. reason, explanation
3. persuasiveness, soundness, accuracy
4. lowest level; low-ranking
5. ended, completed
6. agreement, permission
7. take out; remove; pull out
8. having the same value, equal
9. not fitting together; not matching
10. complete, covering all areas

Check Your Understanding (pp. 80-81)

1. No. Context supplies an approximate definition that allows the reader to understand the sentence, but that definition may not be a perfect match for the one in the dictionary.
2. example, definition, general knowledge, and contrast
3. restatement
4. example
5. contrast
6. general knowledge

Exercise 5: Learning Word Parts (pp. 83-84)

1. rect
2. popul
3. chron
4. per
5. pel
6. bi, lat
7. bi, gam
8. poly, gam
9. mob
10. im, mob

Exercise 6: Using Word Parts and Context Clues (pp. 86-87)

1. *Monotheism* – belief in one god
   Polytheism – belief in many gods
2. moving together in time
3. disgusting, horrible
4. put a hole through; punctured
5. caused not to move; paralyzed, made unable to move
6. brought back to life
7. false or fake names
8. resumé, account of a life
9. criticizing; saying bad things about
10. energy, life force

Check Your Understanding (pp. 87-88)

1. Often knowing what the root or prefix means can help you define an unfamiliar word. Greek and Latin prefixes and roots are particularly important because words used in an academic setting rely heavily on word parts from these two languages.
2. Prefixes come at the beginning of words and they modify the overall meaning. Roots give a word its core or central meaning. Although the addition of prefixes can change the overall meaning of a word, they can't alter the root meaning.
3. Suffixes say more about a word's grammatical function than they do about the word's definition.
4. You double your chances of getting an accurate meaning for the word you don't know.

Exercise 7: Understanding Connotation (p. 92)

1. direct
2. giggled
3. slender
4. preowned
5. husky

Exercise 8: Understanding Connotation (p. 93)

1. blurted
2. disputing
3. stubborn
4. recklessness
5. hurled

Check Your Understanding (p. 93)

1. Words highlighted in these ways are the specialized vocabulary words essential to understanding the subject matter.
2. the glossary
3. The "denotation" is the formal dictionary meaning; the "connotation" is the feeling or association that has become attached to the word with a passage of time.
4. No. Context can dramatically change the meaning of a word.

Exercise 9: Using the Dictionary (pp. 95-96)

1. hey
2. adjective
3. 4
4. two; the first; him
5. 4; the third; spoken; father; an adjective

Exercise 10: Using the Dictionary (pp. 98-100)

1. 2
2. 1
3. 3
4. 1

Check Your Understanding (pp. 100-101)

1. pronunciation, syllabication, and grammatical function
2. the original context for the word
3. word history
4. a; b
5. a; a

Digging Deeper: Word Lovers and Word Histories (pp. 104-106)

1. the search; the panting syllable
2. b
3. They were trying to track down how a word or word meaning originated.
4. *phil*, meaning "love," and *ist*, meaning "person who"
5. c
6. herculean
7. martinet
8. titan
9. chauvinist
10. ostrasized

Making Connections (p. 107)

They were all lexicographers, or makers of dictionaries.

Drawing Your Own Conclusions (p. 107)

He would probably not allow his employees to do that. Where martinets are concerned, rules are not made to be broken or changed. Rules are rules.

Test 1: Using Context Clues (pp. 108-110)

1. c
2. b
3. a
4. d
5. c
6. d
7. d
8. c
9. b
10. d

Test 2: Using Context Clues (pp. 111-112)

1. humorous, sarcastic, comical
2. nearness, closeness
3. mark, fault, embarrassment
4. bottleneck; traffic jam
5. excitement, interest, encouragement
6. honesty, openness, frankness
7. following, additional
8. empty, bleak, sterile, lacking in vegetation
9. arrogant, bored, superior
10. compelling, inspiring

Test 3: Using Context Clues (pp. 113-114)

1. treating unfairly
2. buying, acquiring
3. changed, adapted
4. heavily, mainly, mostly
5. before; prior to
6. began, started
7. theory, idea
8. direct, exact, stated, detailed
9. possible consequences, suggested possibilities
10. changes; up and down

Test 4: Word Analysis and Context Clues (pp. 115-116)

1. cure; medicine against
2. cut up
3. followers, believers
4. extra, unnecessary, useless
5. separate, isolate
6. training; proof of knowledge
7. saying, advice
8. get out of
9. believable, acceptable
10. stick, attach to

Test 5: Word Analysis and Context Clues (pp. 117-118)

1. impossible to please or calm
2. get around, avoid
3. leaning, tendency, response
4. all-knowing
5. number
6. coming between; interfering
7. ready to eat everything
8. numbers; large numbers of people
9. calmed, bribed
10. roundabout, overly long

Test 6: Word Analysis and Context Clues (pp. 119-120)

1. produce
2. loud, outspoken
3. introduction, opening
4. calls up; creates; re-creates
5. origin, source
6. talkative
7. made up; fake
8. unnecessary, extraneous
9. get rid of; put down; control
10. made-up stories

CHAPTER 3: CONNECTING THE GENERAL TO THE SPECIFIC IN READING AND WRITING (pp. 122-163)

Exercise 1: Coming Up with Specifics (pp. 124-125)

Answers will vary.
1. happiness, anger, sadness
2. jazz, rap, classical

Exercise 2: Seeing the Difference Between General and Specific Words (pp. 126-127)

1. churches
2. robbery
3. Usher
4. Congress
5. Constitution

Exercise 3: Seeing the Difference Between General and Specific Words (p. 127)

1. creature
2. planet
3. pollution
4. phobia
5. symbol

Exercise 4: Finding a General Category (pp. 127-128)

1. books or bestsellers
2. female singers
3. female action heroes
4. cartoon characters
5. horror movies

Exercise 5: General and Specific in Context (pp. 128-129)

1. b, a, c
2. a, c, b
3. b, a, c
4. b, a, c

Check Your Understanding (pp. 129-130)

1. General words sum up or connect people, objects, events, and experiences that share some kind of relationship.
2. The number of things they refer to increases, and the things referred to become more dissimilar, or different from one another.
3. The specific words focus more on individual people, places, events, and experiences. They help clarify the meaning of general words.

4. A word can become more general or more specific when seen in relation to other words. Thus, a word considered general might actually seem specific when placed next to a word that is at a higher level of generality.

Exercise 6: Recognizing General and Specific Sentences (pp. 132-133)

1. a. G
    b. S
2. a. G
    b. S
3. a. S
    b. G
4. a. S
    b. G
5. a. S
    b. G

Exercise 7: Relating the Specific to the General (pp. 133-135)

1. c
2. c
3. b
4. b

Check Your Understanding (p. 135)

General sentences are broad in meaning to sum up many different events, but that also makes them open to various interpretations. Thus they require more specific sentences to clarify their meaning and narrow the number of interpretations.

Exercise 8: Relating the Specific to the General (pp. 136-142)

1. 3
2. 2
3. 1
4. 1
5. 2
6. 2
7. 1
8. 3
9. 2
10. 3

Exercise 9: Clarifying General Sentences (pp. 142-144)

1. b, c, e
2. a, b, d
3. a, c, e
4. b, d, e

Exercise 10: Locating the Main Idea (pp. 146-148)

1. 1
2. 1
3. 7
4. 6
5. 10

Vocabulary Check (p. 149)

1. d
2. f
3. a
4. j
5. b
6. g
7. e
8. i
9. c
10. h

Digging Deeper: Going Global (p. 151)

1. c
2. c
3. a
4. c

Making Connections (p. 151)

Answers will vary, but the following are possibilities: "Companies interested in expanding their hold on foreign markets have had to expand their product line *and* beef up their security measures"; "There are benefits and drawbacks to companies expanding their reach into global markets"; "Companies looking to make money from foreign markets face a whole new set of challenges."

Drawing Your Own Conclusions (p. 151)

Answers will vary. It would not seem so because some provide employees security guards whereas others only tell their employees to be careful and to not call attention to themselves.

Test 1: Vocabulary Review (pp. 153-154)

1. asteroid
2. fidelity
3. obscurity
4. anecdotal
5. denominations
6. creed
7. sage
8. discrimination
9. commitment
10. conformity

Test 2: Distinguishing Between General and Specific Sentences (p. 155)

1. a. G
   b. S
2. a. S
   b. G
3. a. G
   b. S
4. a. S
   b. G
5. a. G
   b. S

Test 3: Distinguishing Between General and Specific Sentences (p. 156)

1. a. G
   b. S
2. a. G
   b. S
3. a. S
   b. G
4. a. G
   b. S

Test 4: Recognizing the Most General Sentence (pp. 157-158)

1. d
2. c
3. c
4. c
5. e

Test 5: Recognizing the Most General Sentence (pp. 159-160)

1. b
2. b
3. e
4. c
5. b

Test 6: Identifying General Sentences in Paragraphs (pp. 161-163)

1. 12
2. 1
3. 1
4. 7

CHAPTER 4: FROM TOPICS TO TOPIC SENTENCES (pp. 164-240)

Exercise 1: Determining the Topic (pp. 168-170)

1. a
2. b
3. b
4. a

Exercise 2: Determining the Topic (pp. 170-172)

1. c
2. a
3. b
4. b

Exercise 3: Phrasing the Topic (pp. 174-178)

1. long-term study of ginkgo biloba; study of ginkgo
2. theories about dreaming; meaning of dreams; source of dreams; function of dreams
3. failure of the Homestead Act; disappointment in the Homestead Act
4. new evidence about concussions; changing attitudes toward concussions

Check Your Understanding (p. 178)

1. It's the word or phrase that names the person, place, event, idea, or experience being discussed in the paragraph.
2. It's repeatedly mentioned or referred to throughout the paragraphs.
3. No. The actual word or phrase expressing the topic might appear only once, while the references through pronouns, examples, and associated words are more frequent.
4. The topic should be expressed in a phrase rather than a single word.

Exercise 4: Identifying the Topic and Main Idea (pp. 180-182)

1. *Topic:* causes of depression in adolescents; adolescent depression
   Main Idea: c
2. *Topic:* moon's rise; time of the moon's rise
   Main Idea: a

Exercise 5: Identifying the Topic Sentence (p. 185)

1. a
2. b

Check Your Understanding (p. 186)

1. The topic is the word or phrase that identifies the subject under discussion. The main idea is the message or point the author wants to communicate about the topic.
2. You can find references to the main idea in almost every sentence.
3. Topic sentences are developed throughout the passage and introductory sentences are not.

Exercise 6: Identifying Topics and Topic Sentences (pp. 188-192)

1. *Topic:* c
   Topic Sentence: 1
2. *Topic:* a
   Topic Sentence: 1
3. *Topic:* b
   Topic Sentence: 2
4. *Topic:* c
   Topic Sentence: 2

Check Your Understanding (p. 192)

1. They tell the reader that the author is going to modify or challenge what's just been said.
2. The second sentence is likely to be the topic sentence.

Exercise 7: Locating Topic Sentences (pp. 197-202)

1. 4
2. 2
3. 3
4. 4 and 7
5. 3
6. 1
7. 4
8. 10
9. 2   Point out the presence of a reversal transition in the second sentence. Sentence 2 can also generate some good discussions. Is the statement true?
10. 4

Vocabulary Check (p. 203)

1. h
2. m
3. t
4. j
5. d
6. f
7. p
8. g
9. c
10. e
11. o
12. r
13. q
14. s
15. k
16. l
17. b
18. a
19. i
20. n

Exercise 8: Recognizing an Accurate Reading Paraphrase (pp. 208-210)

1. b
2. b

Exercise 9: Recognizing the Best Reading Paraphrase (pp. 210-211)

1. a
2. b

Exercise 10: Recognizing the Best Paraphrase (pp. 211-215)

1. *Topic Sentence*: 4
   Paraphrase: b
2. *Topic Sentence*: 1
   Paraphrase: c
3. *Topic Sentence*: 3
   Paraphrase: d
4. *Topic Sentence*: 3
   Paraphrase: a
5. *Topic Sentence:* 1
   Paraphrase: a

Vocabulary Check (p. 216)

1. j
2. k
3. m
4. a
5. q
6. i
7. g
8. h
9. b
10. c
11. o
12. t
13. s
14. p
15. f
16. r
17. l
18. e
19. n
20. d

Digging Deeper: Jury Dodgers Beware! (pp. 218-219)

1. c
2. b
3. the process of interviewing jurors to see if they are appropriate

4. c
5. a. relevant, related, central
    b. payment, reward, money

Making Connections (pp. 219-220)

(Part 1) The authors of the longer selection include the reasons why people might want to avoid jury duty.

(Part 2) Although answers will vary, the longer reading points out some of the ways jury-duty scofflaws are punished. This suggests that the states are inclined to pursue those who   ignore a summons to jury duty.

Drawing Your Own Conclusions (pp. 220)

(Part 1)   Answers will vary, but presumably the details of the case might be painful to hear about if, for instance, murder or rape are described.

(Part 2)   Answers will vary.

Test 1: Vocabulary Review (pp. 221-222)

1. dementia
2. placebos
3. consolidating
4. speculators
5. conclusive
6. quarantine
7. analogies
8. traumatic
9. paradoxes
10. innovative

Test 2: Vocabulary Review (pp. 223-224)

1. dignitaries
2. disoriented
3. etching
4. anthropological
5. electors
6. flouting
7. geriatric
8. toxic
9. habitats
10. homage

Test 3: Vocabulary Review (pp. 225-226)

1. staple
2. nocturnal
3. devotees
4. charisma
5. graphic

6. sociopathic
7. precedent
8. instigated
9. productivity
10. genetic

Test 4: Vocabulary Review (pp. 227-228)

1. renovations
2. Liberator
3. cultivated
4. comprehensive
5. random
6. mutilation
7. reproductive
8. subsequent
9. predators
10. pollutants

Test 5: Recognizing Topics and Topic Sentences (pp. 229-231)

1. *Topic:* c
   Topic Sentence: 6
2. *Topic:* b
   Topic Sentence: 1
3. *Topic:* a
   Topic Sentence: 1, 8
4. *Topic:* d
   Topic Sentence: 2
5. *Topic:* c
   Topic Sentence: 2

Test 6: Recognizing Topics, Topic Sentences, and Transitions (pp. 232-234)

1. *Topic:* c
   Topic Sentence: 2
   Transition word: sentence 2 – though
2. *Topic:* b
   Topic Sentence: 1
3. *Topic:* a
   Topic Sentence: 4
   Transitional sentence: 2
4. *Topic:* c
   Topic Sentence: 1

Test 7: Recognizing Topic Sentences (pp. 235-236)

1. 3
2. 1
3. 1, 5
4. 4
5. 1

Test 8: Recognizing the Most Accurate Paraphrase (pp. 237-240)

1. *Topic Sentence:* 2
   Paraphrase: d
2. *Topic Sentence:* 1, 10
   Paraphrase: c
3. *Topic Sentence:* 2
   Paraphrase: b
4. *Topic Sentence:* 2, 8
   Paraphrase: d
5. *Topic Sentence:* 3   Although sentence 2 could qualify as a topic sentence, it functions more effectively as a transitional device, mainly because it does not state the topic directly.
   Paraphrase: a
6. *Topic Sentence:* 3
   Paraphrase: d

CHAPTER 5: FOCUSING ON SUPPORTING DETAILS (pp. 241-313)

Exercise 1: Recognizing Supporting Details (pp. 244-246)

1. a, b, d
2. b, c, e
3. c, d, e
4. a, d, e

Exercise 2: Distinguishing Between Supporting Details and Topic Sentences (pp. 246-248)

1. 4
2. 4
3. 2
4. 3

Exercise 3: Identifying Irrelevant Details (pp. 249-251)

1. *Topic Sentence:* 1
   Irrelevant Detail: 5
2. *Topic Sentence:* 1
   Irrelevant Detail: 4
3. *Topic Sentence:* 3
   Irrelevant Detail: 5
4. *Topic Sentence:* 2
   Irrelevant Detail: 6

Exercise 4: Diagramming Major and Minor Details (pp. 255-257)

1.

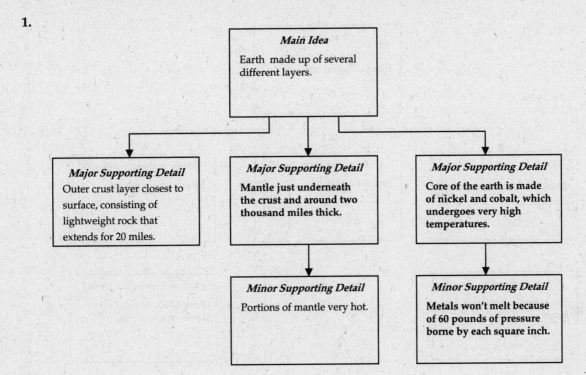

2.

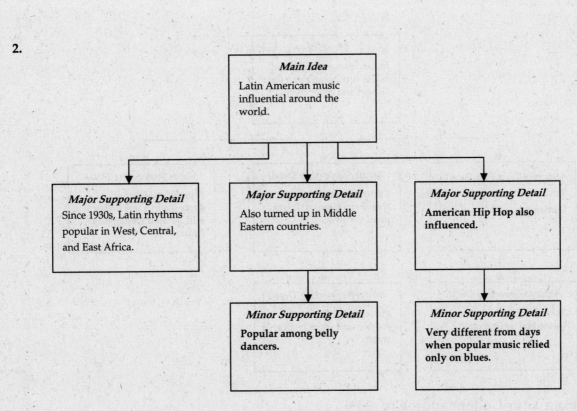

Exercise 5: Diagramming Major and Minor Details (pp. 258-259)

1.

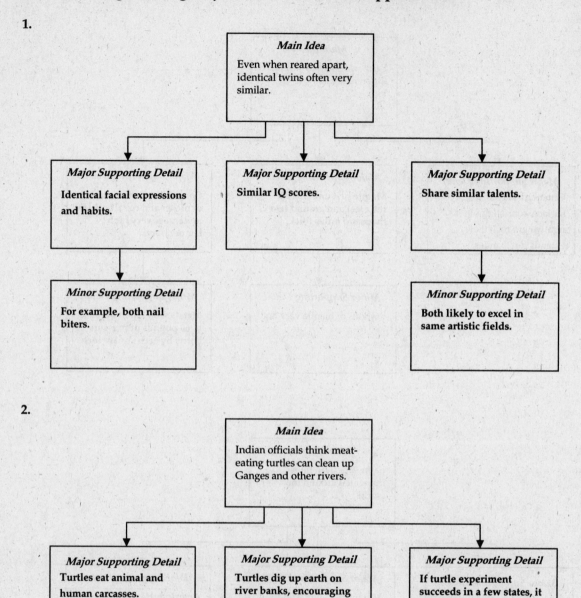

Main Idea

Even when reared apart, identical twins often very similar.

Major Supporting Detail

Identical facial expressions and habits.

Major Supporting Detail

Similar IQ scores.

Major Supporting Detail

Share similar talents.

Minor Supporting Detail

For example, both nail biters.

Minor Supporting Detail

Both likely to excel in same artistic fields.

2.

Main Idea

Indian officials think meat-eating turtles can clean up Ganges and other rivers.

Major Supporting Detail

Turtles eat animal and human carcasses.

Major Supporting Detail

Turtles dig up earth on river banks, encouraging plant survival

Major Supporting Detail

If turtle experiment succeeds in a few states, it will be used throughout India.

Minor Supporting Detail

Some religious groups throw bodies in river.

Minor Supporting Detail

Plants fight river bank erosion and some purify water.

Checking Your Understanding (p. 259)

Major details provide the explanations or evidence topic sentences need to be clear and convincing. Minor details are the more specific sentences that further explain major ones. They also add interest and emphasis.

Vocabulary Check (p. 263)

1. g
2. j
3. e
4. h
5. a
6. b
7. i
8. c
9. f
10. d

Exercise 6: Using Topic Sentences and Transitions to Identify Major Details (pp. 264-266)

1. *Clue to major details:* number of functions
   Transitions: First, Second, Third, Fourth

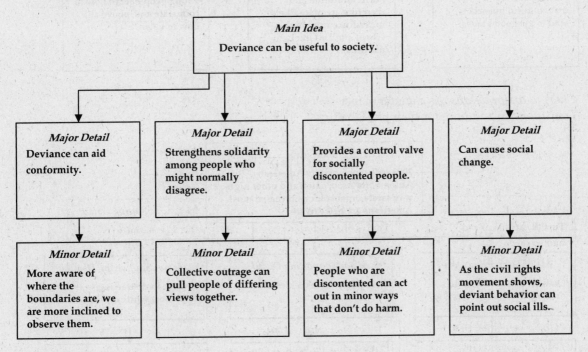

Main Idea
Deviance can be useful to society.

Major Detail	**Major Detail**	**Major Detail**	**Major Detail**
Deviance can aid conformity.	Strengthens solidarity among people who might normally disagree.	Provides a control valve for socially discontented people.	Can cause social change.

Minor Detail	**Minor Detail**	**Minor Detail**	**Minor Detail**
More aware of where the boundaries are, we are more inclined to observe them.	Collective outrage can pull people of differing views together.	People who are discontented can act out in minor ways that don't do harm.	As the civil rights movement shows, deviant behavior can point out social ills.

2. *Clue to major details:* several benefits; one benefit
    Transitions: also, In addition

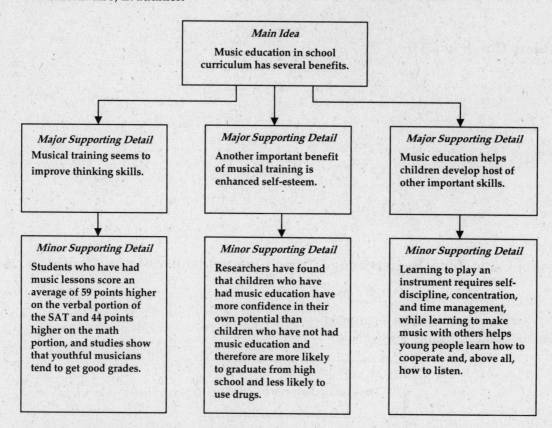

Main Idea

Music education in school curriculum has several benefits.

Major Supporting Detail
Musical training seems to improve thinking skills.

Major Supporting Detail
Another important benefit of musical training is enhanced self-esteem.

Major Supporting Detail
Music education helps children develop host of other important skills.

Minor Supporting Detail
Students who have had music lessons score an average of 59 points higher on the verbal portion of the SAT and 44 points higher on the math portion, and studies show that youthful musicians tend to get good grades.

Minor Supporting Detail
Researchers have found that children who have had music education have more confidence in their own potential than children who have not had music education and therefore are more likely to graduate from high school and less likely to use drugs.

Minor Supporting Detail
Learning to play an instrument requires self-discipline, concentration, and time management, while learning to make music with others helps young people learn how to cooperate and, above all, how to listen.

3. *Clues to major details:* As a matter of fact
    Transitions: In addition, for example, Finally

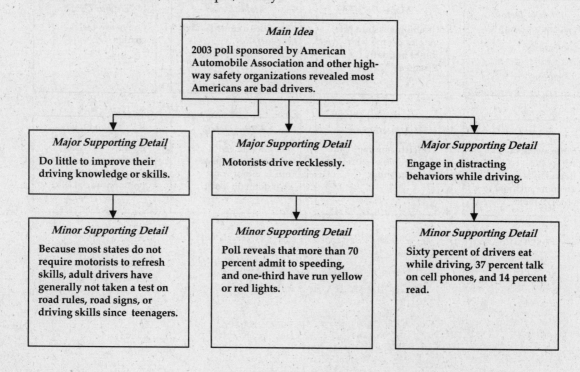

Main Idea

2003 poll sponsored by American Automobile Association and other highway safety organizations revealed most Americans are bad drivers.

Major Supporting Detail
Do little to improve their driving knowledge or skills.

Major Supporting Detail
Motorists drive recklessly.

Major Supporting Detail
Engage in distracting behaviors while driving.

Minor Supporting Detail
Because most states do not require motorists to refresh skills, adult drivers have generally not taken a test on road rules, road signs, or driving skills since teenagers.

Minor Supporting Detail
Poll reveals that more than 70 percent admit to speeding, and one-third have run yellow or red lights.

Minor Supporting Detail
Sixty percent of drivers eat while driving, 37 percent talk on cell phones, and 14 percent read.

Exercise 7: Identifying Topic Sentences and Major Details (pp. 267-270)

1. *Transitions:* for example, for instance
   Point out that "for instance" in this case introduces a minor detail.
   a. 2
   b. a number of special functions
   c. 1. Queen gives birth to all the drones, workers, and future queens.
      2. Worker bees secrete wax, construct honeycomb, gather food, turn nectar into honey, regulate temperature.
      3. Drones have one function: Mate with the queen.

2. *Transition:* for example
   a. 1
   b. several different ceremonies
   c. 1. The Bear Dance associated with growing and distributing food.
      2. The Snake Dance is plea for rain.
      3. The Corn Dance meant to produce a rich crop.

3. *Transitions:* one kind, the second type, the third kind
   a. 2
   b. three main categories
   c. 1. One type of confusion is result of meds taken or stress, emotional or environmental
      2. Second type is result of brain damage from aging.
      3. Third type is result of mental illness, like psychosis.

4. *Transitions:* too
   a. 2
   b. two main advantages
   c. 1. With flow charts, managers of all kinds can identify and sequence the key events and decisions in a process.
      2. Flow charts force people to consider all the key points or stages in a process.

Exercise 8: Identifying Topic Sentences and Minor Details (pp. 270-274)

1. *Topic Sentence:* 3
   b, c, a
2. *Topic Sentence:* 3
   b, a, c
3. *Topic Sentence:* 1
   c, a, b
4. *Topic Sentence:* 3
   b, c, a
5. *Topic Sentence:* 1
   c, b, a

Check Your Understanding (p. 274)

1. words that can be divided into subcategories
2. symptoms, studies, symbols, reasons, factors
3. Transitions that signal addition are clues to major details.
4. moreover, in addition, also, in the same vein, first, second

Exercise 9: Drawing Inferences About Supporting Details (pp. 276-281)

1. *Topic Sentence:* 2
   1. b
   2. b
2. *Topic Sentence:* 1
   1. c
   2. b
3. *Topic Sentence:* 1
   1. a
   2. b
4. *Topic Sentence:* 1
   1. c
   2. c

Exercise 10: Recognizing Concluding Sentences (pp. 283-285)

1. b
2. a
3. b
4. a
5. a

Exercise 11: Recognizing the Function of Every Sentence (pp. 285-289)

1. b, c, c, c, d, f
2. a, b, c, c, c, c, c
3. b, c, c, c, d, d, d, d
4. a, b, c, d, c, d, c, f

Check Your Understanding (p. 289)

1. No. Writers often leave it up to the reader to fill in the gaps in the supporting details, adding to them when necessary.
2. Appearing at the very end of a paragraph, concluding paragraphs don't develop the topic sentence or a major detail. Instead, they explain how some situation mentioned in the paragraph has changed or should change over time.

Vocabulary Check (p. 290)

1. g
2. c
3. f
4. h
5. j
6. i
7. a
8. e
9. d
10. b

Digging Deeper: Debating Private Prisons (pp. 292-294)

1. b
2. Private prisons don't necessarily save money.
3. evidence, mixed
4. Does the Constitution allow private firms to be in charge of correctional facilities?
5. c
6. buildings
7. insignificant, unimportant
8. imprisonment
9. a
10. 1

Test 1: Vocabulary Review (pp. 295-296)

1. injured severely
2. animals that live on land and in water
3. lacking in respectability; disgusting
4. growing, doing well
5. relating to the miraculous or things not of the ordinary world
6. building(s) used as housing and surrounded by walls
7. fight
8. by nature, naturally
9. famous for bad reasons
10. related to the heart and vessels

Test 2: Vocabulary Review (pp. 297-298)

1. satellite
2. purged
3. respiratory
4. commodity
5. orbit
6. barren
7. imperial
8. medium
9. psychosis
10. edict

Test 3: Recognizing Supporting Details (pp. 299-300)

1. b, d, e
2. c, d, e
3. a, b, d
4. a, c, d

Test 4: Identifying Topic Sentences and Supporting Details (pp. 301-302)

1. a
2. e
3. c
4. b
5. c

Test 5: Distinguishing Between Major and Minor Details (pp. 303-305)

1.

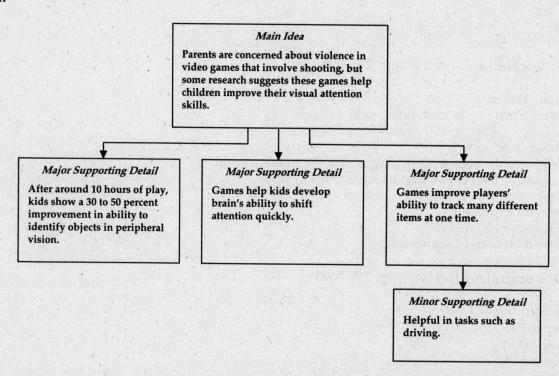

2.

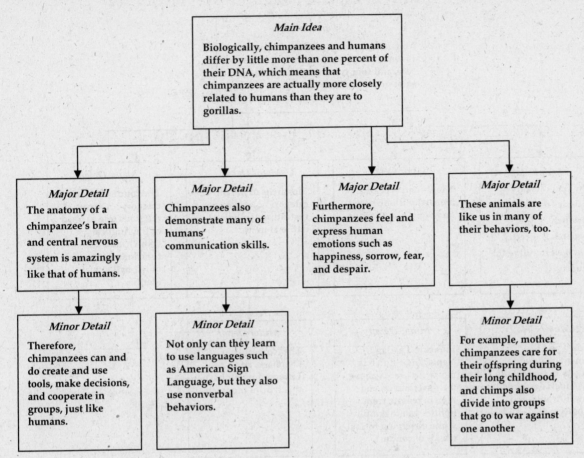

Main Idea

Biologically, chimpanzees and humans differ by little more than one percent of their DNA, which means that chimpanzees are actually more closely related to humans than they are to gorillas.

Major Detail

The anatomy of a chimpanzee's brain and central nervous system is amazingly like that of humans.

Major Detail

Chimpanzees also demonstrate many of humans' communication skills.

Major Detail

Furthermore, chimpanzees feel and express human emotions such as happiness, sorrow, fear, and despair.

Major Detail

These animals are like us in many of their behaviors, too.

Minor Detail

Therefore, chimpanzees can and do create and use tools, make decisions, and cooperate in groups, just like humans.

Minor Detail

Not only can they learn to use languages such as American Sign Language, but they also use nonverbal behaviors.

Minor Detail

For example, mother chimpanzees care for their offspring during their long childhood, and chimps also divide into groups that go to war against one another

3.

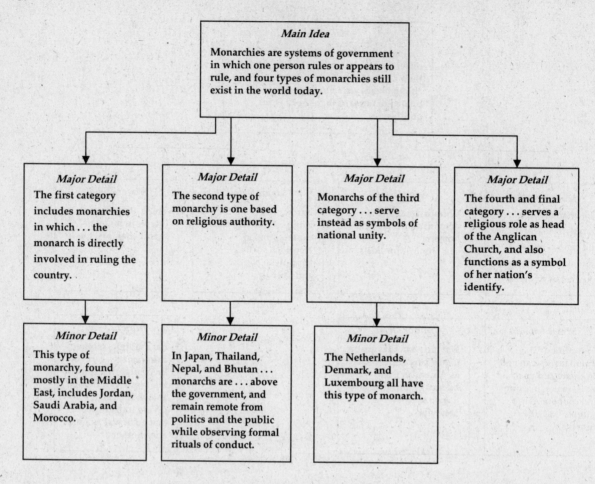

Main Idea

Monarchies are systems of government in which one person rules or appears to rule, and four types of monarchies still exist in the world today.

Major Detail

The first category includes monarchies in which ... the monarch is directly involved in ruling the country.

Major Detail

The second type of monarchy is one based on religious authority.

Major Detail

Monarchs of the third category ... serve instead as symbols of national unity.

Major Detail

The fourth and final category ... serves a religious role as head of the Anglican Church, and also functions as a symbol of her nation's identify.

Minor Detail

This type of monarchy, found mostly in the Middle East, includes Jordan, Saudi Arabia, and Morocco.

Minor Detail

In Japan, Thailand, Nepal, and Bhutan ... monarchs are ... above the government, and remain remote from politics and the public while observing formal rituals of conduct.

Minor Detail

The Netherlands, Denmark, and Luxembourg all have this type of monarch.

Test 6: Recognizing Topic Sentence Clues to Major Details (pp. 306-307)

1. 3
   Clue to Major Details: two different kinds: active and passive
2. 1
   Clue to Major Details: four zones of distance
3. 1
   Clue to Major Details: for a number of reasons
4. 3
   Clue to Major Details: maternal rules

Test 7: Recognizing Supporting Details and Concluding Sentences (pp. 308-309)

1. M, m, M
2. M, m, M, m
3. M, M, m, m, c
4. M, m, M, M, m, c

Test 8: Topics, Topic Sentences, and Inferring Supporting Details (pp. 310-

1. *Topic Sentence:* 4
   Topic: the plight of migrant workers; treatment of migrant workers
   b, c
2. *Topic Sentence:* 1
   Topic: Marian Anderson and the DAR
   b, d
3. *Topic Sentence:* 4
   Topic: first impressions of Wilbur and Orville Wright; the Wright brothers
   c, d
4. *Topic Sentence:* 1
   Topic: José Martí's devotion to Cuban independence
   a, b

CHAPTER 6: MORE ABOUT INFERENCES (pp. 314-380)

Exercise 1: Understanding Inferences (pp. 316-317)

1. We always think other people need to improve, but we forget about improving ourselves.
2. We just can't predict the future.
3. People don't like to admit they don't "get it."
4. The rose may be a symbol of romance, but I'll take the money.

Exercise 2: Understanding Idioms (pp. 318-319)

1. b; Idiom: *shooting from the* hip suggests responding without thought, being impulsive
2. b; Idiom: *egghead* refers to someone very scholarly or intellectual
3. c; Idiom: *dark horse* refers to someone completely unknown who suddenly becomes famous or captures a surprising win.
4. a; Idiom: To *carry water* for someone means "to be in their service."
5. c; Idiom: A *brain trust* is group of experts who are asked for advice.

Exercise 3: Constructing Topic Sentences (pp. 321-323)

1. *Partially Completed Topic Sentence:* 4
   Completed Topic Sentence: When Bela Lugosi died, he had nothing left of the fame and fortune playing Dracula had brought him.
2. *Partially Completed Topic Sentence:* 3
   Completed Topic Sentence: Who got to the North Pole first is still the subject of argument.
3. *Partially Completed Topic Sentence:* 2
   Completed Topic Sentence: New research suggests that coffee may actually offer significant health benefits.
4. *Partially Completed Topic Sentence:* 3
   Completed Topic Sentence: Vahan Simidian thinks his company's magnetic acoustic device, which functions as both alarm and weapon, provides the answer to pirate attacks.

Exercise 4: Recognizing the Implied Main Idea (pp. 326-329)

1. a
2. b
3. a
4. b

Exercise 5: Matching Details and Inferences (pp. 329-332)

1. c
2. a
3. b

Exercise 6: Recognizing the Implied Main Idea (pp. 333-336)

1. b
2. c
3. a
4. b
5. b

Check Your Understanding (p. 337)

1. They should combine the sentences in order to construct a stated version of the main idea.
2. They should look at the specific statements and ask themselves what point those statements make when they are taken all together.

Vocabulary Check (p. 343)

1. d
2. j
3. b
4. a
5. f
6. i
7. h
8. e
9. g
10. c

Exercise 7: Recognizing the Implied Main Idea (pp. 343-348)

1. a; a
2. e; b
3. d; a
4. c; c
5. a; c

Exercise 8: Inferring the Implied Main Idea (pp. 348-352)

1. There are things you can do to stop being an underachiever.
2. Chris Andersen's book, *Free: The Future of a Radical Price*, aroused a heated controversy.
3. Pet owners who dump their pet pythons are undoubtedly behind the growing python population in the Everglades.
4. Deciding who was the best baseball player of all time depends on who you ask or what standard you use.
5. Early differences in language skills between boys and girls seem to be due to a difference in the development of the prefrontal cortex.

Check Your Understanding (p. 352)

1. infer a main idea based on the facts
2. answer it; infer one
3. which one is better
4. similarities and differences
5. what idea or theory the study supports

Exercise 9: Identifying the Implied Main Idea (pp. 355-357)

1. c
2. a
3. b
4. a

Exercise 10: Inferring the Main Idea (pp. 357-359)

1. The fertility rate fluctuates.
2. Many foods and beverages go by different names in different parts of the country.
3. Having Annie Sullivan as a teacher dramatically changed Helen Keller's life.
4. Numerous rock musicians have gotten the inspiration for their music from famous literary works.

Check Your Understanding (p. 359)

Logical inferences are based on the author's words and don't favor the reader's ideas over the author's. They are not contradicted by any statements in the paragraph; they don't divert the reader from the author's intended meaning. **Illogical inferences** rely more on the reader's thoughts than the author's words and are likely to interfere with communication between reader and writer.

Vocabulary Check (p. 360)

1. g
2. i
3. f
4. a
5. d
6. b
7. j
8. h
9. e
10. c

Digging Deeper: Black Baseball (pp. 363-364)

1. b; "To be on," "test" or "prove one's mettle." It means that someone is prepared to accept a challenge and do his or her best.
2. d
3. a
4. a
5. b

Drawing Your Own Conclusions (p. 365)

Baseball used to be the favorite sport of many Americans, but it's no longer such a popular sport.

Test 1: Vocabulary Review (pp. 366-367)

1. chortled
2. distillation
3. palpitations
4. terrain
5. suffrage
6. gravitas
7. quips
8. dissemble
9. hypothermia
10. catapulted

Test 2: Vocabulary Review (pp. 368-369)

1. negative
2. symbols of a company or an institution
3. attack on church teachings
4. interested in political or social change
5. strength; physical well-being
6. original idea; new invention
7. silly, absurd, ridiculous
8. lenient; inclined to spoil
9. people who give up their own lives for others
10. close friend

Test 3: Recognizing the Implied Main Idea (pp. 370-372)

1. b
2. a
3. c
4. a

Test 4: Recognizing the Implied Main Idea (pp. 373-375)

1. d
2. c
3. c
4. d

Test 5: Recognizing the Implied Main Idea (pp. 376-377)

1. a
2. b
3. c
4. d

Test 6: Recognizing the Implied Main Idea (pp. 378-380)

1. Charlie Chaplin modeled the "Little Tramp" on his own life.
2. During the Civil War, journalists didn't just report on the war; they took part in it.
3. Cutting down the rain forest for agriculture is a terrible waste of valuable resources.
4. We now have many different uses for lasers *or* lasers are no longer a solution looking for a problem.
5. Thanks to the work of Karl Landsteiner, blood transfusions became a fairly safe procedure.

CHAPTER 7: DRAWING INFERENCES FROM VISUAL AIDS (pp. 381-422)

Exercise 1: Understanding Pie Charts (pp. 385-388)

1. b
2. b

Check Your Understanding (p. 388)

1. Pie charts let readers see the individual parts, or pieces, that make up some larger whole. Looking at a pie chart, readers can quickly compare how much each share, or piece, contributes to the larger whole.
2. In addition to seeing how much each piece contributes, readers need to understand how the pie chart relates to the overall main idea of the passage it helps explain.
3. They include two separate pie charts.

Exercise 2: Understanding Line Graphs (pp. 393-395)

1. b
2. b; b

Check Your Understanding (p. 395)

1. Line graphs show how a variable, something capable of changing over time, is influenced by the passage of time. They reveal subtle patterns or trends.
2. The x-axis runs horizontally across the bottom of the graph, and it identifies the segments of time used to study the variable tracked by the graph. The y-axis runs from top to bottom, and

it identifies the variable that is being graphed—for example, divorces, marriages, and foreclosures.

3. Those places in the line or lines where there are large decreases or increases in height. This is the time, too, to ask how the graph, particularly the increases and decreases in height, relates to the text it illustrates.

Exercise 3: Understanding Bar Graphs (pp. 402-403)

1. c
2. b   *Note:* The question probably should have read "between the ages of fifteen and twenty-four." Although already at the ages of five to fourteen more boys are in motor vehicle accidents, it's doubtful that they were doing the driving much of the time.

Checking Your Understanding (p. 403)

1. (1) Like line graphs, they track changes over time. (2) They compare differences in quantity or frequency.
2. The height or the length of the bars. They indicate the differences among the things being measured.
3. Take the time to process that information. It will help you remember the author's key point even after the passage of time.

Exercise 4: Understanding Cartoons and Drawings (pp. 407-410)

1. (1) b
      (2) a
2. (3) c
      (4) c

Digging Deeper: Voting Goes High-Tech (pp. 412-413)

1. c
2. the next improvement; fast forward to contemporary times
3. The "hanging chads" illustrated that punch card voting, promoted as a solution to problems with previous voting methods, was also *not* foolproof.
4. b

Making Connections (p. 413)

Answers will vary. My guess would be that they don't feel that any candidate speaks to their needs and interests. It would be interesting to hear what students think.

Test 1: Reviewing Visual Aids (p. 414)

1. a percentage, segment, or piece of some larger whole
2. how each piece compares to the other shares that make up the larger entity or whole
3. variable; influenced by the passage of time
4. tracking subtle changes and revealing trends
5. the x-axis
6. the y-axis
7. what's being measured; increments of time
8. quantities or numbers

9. the length or the width
10. compare what's said in the passage to a similar situation

Test 2: Reading Charts and Graphs (pp. 415-417)

1. Despite the election of Barack Obama, there was no indication of a dramatic rise in the number of people labeling themselves "liberal." The numbers were very similar to those in 2000 when George W. Bush was elected.
2. (1) two hours
   (2) It peaks around the age of twelve
   (3) *Answers will vary.* It shows, in concrete terms, "the extent to which TV has become part of daily life" in the lives of pre-schoolers.
3. Yes. The bars for "beverages" are almost even, but there's a big difference in the bars representing all other products.

Test 3: Understanding Visual Aids (pp. 418-422)

1. c
2. b
3. a. Singapore; Poland
   b. The implication seems to be that, at least by one indicator, the overall health of the nation is not very good. Low birth weight as a source of infant mortality would also suggest that poor nutrition due to a lack of money is a cause.

CHAPTER 8: BEYOND THE PARAGRAPH: READING LONGER SELECTIONS (pp. 423-491)

Exercise 1: Recognizing Main Ideas in Longer Readings (pp. 431-435)

1. c
2. b

Exercise 2: Recognizing Main Ideas in Longer Readings (pp. 435-438)

1. b
2. c

Check Your Understanding (pp. 438-439)

1. Longer readings provide titles and headings that often identify the topic and offer clues to the main idea.
2. You need to identify the overall, or controlling, main idea that determines the content of the other paragraphs.
3. The main differences are length and level of generality. Thesis statements can consist of several sentences, and they can express broader and more general ideas than topic sentences do.
4. What type of specific information does the author supply through supporting details? Does the author use examples, studies, statistics, or reasons? What questions about the overall main idea do the supporting details answer?
5. See if you can come up with an implied thesis statement.

Exercise 3: Recognizing Implied Main Ideas (pp. 441-449)

1. a
2. d
3. d
4. c
5. b   There is a suggestion that *c* is correct, but the author's treatment of the subject becomes more evenhanded at the end.

Exercise 4: Inferring the Main Idea (pp. 449-453)

1. Contrary to popular belief, prison life is not a vacation at taxpayers' expense.
2. For a number of reasons, local televisions news broadcasts don't really serve to inform the public.

Vocabulary Check (p. 454)

1. d
2. q
3. n
4. l
5. m
6. k
7. a
8. b
9. v
10. u
11. c   *Note:* The word *ambiguous* appeared in Chapter 1, but since some instructors skip this chapter, it appears in this chapter as well.
12. s
13. f
14. e
15. p
16. r
17. t
18. j
19. x
20. g
21. h
22. w
23. y
24. i
25. o

Exercise 5: Note-Taking with Informal Outlines (pp. 456-463)

Note: The notes students take will probably look very different, but the content should be similar.

1. *Main Idea:* Less well-known than other famous African Americans, Ida B. Wells is gaining recognition as a journalist and most importantly as a social reformer.

   Supporting Details:
   1. 1883: Long before Rosa Parks, Wells refused to sit in a train car reserved only for black passengers and wrote about her experience.

a. When Wells refused to move, the conductor had her forcibly removed. Wells didn't just bite the conductor, she sued and won, only to have the case overturned on appeal. But the experience started her journalism career.
2. She even bought part-ownership in *Free Speech*, an all-black Memphis paper.
3. 1909: one of the founders of the NAACP.
4. 1913: organized first female suffrage group.
5. 1930: first black woman to run for public office.
    - - seat in Illinois state senate (didn't win).
6. 1830-1930: 3,220 black Americans were lynched; the death of Wells's friend Thomas Moss made Wells join the campaign to abolish lynching.
    a. investigated and wrote about lynching, risking her own life
        - - wrote "Lynching in All Its Phases."
7. She was hated by many for her tactics, but they made a difference.

2. *Main Idea:* Athletes who are severely injured and unable to pursue their sport for a significant period of time may experience something like the five stages Elisabeth Kübler-Ross described in *On Death and Dying.*

Supporting Details:
1. *Denial:* Athlete says the injury is not so bad
    -- trainer needs to emphasize that it is bad, but the player will survive
2. *Anger:* Mad at everyone, including trainer and teammates
    -- needs reminder not to ruin relationship with teammates
    -- needs to have trainer make supportive statements
3. *Bargaining:* Athlete says "I will take it easy *after* I play just a little bit more."
    -- plays one person against another
    -- looks for a doctor who says what athlete wants to hear
4. *Depression:* During long rehabilitation, symptoms like apathy, weight gain, lack of self-esteem emerge
    -- trainer needs to work at reducing athlete's negative thoughts
5. *Acceptance:* Athlete acknowledges both the seriousness of the injury and length of recovery time.
    -- trainer emphasizes motivation and confidence
    -- not everyone experiences stages in same order or way

Exercise 6: Diagramming a Chapter Section (pp. 465-468)

1. *Main Idea:* Jury deliberations can be divided into three basic steps.

2.

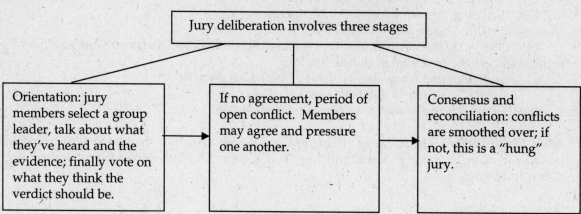

Vocabulary Check (p. 469)

1. e
2. h
3. k
4. g
5. m
6. l
7. a
8. i
9. d
10. b
11. n
12. o
13. j
14. c
15. f

Digging Deeper: Legal Rights for Animals (pp. 472-474)

1. d
2. b
3. b
4. c
5. b
6. c
7. b
8. b
9. b
10. b; a; a

Making Connections (p. 474)

No. The author of the reading on animal law implies that the increase in lawyers is needed.

Drawing Your Own Conclusions (p. 474)

Answers will vary.

Test 1: Vocabulary Review (pp. 475-476)

1. dubbed
2. prodigy
3. incarnate
4. physiology
5. munificent
6. ambiguous   *Note:* The word *ambiguous* appeared in Chapter 1, but since some instructors skip this chapter, it appears in this chapter as well.
7. extroverted
8. wake
9. sumptuous
10. altruism

Test 2: Vocabulary Review (pp. 477-478)

1. authoritarian
2. judicial
3. invigorating
4. plaintiff
5. electoral
6. litigation
7. predisposition
8. specifications
9. credence
10. aspirations

Test 3: Vocabulary Review (pp. 479-480)

1. prediction for cure
2. retraining, healing
3. prove true
4. proven true, accurate
5. opponents of slavery
6. nerve-related
7. originality, imagination
8. straight-forwardly, honestly
9. force, movement, energy, power
10. fatigue; lack of interest
11. agreement
12. unrelated to physical experience; vague
13. seen; viewed; understood to be
14. combined, joined, connected
15. capable of being physically experienced or touched

Test 4: Recognizing Controlling Main Ideas and Supporting Details (pp. 481-486)

1. 1. b
    2. c
    3. c
    4. a
    5. b

2. 1. d
    2. a
    3. c
    4. a
    5. c

Test 5: Recognizing the Main Idea, Supporting Details, and Author's Purpose (pp. 487-491)

1. 1. b
    2. a
    3. a
    4. a
    5. b

2. 1. a
    2. b
    3. c
    4. b
    5. a

CHAPTER 9: RECOGNIZING PATTERNS OF ORGANIZATION IN PARAGRAPHS (pp. 492-578)

Note: All the notes here are models and students' notes may vary although the content should be similar.

Exercise 1: Understanding Definition Paragraphs (pp. 495-499)

1. *Main Idea:*
    The term "self-concept" refers to a person's view of his or her personality.
    Supporting Details:
    1. Self-concept is revealed when answering a question like "What kind of person am I?"
    2. Self-concepts are built out of daily experiences and our responses to those experiences.
        a. If as a child you are a good athlete but a poor team player, you might describe yourself as someone good at sports but not much of a team player.
    3. Self-concepts can and sometimes should be revised.

2. *Main Idea:*
    Because there was little government in the newly settled West, groups of private citizens, called "vigilante groups," dispensed justice.
    Supporting Details:

1. Usually consisted of a few hundred people led by members of upper class.
2. Guilty verdict often resulted in execution.
3. Vigilante groups were well organized.
   a. Even had constitutions.

3. *Main Idea:*
Blood pressure is the force exerted against artery walls while the heart contracts and relaxes.
Supporting Details:
1. Force of blood is measured in millimeters of mercury.
   a. Typical pressure is 120/80.
2. 120 refers to force exerted while heart contracts and is called "systolic pressure."
3. 80 refers to force exerted when heart muscle is relaxed and is called "diastolic pressure."

4. *Main Idea:*
Linguist Salvador Tío coined the word "Spanglish" to describe the mix of Spanish and English spoken by Spanish-speakers in heavy contact with English-speakers.
Supporting Details:
1. Common along the U.S.-Mexico border, in bilingual communities, Panama, and anyplace where English-speaking films or music are popular.
2. Main feature is combining English and Spanish grammar and vocabulary in same sentence or conversation.
   a. "Ya me voy a get up."

Check Your Understanding (p. 499)

1. They almost always begin by highlighting and defining the key term explained in the paragraph.
2. "refers to," "is the name for," "is defined as," and "is said to be"
3. Notes should include the term defined along with the definition. They should also include examples or explanation of origins.

Exercise 2: Understanding Dates and Events Patterns (pp. 504-509)

1. *Transitions:* between 1810 and 1820; In 1848; ten years later; by the Civil War (1861-1865); not until 1880; In 1890; By 1900

   Main Idea:
   It took a while for American colonists to learn how to raise tea.
   Supporting Details:
   1. Between 1810 and 1820: First tea shrub planted
   2. 1848: More experiments with tea production
   3. 1858: Plans to distribute throughout the South
      a. Cut short by Civil War (1861-65)
   4. 1880: Dept. of Agriculture resumes tea production
   5. 1890: Charles Shepard of S. Carolina devoted own fortune to growing tea
   6. 1900: Had planted 60 acres, harvested 5,000 lbs.
   7. Tea never successfully competed with coffee in America.

2. *Transitions:* As a boy; By 1932; By 1934; It was only four years later; by 1945; By 1960; In 1975

   Main Idea:
   Wernher von Braun's life suggests that wrong-doers are not necessarily punished.
   Supporting Details:

1. 1934: Von Braun had received engineering degree and earned a doctorate in physics;   work in rocket science was funded by Adolf Hitler.
2. 1938: He and his team had developed the deadly V-2 missile, later used in air attacks on London.
3. 1945: Nazi government collapsing; von Braun surrenders to American forces.
4. Americans realized how valuable he was, ignored his past—needed him to fight the Cold War.
5. 1960: Von Braun head of NASA's Marshall Flight Center.
6. 1969: Overjoyed at putting a man on the moon; awarded the National Medal of Science in 1975.

3. *Transitions:* As early as 1534; 1880; Thirteen years later; In 1903; in 1904; Over the next ten years; On August 15, 1914; After World War II; In 1977

Main Idea:
By the 16th century, plans were underway for a Panama Canal, but it didn't get built until the 20th century.
Supporting Details:
1. 1534: Holy Roman Emperor says a waterway in Panama would allow ships to travel to Peru and Ecuador.
2. 1880: First construction attempted when French break ground
3. 1893: French give up.
4. 1903: U.S., under Theodore Roosevelt, gets control of the unfinished Panama Canal.
5. 1914: After 10 years, the canal opens.
6. 1945: After World War II, canal is source of controversy over who the rightful owners   were.
7. 1977: President Carter returns canal to Panamanians.

4. *Transitions:* in 1961; In 1966; Even today; In 1967

Main Idea:
In the 1960s, there were marked advances in women's rights.
Supporting Details:
1. 1961: President Kennedy created a "Commission on the Status of Women."
    a. Commission's report openly criticized women's inferior status and led to other similar commissions being established.
2. 1966: Betty Friedan helped start a national feminist organization.
    a. Called National Organization for Women (NOW)
3. 1967: Because of pressure from NOW, Lyndon Johnson prohibited sex discrimination among federal employees.
4. In terms of women's rights, no decade has equaled the sixties.

Check Your Understanding (p. 509)

1. the order of events as they happened in real time
2. They will (1) describe the smaller events that preceded a more major one, (2) chart the career of a famous person, or (3) explain how some activity, invention, or institution entered the culture.
3. *Answers will vary.* Transitions like "Before the revolutionary war," "After World War II," and "Following the election of 2008" are typical of this pattern.
4. *Answers will vary.* "The Brazilian union organizer Francisco `Chico' Mendes had a brief but incredibly courageous career as a labor leader.
5. Timelines often accompany passages that trace a sequence of dates and events.

6. Details with dates are important, but undated details that help explain the main idea are also important.

Exercise 3: Understanding Process Patterns (pp. 512-516)

1. *Transitions:* first; Three to five days after hatching; When she is far enough; Once a drone arrives; Following

   Main Idea:
   The first thing a newly hatched queen bee does is seek a mate.
   Supporting Details:
   1. 3–5 days after hatching, flies far from the hive to avoid inbreeding.
   2. Far enough away, gives off a scent that attracts drones.
   3. Once a drone arrives, queen mates at an altitude of around 50 ft.
   4. Following mating, queen flies home and lays her eggs.
      a. If queen does not mate by the time she is 2 weeks old, incapable of reproducing.

2. *Transitions:* At the illness's onset; At this point; In the third stage; In this final stage

   Main Idea:
   Victims of paranoia usually go through four separate stages.
   Supporting Details:
   1. At beginning, victims distrust others.
      a. Always looking for hidden motives
   2. In the next stage, personal failure is fault of others; victims take no responsibility.
   3. Stage three, victims grow angry and hostile.
   4. Stage four, victims suddenly know for sure there is a conspiracy to destroy them.
      a. The paranoid person now sees enemies everywhere.

3. *Transitions:* then; In the next stage; At this point; After a final massive explosion of lava; During the cooling stage; Eventually

   Main Idea:
   There are several stages in the eruption of a volcano.
   Supporting Details:
   1. Eruption begins when lava—liquified rock—becomes charged with gas and steam.
   2. Lava shoots up, then falls back to earth in pieces of stone.
   3. Next, lava in center of volcano flows over rim.
      a. Volcano is at its crisis.
   4. After a huge explosion, the volcano starts to cool.
      a. Produces gases and vapors.
   5. Explosion often followed by appearance of geysers or hot springs.
   6. Sometimes when last traces of heat are gone, cold springs appear near volcano.

4. *Transitions:* within a year after hatching; During; Then; When; Once; Within days

   Main Idea:
   Shortly after hatching, young king salmon head out to sea on a dangerous journey.
   Supporting Details:
   1. During journey, bears, ducks, raccoons, and industrial pollution kill large numbers of salmon.

2. Only a small portion reaches the sea.
3. Those who reach sea stay 4 to 6 years.
4. At the end of period, start on journey back to the river where hatched.
5. Reaching the river, lay thousands of eggs.
6. Life is over for them.
7. Change color and turn slimy.
8. Float downstream with tails forward and die in a few days

Exercise 4: Understanding Simple Listing (pp. 519-523)

1.

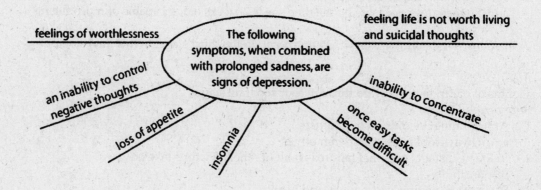

2.

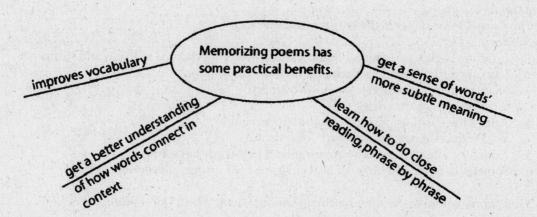

3.

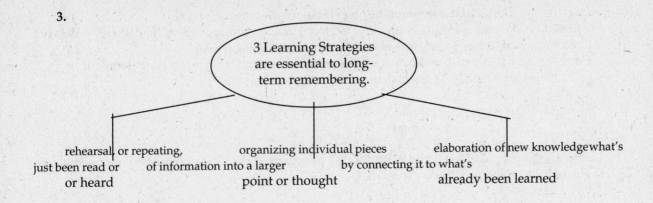

4.

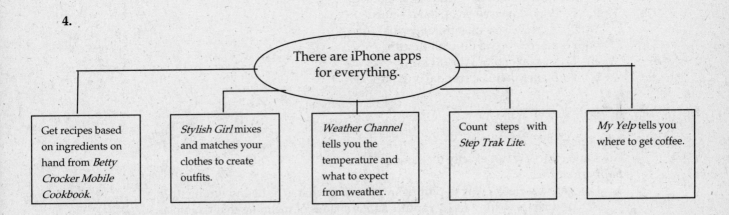

Check Your Understanding (pp. 523-524)

1. The process pattern requires the supporting details be explained according to the order in which they occurred in real time. The supporting details in the simple listing pattern don't need to be explained in any special order. They can be rearranged to suit the writer's preference.
2. In the simple listing pattern, the topic sentence is most likely to occur at the beginning or the end of the paragraph.
3. In the simple listing pattern, many topic sentences will include a plural word like "signs" or "characteristics" that require specific examples to be meaningful.
4. This pattern is likely to use transitions such as "for instance"; "for example"; and "first," "second," and "third."

Exercise 5: Understanding Comparison and Contrast Patterns (pp. 528-533)

1. *Transitions:* however; Unlike; Yet despite

   c

   Main Idea:
   Different in many ways, Plato and Aristotle had a similarly negative effect on scientific thought.
   Supporting Details:
   1. Plato valued intuition rather than fact.
      a. Nature only a dark reflection of higher, more spiritual world.
   2. Aristotle valued fact and evidence.

   a.   Believed truth found through the observation of the natural world.
3.   Both insisted that all motion traced a perfect circle at uniform speed and thereby delayed recognition of Kepler's discovery about the movement of the planets.
   a.   Kepler's discoveries and Newton's laws might have appeared a good deal sooner if Plato and Aristotle had not been so influential.

2.   *Transitions:* Like; also
a
Main Idea:
To increase his popularity, Gerald Ford, the 38th president of the U.S., emphasized his resemblance to one of his predecessors, Harry Truman.
Supporting Details:
1.   Both became president by chance.
   a.   Truman took over when Roosevelt died.
   b.   Ford took over when Nixon resigned.
2.   Both played the role of anti-intellectual.
3.   Both came to office at difficult times.
   a.   Truman at end of World War II
   b.   Ford after political scandal of Watergate

3.   *Transition:* However
b
Main Idea:
Laws and ethics are not exactly the same.
Supporting Details:
1.   Laws are a society's way of putting into writing what is right and wrong.
   a.   Written laws don't really capture subtle shades of meaning that go into an ethical code.
2.   Ethical concepts are more complicated; they are ideas about right or moral conduct.
   a.   Often hard to express them in language of law.

4.   *Transitions:* But; While; Although; however
b
Main Idea:
Nigeria has changed dramatically since the beginning of the nineteenth century.
Supporting Details:
1.   Political power has shifted from local leaders to business and military men.
   a.   Local leaders once waged war to increase their territory but now wield power behind the scenes.
   b.   Community leaders still regarded as last word on values.
2.   Courtship behavior another area of dramatic change.
   a.   In cities, couples now allowed to date even if they don't plan to marry.

Check Your Understanding (p. 534)

1.   The comparison and contrast pattern requires the presence of two topics, and the paragraph has to focus on similarities, differences, or both.
2.   *Answers will vary,* but four listed on page 000 are *likewise, similarly, but,* and *however.*
3.   The topic sentence in this pattern will very likely point out how two people, events, things, or ideas are similar, different, or both similar and different.
4.   Notes on this pattern need to include the two topics being compared and contrasted, along with the similarities and differences that develop the topic sentence or imply the main idea.

5. They carefully record the similarities and differences and forget to include the main idea those details explain.

Exercise 6: Understanding Cause and Effect Patterns (pp. 538-542)

1. *Transitions:* Consequently; As a result; Yet another consequence; Thus

   Main Idea:
   In *The Bounty of the Sea,* Jacques Cousteau painted a scary picture of what will happen if we let the ocean "die" from pollution.
   Supporting Details:
   1. Ocean would become a rotting grave.
   2. Decaying bodies would cause a horrible smell.
   3. People would abandon their homes.
   4. Seas would no longer be able to maintain balance of gases.
   5. Carbon dioxide would increase and trap heat on Earth.
   6. Sea-level temperature would dramatically increase.
   7. Ocean's surface would be covered with a heavy film of decayed matter.
   8. Rain would be rare.
   9. Drought would prevail and many people would starve.

2. *Transition:* Thus

   Main Idea:
   People join groups for two reasons.
   Supporting Details:
   1. Group's activities provide person with chance to fulfill religious or civic obligations.
      a. For example, working in a soup kitchen to fulfill sense of responsibility to society
   2. Group includes people we like.
      a. For example, someone might join a bowling group to be with friends, not because he cares about the activity.

3. *Transition:* thanks to

   Main Idea:
   In the 1830s and 40s, the growth of both cities and literacy altered the appearance of American newspapers.
   Supporting Details:
   1. At first, newspapers written largely for the wealthy interested in art, social events, and trade.
   2. More cities and more people who could read encouraged papers like the New York *Sun* to mass produce cheap newspapers.
   3. New "penny press" broadened the kind of topics covered, describing everyday events, crimes, sports, and gossip.
      a. By 1890s, some penny papers had one million readers.

4. *Transitions:* because; As a result; Thus

   Main Idea:
   Only one theory of dinosaur extinction seems really sound.
   Supporting Details:

1. Theory claims dinosaurs became extinct because a comet or asteroid crashed into Earth and produced huge amounts of dust.
2. Dust blocked sunlight for months and plants that needed sunlight died.
3. Dinosaurs, who survived mainly on vegetation, were left to starve.
4. Lack of sunlight also caused temperatures to drop, leaving dinosaurs to freeze.

Exercise 7: Understanding Classification Patterns (pp.545-549)

1. *Main Idea:*
    Blood vessels consist of 3 types.
    Supporting Details:
    1. Arteries carry blood away from heart to all parts of body.
        a. Aorta is largest artery.
        b. Due to oxygen, blood in arteries appears bright red.
    2. Blood in veins looks purple because it carries no oxygen.
        a. Veins carry blood back to the heart.
        b. Valves in veins keep blood from flowing backward.
            1) Important for lower parts of body where blood fights gravity.
    3. Capillaries are tiny vessels connecting arteries and veins.
        a. Walls are thin.
        b. Thin walls make it possible for digested food to pass through to cells of body.

2. *Main Idea:*
    Learning can be divided into two different kinds.
    Supporting Details:
    1. Incidental learning takes place by chance.
        a. Student who helps a friend learn first 16 presidents of U.S. may, by chance, learn them too.
    2. Intentional learning takes place when purpose is present from very beginning.
        a. Student sits down intending to learn the states' capitals
    3. Intentional learning stays with us over time.

3. *Main Idea:*
    D. Katz and R. Kahn have identified five different kinds of downward communication within organizations.
    Supporting Details:
    1. Job instructions: messages specifying how tasks should be done.
    2. Job rationale: messages that explain why a task needs to be done and how it relates to other organizational activities.
    3. Procedures and practices: messages that tell members about organization's responsibilities, obligations, and privileges.
    4. Feedback: messages that tell employees how they are doing.
    5. Instruction about goals: messages that describe mission and goals of the organization.

4. *Main Idea:*
    Sociologist Max Weber identified three different types of authority.
    Supporting Details:
    1. Traditional authority based on custom and practice.
        a. In England, it's customary for a person to inherit the right to be king or queen.

2. Charismatic authority comes from individual's personal appeal.
   a. Salvador Allende, Martin Luther King Jr., Princess Diana are all examples of people with some charismatic authority.
3. Legal-rational authority comes from rules or laws designed to make institutions function effectively.
   a. Government officials have this kind of authority.
4. Weber's categories are neatly divided, but in real life they often overlap. *Note:* This sentence probably qualifies as a concluding sentence.

Check Your Understanding (p. 550)

1. Unlike the simple listing pattern, which can be used to make a number of different points, the classification pattern always explains how some larger group is broken down into smaller subgroups.
2. It identifies the number of subgroups that make up the larger whole.
3. Notes should include names of the categories and the characteristics used to describe each one.

Exercise 8: Recognizing Primary Patterns of Organization (pp. 550-556)

1. a
2. a
3. d
4. c
5. b
6. b
7. c
8. b
9. b
10. b

Vocabulary Check (p. 557-558)

1. d
2. h
3. i
4. j
5. n
6. p
7. o   *Note:* The word *chromosomes* appeared in Chapter 1, but since some instructors skip this chapter, it appears in this chapter as well.
8. g
9. q
10. t
11. r
12. b
13. a
14. x
15. y
16. e
17. s
18. m

19. u
20. w
21. f
22. k
23. v
24. l
25. c

Digging Deeper: Types of Love (pp. 561-562)

1. c
2. classification
3. a
4. d
5. pragma lovers; love

Making Connections (p. 562)

Answers will vary. Either *storge* or *pragma* would be appropriate; *storge* because it suggests love develops slowly over time and *pragma* because arranged marriages focus on matching people based on hobbies and interests.

Drawing Your Own Conclusions (p. 562)

Answers will vary.

Test 1: Vocabulary Review (pp. 563-564)

1. synthesize
2. coercive
3. stench
4. illumination
5. utterance
6. ousted
7. alluding
8. literacy
9. province
10. provocation

Test 2: Vocabulary Review (pp. 565-566)

1. dubious
2. socialist
3. adversarial
4. inbreeding
5. activists
6. civic
7. chromosomes   *Note:* The word *chromosomes* appeared in Chapter 1, but since some instructors skip this chapter, it appears in this chapter as well.
8. graphics

9. extensive
10. genetic
11. compassionate
12. ascent
13. commerce
14. hindrance
15. ranged

Test 3: Recognizing Primary Patterns (pp. 567-569)

1. d
2. b
3. d
4. b
5. c

Test 4: Recognizing Primary Patterns (pp. 570-572)

1. e
2. c
3. e
4. a
5. c

Test 5: Recognizing Primary Patterns (pp. 573-575)

1. b
2. b
3. e
4. d
5. a

Test 6: Recognizing Primary Patterns (pp. 576-578)

1. c
2. d
3. b
4. e

CHAPTER 10: COMBINING PATTERNS IN PARAGRAPHS AND LONGER READINGS (pp. 579-617)

Exercise 1: Recognizing Combined Patterns (pp. 582-586)

1. b, e
2. c, d, e
3. b, d, e
4. b, f
5. a, c, d, e

Check Your Understanding (pp. 586-587)

1. The needs or requirements of the main idea dictate the choice of patterns.
2. No. The important patterns are the ones needed to explain the main idea. There might well be an introductory sentence or two using an organizational pattern that does not develop the main idea. The elements of this pattern don't need to be recorded in notes.

Exercise 2: Identifying Patterns in Longer Readings (pp. 589-596)

1. b, e   The primary pattern here is cause and effect, but dates and events along with process play a role in describing the explosion and the disaster as a whole.
2. b, e
3. a, d, e, f
4. a, c, e

Exercise 3: Identifying the Primary Patterns (pp. 596-605)

1. (1) c
    (2) a, e, f   The last two paragraphs introduce cause and effect.
    (3) definition; classification
         The writer needs the definition pattern to tell readers about schizophrenia. Classification is essential to explaining the disease's different forms. Cause and effect is important only in describing the effects of the disease, which are already covered by classification.

2. (1) c
    (2) a, d, e, f
    (3) definition; classification
         The definition pattern is essential to tell readers what the Johari Window is. Classification is equally important to describe it. Comparison and contrast governs only one sentence, and only the last paragraph hints at cause and effect.

3. (1) d
    (2) a, b, c, e   In this case, simple listing *and* cause and effect overlap, so I'd accept three or four patterns as an answer.
    (3) cause and effect; simple listing
         The reading focuses on explaining why the attempts at farming in the Amazon Basin have failed. That makes the cause and effect pattern the crucial one. However, because the first paragraph identifies what are, in effect, causes as "problems," I'd also accept simple listing as correct. Students who thoroughly understand the patterns will probably vote for both cause and effect and simple listing, which, to me, is the perfect response.

4. (1) b
    (2) d, e
    (3) comparison and contrast; cause and effect
         Although there's an implied cause and effect, suggesting that gender determines people's responses to older parents, the primary pattern is comparison and contrast, and I'd also accept as correct that one answer.

Vocabulary Check (p. 606)

1. h
2. e
3. g
4. j
5. f
6. i
7. a
8. b
9. d
10. c

Digging Deeper: The Development of Self in Childhood (pp. 608-609)

1. *Answers will vary somewhat.* In Europe and the United States, people form their identity, or sense of self, in stages that occur at different times.
2. b
3. c
4. d, f
5. a

Making Connections (p. 609)

the open area

Drawing Your Own Conclusions (p. 609)

Answers will vary. The reading suggests young children would insist that someone can be in two places at one time. Since they think they can "throw off human identity," it seems probable that very young children also assume they can split themselves into two different identities.

Test 1: Vocabulary Review (pp. 610-611)

1. convulsions
2. lax
3. synthetic
4. diluted
5. giddiness
6. incomparable
7. biographical
8. posh
9. diversion
10. propaganda

Test 2: Identifying Main Ideas and Patterns of Organization (pp. 612-614)

1. (1) b
   (2) b, d, e
2. (1) a
   (2) a, d, e

Test 3: Identifying Main Ideas and Patterns of Organization (pp. 615-617)

1. (1) d
   (2) b, e
2. (1) b
   (2) c, d

CHAPTER 11: MORE ON PURPOSE, TONE, AND BIAS (pp. 618-688)

Exercise 1: Identifying the Main Idea and the Primary Purpose (pp. 626-632)

1. (1) c
   (2) b
2. (1) c
   (2) b

Check Your Understanding (pp. 632-633)

1. Writers can't always control their biases, try as they might to do so. Thus, readers need to be alert to those places where supposedly informative writing reveals a bias.
2. factual statements
3. neutral; objective
4. If the writer can't seem to acknowledge that an opposing point of view might have *some* value, then readers need to be wary of the writer's claim overall.
5. The writer includes facts, but they are usually facts that support the author's point of view.
6. They point out the flaws in the opposition's argument.
7. They use a variety of tones, depending on the effect they want to have on their audience.

Exercise 2: Labeling Facts and Opinions (pp. 636-637)

1. F
2. O
3. O
4. O
5. F
6. F
7. F
8. O
9. O
10. O

Exercise 3: Recognizing Opinions in Factual Statements (pp. 639-640)

1. F
2. O
3. F
4. M
5. M
6. F
7. M
8. M
9. M   *Note:* Some people might not admit or believe that there were gender barriers.
10. M   Because it's a time-order transition, students may not see the significance of *finally* as an indicator of opinion.

Exercise 4: Drawing Conclusions About the Author (pp. 640-644)

Note: Point out that the excerpts used here are from textbooks.

1. M, c
2. M, b
3. V, d
4. M, b
5. M, b

Check Your Understanding (p. 644-645)

1. Statements of fact describe or explain topics and issues without the writer offering any personal evaluation.
2. They can be verified by outside sources.
3. Writers making factual statements use a coolly neutral tone.
4. No. To be taken seriously, opinions on issues other than one's personal state of mind need to be grounded in evidence, experience, and logic.
5. Writers expressing opinions can assume any number of tones. The tone they choose depends on how they feel about the subject matter as well as their audience.
6. Yes. If the word or phrase carries positive or negative associations, it mixes an opinion into what is otherwise a factual statement.

Exercise 5: Recognizing Excessive Bias (pp. 650-654)

1. c, a, a
2. a, a, a
3. c, a, b

Check Your Understanding (p. 654)

1. Bias in persuasive writing is a drawback when the writer uses a bullying tone and refuses to acknowledge any opposition. It's also considered a drawback when the writer misrepresents opposing points of view in order to discredit them.

2. Instead of criticizing the opposing argument, the writer attacks the person or group voicing the argument. The writer uses as "evidence" the opponent's character, experience, or beliefs and avoids analyzing the opposing point of view.
3. The writer who insults the opposing point of view has stepped over the line.

Exercise 6: Recognizing Faulty Logic (pp. 662-665)

1. c
2. e
3. d
4. c
5. a

Exercise 7: Recognizing Faulty Logic (pp. 665-668)

1. c
2. b
3. e
4. d

Vocabulary Check (p. 669)

1. d
2. g
3. e
4. a
5. h
6. j
7. i
8. c
9. f
10. b

Digging Deeper: Critical Thinking and Pseudo-psychologies—Palms, Planets, and Personality (pp. 672-)

1. We need to be more skeptical about pseudo-psychologies like palmistry, graphology, and astrology.
2. pseudo
3. We tend to remember or pay attention to information that fits our worldview.
4. a
5. c

Test 1: Vocabulary Review (pp. 674-675)

1. alarmist
2. forensic
3. oratory
4. indigenous
5. crustaceans
6. zealous

7. equitable
8. imperiled
9. segregationist
10. bureaucratic

Test 2: Fact, Opinion, or Both (pp. 676-677)

1. M
2. F
3. F
4. O
5. M
6. O
7. F
8. M
9. M
10. F

Test 3: Identifying Tone (pp. 678-680)

1. b
2. b
3. a
4. b
5. c

Test 4: Recognizing Tone and Excessive Bias (pp. 681-684)

1. a, b
2. d, a
3. c, a
4. c, b

Test 5: Locating Errors in Logic (pp. 685-688)

1. a, b
2. c
3. d
4. a
5. e

PART VIII

Answer Keys for Putting It All Together

ANSWER KEYS FOR PUTTING IT ALL TOGETHER

Reading 1: Beyond Time Management (pp. 693-696)

1. b
2. b
3. The obituary will define long-term goals a person hopes to reach, making it easier to plan for and work toward them on a daily basis.
4. Although the author doesn't say it, he seems to be suggesting that repeatedly visualizing goals might make them more achievable.
5. It will give you a feeling of renewed energy and purpose.
6. b
7. We can't control time, but we can control ourselves and act in ways to make better use of time.
8. a, c, d
9. b
10. b

Drawing Your Own Conclusions (p. 696)

Answers will vary. The reading suggests the author would tell the student to concentrate less on managing time and more on overall planning, especially in terms of her life's goals. He might well suggest the obituary exercise (paragraph 5) so that she can figure out what she wants to achieve and how taking specific steps now would help her accomplish her future goals.

Reading 2: Arriving at a Crossroads (pp. 700-701)

1. c
2. *Answers will vary.* The author realizes that she, too, might no longer have a job as a reporter and she has to think about what else she might do for a living.
3. figuratively
   There were no real seeds planted that night, but her daughter's comment figuratively gave her the seed of an idea that was to develop into a life-changing decision.
4. c
5. "That night," Just three weeks after," "After years of writing"
6. figuratively.
   Answers will vary. There is no bullet, but there was a chance of something happening that was just as deadly as a bullet: The author might have had cancer. However, if she escaped a deadly threat, her mother did not.
7. The meeting was fate rather than chance. (Point out that the question is rhetorical. The author doesn't really expect an answer.)
8. If a man who suffered that kind of tragedy can survive to refashion his life, so can she.
9. c
10. b

Drawing Your Own Conclusions (p. 701-702)

Answers will vary, but the overriding theme of the reading is that things do not happen by chance, and the author specifically challenges the notion of events in life being a series of random events in paragraph 7. She suggests that everything happens for a purpose.

Reading 3: Marla Ruzicka: An Activist Angel (pp. 706-707)

1. b
2. c
3. a
4. d
5. a
6. a
7. The soldiers were on edge and fearful for their own safety, so they were too quick to open fire even when there was no real threat.
8. c
9. b
10. admiring; *Answers may vary.*

Drawing Your Own Conclusions (p. 708)

She would have agreed because she obviously believed that her own actions made a difference.

Reading 4: The Altruistic Personality (pp. 713-715)

1. b
2. c
3. c
4. d
5. People with a genetic predisposition toward altruism are inclined to help others.
6. a
7. Research has been able to tell which specific situations produce helping behaviors, but they are less clear about which personality traits produce them.
8. Americans are more likely to help if they see people in extreme need. Indians are more likely to help people in need, mild or extreme.
9. a
10. d

Drawing Your Own Conclusions (p. 715)

The authors, who strongly suggest a genetic component to altruism, might not be optimistic about preschools' attempts to nurture altruism.

Reading 5: Where Does Free Speech End? (pp. 718-720)

1. c
2. They fear that another Holocaust could occur if people are allowed to minimize or forget the horror of the Holocaust.

3. (1) Freedom of speech gave Irving the right to say what he said; (2) preventing the expression of a dangerous idea does not effectively expose the flaws of that idea; (3) imprisoning him made him a martyr.
4. If we take the Holocaust lightly and diminish its horror, we pave the way for it to happen again.
5. c
6. *Answers will vary.* The Holocaust is akin to a myth or fairy tale
7. b
8. c
9. b No. At the every end, the tone reveals more personal involvement. The very last sentence is not attributed to someone else. It appears to be the authors' point of view.
10. c

Drawing Your Own Conclusions (p. 720)

Voltaire would seemingly be siding with those who don't believe in censorship like the historian Deborah Lipstadt. That seems to be the whole point of defending to the death even statements that merit personal disapproval or disgust.

Reading 6: Is Facebook Growing Up Too Fast? (pp. 725-727)

1. b
2. b
3. a
4. b
5. b
6. Many people are not happy with changes to the site.
7. The people in charge of Facebook have their own views of what the site should accomplish, and those views may not always be in accord with what the membership wants.
8. *Answers will vary.* The inclination of people to seek out others like themselves.
   Against. Facebook seeks to connect people around the globe, while the sociologists who coined the term *homophily* believe that individuals like to stick with people similar to themselves. They don't want to be connected to people very different from themselves.
9. a
10. c *Note:* There is no break in the tone as there is in the previous reading.

Drawing Your Own Conclusions (p. 728)

Based on the reading, Cox would have little interest in this argument. He is pretty clear on the subject of who makes decisions about the site, and it's not the members. He says explicitly, "It's not a democracy" and, in his words, "we," meaning management, are the "caretakers."

Reading 7: Memory, Perception, and Eyewitness Testimony (pp. 733-735)

1. b Although the authors come very close to stating the overall main idea, it is implied rather than stated.
2. c
3. d
4. b
5. b
6. b

7. b
8. a   (This is a tough one, and the textbook context is the deciding factor.)
9. neutral, objective
10. a

Drawing Your Own Conclusions (p. 735)

Given that they know how many mistakes can be made in a courtroom, it's likely that they do not support the death penalty.

Reading 8: Is a Monster Pandemic Around the Corner (pp. 742-744)

1. c
2. its wide geographic range
3. d
4. It hits but seems to go away, only to return all the stronger.
5. The government of Hong Kong took action and slaughtered all the chickens in the area so that the virus could not keep spreading through birds.
6. It mutates easily and can assume new forms.
7. a
8. a
9. a
10. c

Drawing Your Own Conclusions (p. 744)

Answers will vary, but it seems extremely likely that efforts to find a vaccine will intensify dramatically.

Making It Personal (p. 744-745)

Answers will vary, but it seems pretty clear that slaughter of the farmer's entire flock could be a consequence of the admission, bringing with it economic disaster, and that's not an easy consequence to accept. It's probably much easier to pretend that the chickens are not sick with avian flu.

Sources of Quotations and Statistics

Barry, John M. *The Great Influenza.* New York: Penguin Books, 2005, pp. 98-115. (Source of information about influenza viruses and disease's symptoms.)

Davis, Mike. *The Monster at Our Door: The Global Threat of Avian Flu.* New York: Henry Holt and Company, 2005, pp. 3-51.

Kilbourne, Edwin D. Interview. www.who.int/csr/disease/avian_influenze/avian_faqs; www.multinationalmonitor.org/mm2006/interview-ki.

Kolata, Gina. *Flu: The Story of the Great Influenza Pandemia of 1918 and the Search for the Virus That Caused It.* New York: Farrar, Straus and Giroux, 1999, pp. 219-43. (Source of claim about Alfred Crosby, description of 1997 aborted pandemic, and quote from Stephen Ip.)

www.cidrap.umn.edu/cidrap/content/influenza/avianflu/news/jan2604birdflu.html. (Source of information about avian flu incidents in Southeast Asia.)

Reading 9: Whaddya Have to Do to Get a Kidney Around Here? (pp. 751-753)

1. b
2. If you need something, ask for it.
3. c
4. d
5. (1) People are keeping their kidneys in case they need to help family members.
   (2) Some were discouraged from being an organ donor by other family members.
   (3) Transplants are still thought to be scary, complicated, and dangerous.
   (4) People who need kidneys don't talk about it.
6. The author seems to be referring to the more established agencies that are formally in charge of matching donors with people in need of a transplant.
7. She seems to be pestering the established agencies to do things differently and annoying them in the process. In other words, she is causing them discomfort similar to the irritation a thorn in one's flesh would cause.
8. b *Note:* The allusion suggests that while a tragedy is occurring, members of the kidney establishment are doing something pointless.
9. a
10. b

Drawing Your Own Conclusions (p. 753)

Answers will vary, but the reading suggests that she would think it was a wonderful decision on the part of the donor.

Reading 10: Debating Parental Notification Laws (pp. 757-760)

1. c
2. a
3. Some person or group claims that the law is not provided for by the Constitution and forces the state to go to court in order to prove that the legislation is legal.
4. c
5. simple listing, definition, cause and effect
6. One, Another
7. (1) Parents are the ones responsible for their child's well-being and therefore have a right to know when a child is going to make an important medical decision.
   (2) Parents need to know so that they can provide emotional support.
   (3) Parents are more experienced and can help the child make the right decision.
   (4) Not notifying parents if a child is planning to have an abortion undermines parental authority.
   Transitions: for example, also, finally
8. (1) Teenagers often have good reasons for not wanting to tell their parents (later on the author mentions that some parents might become abusive).
   (2) In taking the time to convince teenagers to notify their parents, there's a delay in the abortion procedure that increases the risk.
   (3) States allow teenagers to receive other kinds of medical treatment and services without parental consent.
   Transitions: in addition, also
9. a
10. c

Drawing Your Own Conclusions (p. 760)

(1)   The members, at least based on the website, seem to support such legislation.

(2)   There are numerous statements stressing the importance of confidentiality rules applying to all interactions between physicians and patients. There are similar ones stressing that adolescents who think their parents will be informed of their desire for an abortion will not seek out medical help. Thus the logical conclusion is that NARAL supporters would probably not approve of parental notification legislation.

PART IX

Answer Keys for Author's Website Materials (laflemm.com)

Chapter 1: Strategies for Textbook Learning

Questionnaire 1: Textbook Clues to Meaning

Answers will vary.

Questionnaire 2: Strategies for Reading

Answers will vary.

Questionnaire 3: Improving Concentration

Answers will vary.

Chapter 2: Building Word Power

Quiz 1: Using Context Clues

1. b   2. c   3. a   4. a   5. b   6. c   7. c   8. a   9. b   10. a

Quiz 2: Using Word Parts

1. cred   2. dis   3. re; vit   4. corp   5. temp
6. viv   7. corp   8. viv   9. temp   10. cred

Quiz 3: Vocabulary Test

1. ominously   2. Devotees   3. radical   4. exhume   5. irrational
6. doctrine   7. lore   8. commitment   9. abhorrent   10. discrimination

Quiz 4: Vocabulary Test

1. plagiarized   2. Heredity   3. nocturnal   4. perpetuated   5. impunity
6. Flouting   7. despicable   8. homage   9. appalled   10. instigated

Quiz 5: Vocabulary Test

1. stamina   2. meteorological   3. geriatric   4. Ironically   5. irreparable
6. liberation   7. geological   8. turmoil   9. Respiratory   10. abated

Quiz 6: Vocabulary Test

1. scavenging   2. inherently   3. punitive   4. corruption   5. looting
6. excels   7. thrive   8. linguistic   9. disreputable 10. commodity

Chapter 3: Connecting the General to the Specific in Reading and Writing

Quiz 1: Creating General Categories

1. General Category: Things with bristles
2. General Category: Supernatural beings, figures in horror movies, scary characters
3. General Category: Things that undergo change, transformation or metamorphosis
4. General Category: Things that smell or have an odor
5. General Category: Things that are stuffed
6. General Category: People who wear uniforms
7. General Category: Things that can be broken
8. General Category: Events that cause anxiety; also tension producing situations
9. General Category: Things that shed
10. General Category: Things that run

Quiz 2: General and Specific Sentences

1. a   4. b   7. b   10. a
2. b   5. b   8. a
3. a   6. a   9. b

Quiz 3: Getting Specific

Answers will vary.

1. If you are feeling stressed, playing with a pet can help you unwind.
2. Often, the children involved mistakenly think they caused the divorce.
3. The oldest child usually has to take responsibility for the younger ones.
4. Some restaurants refuse to allow diners to smoke.
5. With her natural warmth and charm, Princess Diana won the hearts of the British public.
6. Because they get a lot of money for celebrity pictures, some photographers think nothing of stalking celebrities wherever they go.
7. Money isn't much good if you have no family or friends who care what happens to you.
8. You can say the dumbest things, but if you say them with a British accent, someone is bound to think you are clever.
9. In soap operas, villains always get punished; in real life, they often get off scot-free.
10. In some countries, women are not allowed to show their faces in public; everything except their eyes much be covered.

Chapter 4: From Topics to Topic Sentences

Quiz 1: Identifying Topics

1 a   4. b   7. b   10. c
2. b   5. b   8. b
3. c   6. a   9. a

Quiz 2: Topics, Topic Sentences, and Paraphrasing

1.   Topic: C

Topic
Sentence: "Although not all medical researchers are quite as vehement as Stuart Levy, most
agree with his general point - Americans have overused antibiotics and may, in the
long run have done themselves more harm than good."

Paraphrase: a

---

2.   Topic: c

Topic
Sentence: "Indian leader Mahatma Gandhi believed strongly in the principle of non-violence.
He refused to be shaken in his belief, even when he had to pay dearly for it." (Note: I
would also count just the first sentence as a correct answer.)

Paraphrase: b

---

3.   Topic: b

Topic
Sentence: "Next to salsa, swing music is probably the hottest dance craze around, but swing
music is hardly new."

Paraphrase: b

---

4.   Topic: c

Topic
Sentence: "It seems like everyone has a web page these days, so it should come as no surprise to
discover that the Crips and the Bloods, two of the most violent youth gangs to emerge
in the last twenty years, have their own web sites. Yet despite the threatening gun
icons one has to click to navigate these sites, there are some signs that the web sites
may offer a more peaceful message than one might at first imagine."

Paraphrase: b

---

5. Topic: b

    Topic
    Sentence: "It took over one hundred years, but in 1999 Henry O. Flipper and his descendants finally got the justice they deserved."

    Paraphrase: b

---

6. Topic: c

    Topic
    Sentence: " Diet and health food fads usually come and go in a year or two; however, the food fad associated with nineteenth century health guru, Horace Fletcher had a considerably longer run."

    Paraphrase: b

---

7. Topic: b

    Topic
    Sentence: "Some brandy lovers like their liquor flavored by a whole pear, but since you can't squeeze a whole pear into a bottle, pear growers had to be creative."

    Paraphrase: b

---

8. Topic: b

    Topic
    Sentence: " Actually, television has been around almost as long as radio. It just took a much longer time getting established."

    Paraphrase: b

---

9. Topic: a

    Topic
    Sentence: "In the days when unions were young, bloodshed during a strike was not unusual."

    Paraphrase: a

---

10. Topic: b

    Topic
    Sentence: "All around the world, the rocky deposits known as coral are dying, and many experts believe that global warming is the culprit."

    Paraphrase: b

Quiz 3: Paraphrasing the Topic Sentence

Paraphrases will vary.

1. Topic Sentence: 2
    Note: Although I think sentence 2 is a better answer, I would also accept sentence 1, which is a more general version of 2.

    Paraphrase: Computers are changing the practice of architecture in several different ways.

---

2. Topic Sentence: 3
    Note: Here again, sentence 2 is a possible answer although it is not as precise as sentence 3, which I consider the better answer.

    Paraphrase: Basketball is a Canadian invention.

---

3. Topic Sentence: 1

    Paraphrase: The Monroe Doctrine has been a critical part of U.S. history.

---

4. Topic Sentence: 2

    Paraphrase: The last words of some people were intriguing enough to be recorded.

---

5. Topic Sentence: 1

    Paraphrase: When proper Brooklyn matron Gertrude Lintz decided to raise two young gorillas as if they were her own children, she became an outcast to her neighbors.

---

6. Topic Sentence: 6

    Paraphrase: Although women do live longer than men, they are more prone to a number of serious diseases.

---

7. Topic Sentence: 2

    Paraphrase: Juries can be manipulated in ways that prevent them from making the right decision.

---

8.   Topic   3
       Sentence: Note: I would also count sentence 1 as a correct answer. It's less precise than 3, but it does, in very general terms, sum up the paragraph.

       Paraphrase: Temperament seems to be the major factor in achieving happiness.

---

9.   Topic   1
       Sentence: Note: Sentence 2 would be a less complete but still adequate answer.

       Paraphrase: Thousands of Americans are following the example of "life extensionists" like Larry Wood: They are doing everything they can to avoid dying.

---

10.   Topic   3
       Sentence:

       Paraphrase: A newly discovered memoir of a Mexican soldier who was also at the Alamo has challenged the legend of how Davy Crockett died.

Chapter 5: Focusing on Supporting Details (10th edition: Chapter 6)

Quiz: Spotting Irrelevant Details

1.   T.S. <u>1 and 2 or just 2</u>; I.D. <u>X</u>
     Note: The real point of the passage is that Clemente made full use of his time on earth, but some students may feel that sentence 2 alone, with its reference to "these words" is incomplete.<>

2.   T.S. <u>2</u>; I.D. <u>11</u>

3.   T.S. <u>3</u>; I.D. <u>5</u>

4.   T.S. <u>3</u>; I.D. <u>8</u>
     Note: Sentence 1 is also possible as a topic sentence.

5.   T.S. <u>1</u>; I.D. <u>X</u>
     Note: A case could also be made for sentence 5 being the topic sentence although I would count sentence 1 as the better answer because the whole paragraph is devoted to explaining the paradox of teenagers' natural health being undermined by increasing health problems.

6.   T.S. <u>1</u>; I.D. <u>5</u>
     Note: Sentence 12 as the topic sentence would also be correct. This is a good example of a paragraph that introduces the main idea at the beginning of the paragraph and then repeats it at the end. Although it is less precise, you could even argue, correctly I think, that sentence 11 is a topic sentence. As long as students could interpret the clause "the jury is still out," I would also accept sentence 11 as a correct answer.

7.   T.S. <u>3</u>; I.D. <u>4</u>

8. T.S. <u>1</u>; I.D. <u>2</u>

9. T.S. <u>1</u>; I.D. <u>9</u>
    Note: I would also accept sentence 2 as a topic sentence that could sum up the paragraph.

10. T. S. <u>1 and 2</u>; I.D. <u>3</u>
    Note: This is a case where I think you need to have both sentences to create a complete topic sentence. However, some instructors would consider sentence 2 as correct as long as students knew they had to mentally plug in the phrase "during World War II." That's fine with me.

Chapter 6: More About Inferences (10th edition: Chapter 5)

Quiz 1: Selecting the Better Inference

1. b   2. b   3. a   4. b   5. a

Quiz 2: Drawing the Appropriate Inference

Answers will vary.

1. The hognose snake may look and act dangerous, but it is essentially harmless.
2. In the early part of the twentieth century, the growing popularity of the automobile created a whole new vocabulary.
3. The new "G.I. Joe Extreme" doll sends the disturbing message that little boys should grow upto be muscle-bound men.
4. Given what he hoped television would accomplish, David Sarnoff would undoubtedly be disappointed by what the medium has become.
5. Many of the popular dishes we think were invented in a foreign country actually originated here in the United States.

Quiz 3: Drawing Inferences

Answers expressing the main idea will vary.

1. Main idea: Although extremely low-calorie diets seem to extend the life span, they may have major drawbacks for humans.
    Pattern: e

2. Main idea: For several everyday tasks, the tried-and-true, older method of doing things is actually quicker than newer methods.
    Pattern: d and e

3. Main idea: One study suggests that laparoscopic surgery for colon cancer patients is as effective as—or maybe even a little more effective than—conventional surgery.
    Pattern: d and e

4. Main idea: Teenagers' positive perceptions of smokers seem to be influenced by portrayals of smokers in advertisements and the media.
Pattern: b and e

5. Main idea: Due to a lack of earthquake engineering, the death tolls from earthquakes are higher in the developing world than in more industrialized countries.
Pattern: d

Chapter 8: Beyond the Paragraph: Reading Longer Selections (10th edition: Chapter 7)

Quiz 1: Identifying the Main Idea

1.   b
2.   a

Quiz 2: Recognizing Thesis Statements

1. *Thesis Statement*: On May 5, 1862, the Mexican government announced to the world that foreign intervention in its affairs would no longer be tolerated. Although the Mexican-American War (1846 -- 48) might have left the country weary and bankrupt, that did not mean foreign intrusion would be met with no resistance. The fifth of May, or *Cinco de Mayo*, proved that once and for all.
Note: I would also accept as correct just the first sentence beginning with On and ending with tolerated. It doesn't sum up the reading as effectively, but it can act as a summary statement, which is the essential requirement of a thesis statement.

2. *Thesis Statement*: Numerous psychology textbooks have dutifully passed on to students the notion that the "Hawthorne effect" was a scientific finding grounded in solid research. Yet, in reality, the Hawthorne effect was based on very shaky evidence.

Chapter 9: Recognizing Patterns of Organization in Paragraphs (10th edition: Chapter 8)

Quiz 1: Predicting Patterns

1. c
2. f
Note: Answer d is also possible since writers often compare and contrast within the framework of the classification pattern.
3. b
Note: Answer e is also a possibility since the heading could suggest the author will discuss why the blues came into being.
4. c

5. e
6. b
Note: The better answer is b, but e is also possible.
7. d
8. a
9. d
10. a

Quiz 2: Sentence Relationships I

1. c 2. a 3. d 4. c 5. c

6. b 7. c 8. b 9. a 10. c

Quiz 3: Sentence Relationships II

1. c 2. a 3. b 4. c 5. d

6. a 7. c 8. b 9. c 10. b

Quiz 4: Looking for Patterns

1.   b, e
2.   a, d, e
3.   e
4.   d, f
5.   d, e
6.   a, c
7.   a, f
8.   a, e
9.   c
10.   a, d

Chapter 10: Combining Patterns in Paragraphs and Longer Readings (10th edition: Chapter 9)

Quiz 1: Recognizing Patterns

Answers will vary in places.

1.   *Thesis Statement:* Cybercolleges are achieving growing acceptance.
     Patterns: a, d, and e
     Note: Students may miss the comparison and contrast pattern because it is very subtle, but the last paragraph does contrast real schools with cyberschools.

2. *Thesis Statement:* Each hemisphere in the brain controls different activities.
   Patterns: d and e.
   Note: If students add the definition pattern because the reading does, in effect, define the two hemispheres, I would give them credit for that answer.

3. *Thesis Statement:* Combining romance and marriage is a fairly modern idea.
   Patterns: b, d

4. *Thesis Statement:* Volcanic eruptions follow a general sequence of steps.
   Patterns: a, c, and e

Quiz 2: Patterns and Thesis Statements

1. Cause and effect is the most obvious choice, but definition is also possible, since the revised notion of the family would require a definition.

2. Definition for sure, although comparison and contrast is also a good bet.

3. Cause and effect

4. Sequence of dates and events is the most likely answer, although this is a tricky one because students have to realize that the phrase "hard-won victory" implies a struggle that took place over time. I would also accept cause and effect if students argued that the paper would have to show why the victory was hard-won.

5. Comparison and contrast is an obvious answer. However, if students argued for definition, too, because the two men's views of nature needed to be defined, I would accept that answer as correct.

6. Definition

7. Comparison and contrast

8. Definition and cause and effect

9. Definition and cause and effect

10. Process and definition

Chapter 11: More On Purpose, Tone and Bias (10th edition: Chapter 10)

Quiz 1: Blending Fact and Opinion

1. *F*
2. *B*

Note: It's impossible for anyone to know exactly what Polk knew or how well he knew it, so some opinion informs this statement despite the presence of factual information.

3. *F*
4. *B*
5. *F*
6. *B*
7. *B*
8. *O*
9. *O*
10. *O*

Quiz 2: Recognizing Tone and Purpose

1. b; c
2. a; a
3. b; c
4. b; c

Note: Some students might select answer a, but that answer ignores the author's personal involvement reflected in the use of the first person plural.

5. b; a

Quiz 3: Looking for Errors in Arguments

Answers will vary in places.

1. c

2. a   *Note:* That's not to say there aren't some good reasons here, but some statements are pure repetition: "In addition, fewer people would be locked up for shorter periods of time" is a given, not a new reason.

3. d

4. c

5. a

Exercise: Expressing Opinions

Answers will vary.